Complementarities

Complementarities

Uncollected Essays

I. A. Richards

Edited by John Paul Russo

Harvard University Press
Cambridge, Massachusetts
1976

Copyright © 1976 by the President and Fellows of Harvard College
All rights reserved
Printed in the United States of America
Library of Congress Cataloging in Publication Data

    Richards, Ivor Armstrong, 1893-
      Complementarities.

      Includes bibliographical references and index.
      1. Criticism—Collected works. I. Title.
    PN85.R5   809   76-19044
    ISBN 0-674-15520-3

Contents

Introduction

The contribution of I. A. Richards to modern criticism began in the early 1920s when he was teaching in the newly founded English School at the University of Cambridge and publishing *The Meaning of Meaning* and *Principles of Literary Criticism*. The first was a pioneer study in semantics, the second an account of value in psychological terms, a theory of communication, and an analysis of poetry. The word "principles" was something to note; as it was said of his teachers in philosophy, Moore and Russell, he was seeking foundations in criticism and was taking off from "a new and initially uncommitted beginning." Richards' most influential book, *Practical Criticism: A Study of Literary Judgment*, appeared in 1929. In it he presented hundreds of reports by undergraduates on poems he had set for them; he analyzed their responses, classified them according to type of error, and drew up a methodology of criticism as a serviceable corrective. The whole experiment had a scientific approach, and the method was suited to the various problems that were diagnosed. This book, with its critical strategies for "close reading," its discussion of authorial tone, feeling, doctrine or belief in poetry, and sincerity, had a potent effect on the subsequent generation of teachers and students in England and America; later studies, *Coleridge on Imagination* and *The Philosophy of Rhetoric* in the mid-1930s, added to Richards' influence. The New Criticism, as John Crowe Ransom acknowledged, stemmed largely from his work. Even today, when the influence has been absorbed and may pass unnoticed, one will occasionally hear Richardsian echoes in the classroom and read of his terms and concepts in critical books or note their effect in contemporary literary discussion.

What sets Richards among the finer critics of the century is that he was from the beginning concerned with expanding the perimeter of criticism and relating it to developments in other disciplines. Before 1920 he was taking tools, as he said, from the workshops of Cambridge philosophy. He was extraordinarily innovative in the field of semantics and anticipated the linguistic investigations of the logical positivists. He studied neurophysiology and borrowed a model of integration from C. S. Sherrington. Psychological concepts from behaviorism and the Gestalt group were employed for what they could say about reader response. Yet he was no less aware of what was being responded to, the poem or prose work, and his criticism emphasized the status of the literary object and had a large formalistic component. There were, to be sure, some areas of criticism he avoided, perhaps out of reaction to their predominance in his time—for example, historical backgrounds and the "life and times" biography. In the 1930s and 1940s he was writing on educational method, on learning a second language, on the theory of translation (he wrote a book on the Chinese philosopher Mencius), and on the experimentally simplified version of English known as Basic. He was and is still translating from classical and biblical literature (the *Iliad*, Plato, the Book of Job); he published a humanistic inquiry *Beyond* in 1974 and is currently collecting a fourth volume of poetry. Scientific models were not abandoned in his middle years; and the title essay of this collection, written in 1972, takes its name and concept from the physical theory of Niels Bohr.

Above all, Richards has been concerned with values, and in this respect he is an heir of Matthew Arnold's humanistic criticism. As an epigraph for *Science and Poetry* in 1926 he cited Arnold's "The Study of Poetry," *The future of poetry is immense,* believing that if the future of poetry is immense, the future of man can be immense too. Yet Richards had the plain sense to admit that the future of poetry appeared nil.

I have collected here only Richards' literary essays, with the few exceptions in part III. Excluded are essays on education, science, Basic English and language training, and other subjects, and so one cannot treat the collection as representative. The essays fall into three categories, although needless to say some of the essays could be put in any of the categories. (1) Historical: essays that help to show Richards' philosophical and critical background (1-3, 12, 26, and the interview) and his relations to other disciplines (4, 7, 8,

9). These may also fill in gaps for future students of early modernist criticism. (2) Practical criticism: since Richards usually saved his "practical" work for the classroom or lecture hall and there have been requests to see more of his few published pieces in this area, I have sought in part II to place as many of these uncollected pieces as possible. (3) Humanistic essays of general interest: essays 5, 6, 12, 13, 22-24, and the interview, serve as a bridge to Richards' recent humanistic criticism and poetry.

Richards was born in Sandbach, Cheshire, in 1893. He was a student at Clifton College, near Bristol, and went up to Cambridge in 1911 as an exhibitioner in history at Magdalene College. After turning from history to moral sciences at the end of his first year, he was supervised by the idealist philosopher J. M. E. McTaggart and the logician W. E. Johnson. Unquestionably the most powerful influence at this time and in the years immediately following was G. E. Moore, who lectured on the philosophy of mind thrice weekly. Richards earned first-class honors in part one of the tripos examination in moral sciences in 1915, left Cambridge, and shortly afterward suffered a severe bout of tuberculosis (his third). He recuperated in northern Wales and in the Alps and took up what became a lifelong sport, mountaineering. Before the end of the war he returned to Cambridge and studied biology and chemistry with the intention of going into medicine and eventually psychoanalysis. Dropping these studies, he was invited by Mansfield Forbes of Clare College to lecture on the contemporary novel and the theory of criticism in the English School. Richards had been laying plans with C. K. Ogden for *The Meaning of Meaning* when he published his first literary essay, "Art and Science," in June 1919. He was appointed Lecturer in English and Moral Science in 1922 by Magdalene College and became a Fellow of the College four years later.

"Art and Science" was a philosophical reply to Roger Fry in *Athenaeum.* Just a few months before Richards started lecturing on modern novels and the theory of criticism he was setting down ideas on what became an important polarity—or pairing—throughout his career, poetry and science. With its "propositions," its theory of meaning as a concept (not an object or a use), its philosophical psychology, and its treatment of art as conveying propositions "worth contemplating for their own sake," this essay revealed

Richards' reliance on Moore and the philosophical background of Cambridge realism. Richards was already borrowing philosophical instruments for his literary criticism, and some of his innovative spirit derived from the revolution in British philosophy that had been effected by Bertrand Russell and Moore at the turn of the century.

Many of the issues that Richards examined in later books come up in the three early pieces included in this book: the concept of the "vehicle"; the need for method in criticism; multiple definition of words; emotion and the critique of expressionism and of personality theories of poetry; the emphasis on works of art as "vastly complex systems" and "wholes"; the notion of truth in poetry; and the relation between art and science, a topic that warrants attention as one of Richards' long-standing preoccupations.

The split between an aesthetic and a scientific view of the world was important to Richards as a young man and though he later modified his view, he never really abandoned it. This division had long been a part of Romantic-Symbolist criticism, and a number of writers important to Richards—Coleridge, Shelley, Arnold —had grappled with it and sought to relate the one to the other. The aesthetic view was holistic, vital, synthetic; the scientific view was separatist, analytic, discursive. Science was *abstractive;* its presentation of the universe necessarily distorted and thereby falsified it. Art provided an enactment of a world; it was a dynamic organism and so was a closer approximation of the essential being of the universe. The aesthetic view was concerned with the experiencing of something of import; the scientific view, with the analysis of the experience or the import. This is the difference, as Richards remarks in "The Conduct of Verse," between poetry and poetics; it is the difference between *what* something does to the mind and *how* it is doing it.

How does one test the truth-value of a scientific theory or an aesthetic experience? What makes one scientific theory more valuable than another? What are these theories and experiences tested against? These questions are treated directly in the Fry-Richards debate ("Art and Science") and the Murry-Richards debate ("Between Truth and Truth"), and they come up indirectly in "Belief," "Emotive Language Still," and "Complementarities." I shall examine briefly the first of these debates; although some of the terms and concepts in Richards' contribution offer special problems, they do usefully introduce central themes of this book.

Roger Fry had argued that the aesthetic value of a theory of science did not depend on the truth or falsity of the propositions wherewith it was built. Indeed, the "highest pleasure" in observing a scientific theory or in appreciating a work of art was identical, namely a "unity-emotion," an emotion accompanying the "clear recognition of unity in a complex." He distinguished this unity-emotion from a lesser but specifically aesthetic emotion by which "the necessity of relations is apprehended, and which corresponds in science to the purely logical process," and from the various physiological pleasures of, say, seeing certain colors or hearing certain sounds. Fry betrayed his suspicion, however, that even the aesthetic value of a scientific theory must come to terms with truth: "I suspect that the aesthetic value of a theory is not really adequate to the intellectual effort entailed unless, as in a true scientific theory (by which I mean a theory which embraces all the known relevant facts), the aesthetic value is reinforced by the curiosity value which comes in when we believe it to be true."

For Richards in "Art and Science," "the notion of truth is the decisive notion, not only for the scientific value of theory, but for its aesthetic value as well . . . any aesthetic worth considering must use truth as a main instrument." Richards always has maintained this position, but he might well have said "truths," for truth in scientific theory and truth in art have different modes of verification, one against empirical evidence, the other against individual experience. Richards' initial discussion owed a considerable debt to G. E. Moore's definition of propositions and his concept theory of meaning. Like Moore, Richards defined the term "proposition" negatively, as neither a mental state nor a fact nor a sensible form (word or image). Not a mental state: Richards followed Moore and Russell in rejecting the "Idea-ism" of Locke, Hume, and Mill whereby propositions are a "part of our minds, or produced by our minds." Not facts: "for we may apprehend what is false, and then there is no fact for us to apprehend." Not a sensible form: for the form is only that by which the proposition is apprehended. Otherwise, positively, a proposition is defined as a objective "complex of terms" in relation to one another; it is the *meaning* of a sentence independent of the sensible form of its words. The terms may be called ideas provided that "no confusion is allowed between images and sensations which are in some sense 'occurrences in our minds,' and ideas which are not in our minds in this sense, but things which by means of these occurrences the mind gains access to, or thinks of."

How does the mind gain access to propositions, to "complexes of terms," before their truth can be tested? For both art and science, "vehicles" are required: some sensible form, "either of words or of imagery or of sensations." Richards thus introduced the term "vehicle," which gained wide currency in literary criticism of the thirties and forties. Since science is the "systematic connection of propositions," it deals with propositions whose connections can be traced accurately back to empirical reality, to the hard facts. "The vehicles of science for this reason are composed of signs, words for the most part, arbitrarily assigned as names to defined ideas." Scientific theory employs connected terms or complexes of terms to which objects or complexes of objects correspond, and this correspondence is the theory's test of truth.

In the case of art, on the contrary, the truth of propositions does not depend on any systematic connection between them. (The propositions may, one notes, be systematically connected, but this is not their test of truth.) Art "is interested in propositions for their own sake, not as interconnected." The two phrases bear examination: "for their own sake" and "not as interconnected." The first is almost certainly derived from Moore's discussion of goodness in *Principia Ethica*. Goodness is, finally, unanalyzable; it cannot be broken down into any parts more basic; it can be known only by direct intuition. So Moore argued, adding that there are some things "worth having *purely for their own sakes*" (Moore's italics). These are "certain states of consciousness which may be roughly described as the pleasures of human intercourse and the enjoyment of beautiful objects." That such states are unanalyzable means that they too cannot be broken down and reduced to something else. As Richards asserted in "Art and Science," those propositions "which are most worth contemplating for their own sake are not those whose connections we have the best hope of tracing." The truth of art is tested against the whole dynamic of mind and feeling, a single individual's interiority. Richards' psychological criticism was but a short step away.

The second phrase, "not as interconnected," is formidable. In what sense are aesthetic propositions not necessarily connected? Should one try to trace the connections, like a good scientist, and give up only after great effort? According to this statement, the work of art is the more successful the more difficult it is to trace fully its connections in order to test its truth-value. This seems fairly opaque, and Richards offered no elaborate commentary. Should one try to trace connections and, having found them, count the work of art as negligible? How hard should one try to trace these connections—before conceding importance to the work of art? By this principle, obscurity and ambiguity in themselves become criteria of important art. So too do works of art with a complex textual organicity. We may fault Richards on this point, though it must be conceded that he was moving with the times; ambiguity and obscurity were becoming poetic values. How then does one finally test the truth of a work of art? In his earliest essay Richards fell back on Moore's dogmatic position; it became a matter of direct intuition, something "self-evident" and "inevitable."

Fortunately Richards did not follow Moore (and the Bloomsbury circle, whom Moore had influenced) farther down the road of aesthetic purism. Indeed, you have not much farther to go when you have arrived at intuition. There is, however, a significant value to be learned here. What Moore and Richards meant by "intuition" was a faculty independent of any determinative, scientific, or logical system or theory that might impose its own exclusive standard or requirement over one's final judgment as to the truth-value of a work of art. Such truth is tested by the whole mind in a state of contemplation.

Richards began reacting to this intuitionism almost immediately, and in his early psychological studies he attempted to find ways of tracing connections between a work of art and an individual psychology. In contrast to Moore, he came to reject the absolute split between aesthetic and nonaesthetic experience. However, he always saved intuition as a final test of truth, and gave his classic position on the subject in "Doctrine in Poetry" in *Practical Criticism*. However, intuition is "guarded" from pure relativism by a "frame of feelings whose sincerity is beyond our questioning": (1) man's loneliness, (2) facts of birth and death "in their inexplicable oddity," (3) the immensity of the universe, (4) man's place "in the perspective of time," and (5) man's ignorance. Richards called this a "technique or ritual for heightening sincerity."

The distinction between poetry and science remained significant in Richards' criticism. The tendency of many writers was to reject one or to subordinate one to the other. Max Eastman elevated science over poetry, Middleton Murry poetry over science; and in his review of Eastman and his reply to Murry, both reprinted here, Richards considered the insufficiency of their solutions. He wrote against Eastman that poetry is not exquisite euphoria: "If 'heightened consciousness' is all we are to ask for, what is wrong with lumbago?" Poetry may perhaps be the "impassioned look upon the face of Science" (Wordsworth), but the two disciplines have nonetheless their own spheres, their own "very different procedures of verification." He chided Murry for thinking that the poet and the scientist could be in a contest for the best description of a primrose. Richards hoped to find in psychology some common area between science and art, some third term capable of relating them to each other. *Principles of Literary Criticism* represented his most sustained endeavor to explore this relation in psychological terms. Another approach was his method for analyzing contexts, to which a number of essays in this collection address themselves.

In his early essays there are hints that Richards would direct attention toward close language analysis. The method he eventually developed was his major contribution to criticism. One proof of this method was soon apparent; it could cope with the special uses of language and thematics in modernist poetry of the Pound-Eliot stamp and the experiments in consciousness and time in the novels of Joyce, Proust, Faulkner, and Mann. It is well known that a chief goal of the 1910-1925 avant-garde was to secure the technical and formalistic underpinnings of their poetics and to defamiliarize artistic content. The reader of A. E. Housman's *A Shropshire Lad* or Rupert Brooke's patriotic war elegies was not prepared for the tonal and rhythmic complexity of Pound's *Homage to Sextus Propertius* ("When, when, and whenever death closes our eyelids") or Eliot's *Hollow Men* or the formal experiments in Molly Bloom's soliloquy or Proust's *Le temps retrouvé*. Modernist literature made large, some would say excessive, demands upon its readers. It was not simply unpopular art destined, like its nineteenth-century predecessors, to win gradual acceptance by a broad audience. So went the argument of Ortega y Gasset in "The Dehumanization of Art." This new "artistic art" did not cultivate an open and easily communicable idiom; for some it seemed positively antipopular. Whether or not we agree with the rest of Ortega's thesis, that such art was a dehumanization (because it stylized and so derealized), is quite another matter. The modernist writers had come down firmly against making the poem the servant of "other" interests. They spoke of something dense, definite, and carefully crafted, an inclusive form (as Richards wrote in *Principles*) that protected itself from the reader's irony by being itself ironic. A poem was a lyrical object as durable and admirable as a sculptured form. It is true, they were employing classical metaphors to support Romantic-Symbolist ends. However, the demand for "hard, dry verse" was taken as the necessary antidote to the soft, wet emotionality of a prevailing taste in poetry and impressionistic criticism. It was *craft* and the *thing*, as Pound insisted in 1914, but whether it was an objective or a subjective *thing* did not really make a difference.

Modernist art was obscure, ambiguous, allusive, and, in Eliot's prescriptive term, difficult. And the Richardsian method of language analysis—sense, tone, form, intention, linguistic functions, attitude, irony—was developed in the 1920s to encounter obscurity, ambiguity, and allusiveness. It also dealt with "sincerity," stock responses, irrelevant associations, and doctrine in poetry. Of course this was not the sole justification of the method, only its immediate historical context; Richards wanted to make this new "difficult" art easier of access. Generally, the method aimed at clearing blockage in the communication of any writer, past or present. Since poets have been the master manipulators of language, only by "close reading" could error be reduced or avoided, or at any rate not counted against the writer. Many of the contributors to *Practical Criticism* blamed the writers for their own faulty interpretations. (Sometimes, to be sure, the stock or conventional, ready-made response was not the reader's but the poet's own, foisted upon a reader by tradition or bad teaching).

In "Emotive Language Still" and "Semantics" Richards explained the rationale behind and some procedures for the method of close reading. He was trying to dislodge the sense of a word's definition as standing among a strict group of dictionary definitions. Words were not "rigid crystals," he insisted. On the contrary, they were workers, had functions, performed within a given context. Lexicographers recorded only the most general senses of the meanings of words over time ("Multiple Definition"). The point was to begin by examining the particular context in which the word was found, lending and receiving its own nuanced meaning in a fluid transaction. Richards wrote three books to show how multiple and contrasting were current definitions of key words. Only by slowing down the reading process could one observe the "behavior" and "resourcefulness" of words in contexts. He challenged Mortimer Adler's *How to Read a Book* (1940) with his own *How to Read a Page* (1942).

As early as *The Meaning of Meaning* (written with C. K. Ogden) Richards distinguished five functions that language could have in a given context: (1) symbolizing a reference, (2) expressing an attitude toward a listener or reader, (3) expressing an attitude toward the object spoken of or written about, (4) promoting certain intended effects through the statement, (5) managing or supporting the whole statement effectively. In "Emotive Language Still" there were six functions, in "Semantics" seven. At a public lecture I once heard someone ask Richards why the number of functions went up and he replied (this is nearly verbatim) that there was "nothing magical" about the number; one may choose "as many functions as one likes provided each is given its specific work within the context."

In "Semantics" we are given a schema of seven functions or "jobs," "all in some measure in progress simultaneously, and interdependently, whenever we use language": (1) selecting, or pointing to, indicating; (2) characterizing, or saying something about; (3) presenting, or realizing, "vividly or plainly, excitingly or quieteningly"; (4) valuing, or giving worth to, making it more or less on a given value scale; (5) adjusting, getting someone (maybe the speaker) to take an attitude toward; (6) managing, or keeping the preceding five functions working effectively for, to some end;(7) purposing, the overall intention or endeavor of the statement. No single word, out of a context, may be said to have or to be serving any one of these functions. In context "here" or "there" may be simply *selecting* words; while words like "and" and "or" may be just *managing* words. For conveying a laboratory report, a sociological analysis, or cooking directions, one would expect uses 1, 2, and 6 to be dominant. Likewise for a mathematical theory. But in swearing, 4 and 5 prevail; in a political speech perhaps 2, 3, and 4, depending on the speaker. "But almost all our words and phrases commonly exercise a simultaneous multiplicity of functions." By separating, describing, and analyzing the processes and the objects of the various functions in a given context, one gets under the skin of language, draws out the rich associations methodically, and unlocks what Richards calls the "interinanimation of words." One test of the usefulness of such analysis is translation: How does an utterance carry out the several functions in the two languages?

Neither Richards nor anyone else, so far as I know, has followed the method to the letter. One reason for the success of *Practical Criticism* is its very openness; it invites readers to move out with some basic strategies and to find their own territory. William Empson, Richards' student in 1928-1929, focused on the ambiguities of whole poems, phrases, single words. Cleanth Brooks explored paradox and irony in (and *as*) the structure of a poem. Allen Tate analyzed the "tension" with and through which the associations of words, sounds, and images win their unity. The nature of tone and allusiveness concerned Reuben Brower and Earl R. Wasserman; their criticism was receptive to historical and classical sources, remedying a flaw in the original theory.

Besides the functions, there are also two broad *uses* or "principles of structuring or organization" to which all the functions in varying degrees may be put: the referential and the emotive. As such the uses correspond to the division between science and art. Referential language is defined as a certain type of expository prose, a prose cleaned of the subjective element to serve as the ideal medium for scientific communication. Such language conveys knowledge, not only the hard facts but theoretical knowledge as well. Economy, clarity, and an explicitness in the relation of word (or sign) to referent (or object, concept) are essential. Language is referential if the question "Is this true or false in the ordinary strict scientific sense?" is relevant. *Selecting* and *characterizing* functions hold sway here. Paraphrase is relatively simple since this is a pointing and describing language.

What concerns Richards as a literary explicator is, of course, emotive language. Here language is used to stimulate attitudes and enact states of awareness, to engage the will and promote interests. It is a poetic vis-à-vis a matter-of-fact use of language. Strict reference (functions 1 and 2) may be present, but reference is employed not for what it can "say" about the world so much as what it can release or trigger in the emotional and intellectual components of the poem. Such emotive communications—the emphasis falls on the *presenting, valuing,* and *adjusting* functions—are "deeper than those with which references are concerned." Richards describes emotive language as "more massive," more dense with association (and interinanimation), than referential language, where the virtue is terseness and thinness of association. Emotive language has body to it; it employs all the devices of language, sound, rhythm, image, stanzaic pattern, typography, and so forth. Moreover, use of language in this way ties the writer to *history:* "What are awakened are feelings, attitudes, impulses to action which were on the move in those past situations with which the emotive words were conjoined." The scientific or referential use comes later: emotive "modes of influence, these urgings this way and that, are . . . a matrix out of which referential language forever develops—in the race and in the child." Such are the underground emotive influences in our language which entail "no small part of the guiding and shaping means by which we damn or save ourselves."

Psychologically, such emotive attitudes in literature stimulate broad areas of mental experience, organizing them and achieving a temporary equilibrium, a stable and "balanced poise," which "we suspect to be the ground-plan of the most valuable aesthetic responses." Aesthetic equilibrium "brings into play far more of our personality than is possible in experiences of a more defined emotion. We cease to be oriented in one definite direction; more facets of the mind are exposed and, what is the same thing, more aspects of things are able to affect us." To respond in this way is to be truly disinterested. This "balanced poise" is a reaction to the poem, and so one can trace the formal and structural elements that are responsible. Richards likens a poem—a significant poem—to an "energy system" of varied or opposing attitudes, subtly interpenetrating one another. He is fond of citing Coleridge's definition of a poet: "The poet, described in *ideal* perfection, brings the whole soul of man into activity, with the subordination of its faculties to each other, according to their relative worth and dignity. He diffuses a tone and spirit of unity, that blends, and (as it were) *fuses*, each into each, by that synthetic and magical power, to which we have exclusively appropriated the name of imagination" (*Biographia Literaria*, chapter 14). Since emotive language is as much the tool of propagandists and advertisers as of poets (as Plato warned, the three are not always distinguishable), part of the critic's task is the exacting exercise of ethical judgment.

Judgment and the search for values grounded in truth have been themes in Richards' criticism from that first essay where he called truth the "decisive notion." I have stressed this theme through my choice of essays for this collection, notably the two on belief and truth (5 and 6) and the later essays in practical criticism. An autobiographical essay on this topic is "The Secret of 'Feedforward,' " and there are further reflections in the interview.

In *Principles of Literary Criticism* Richards won a certain notoriety by his use of behaviorist psychology and neurophysiology to explain modes of judgment and value. He had been interested in these questions for some time; his first paper, read before the Moral Sciences Club at Cambridge about 1915 (his teacher G. E. Moore was present), was an analysis of John Henry Newman's *Grammar of Assent*. Richards' writings in the period of 1922-1931 reveal a large debt to the nineteenth-century British philosophers who had undermined the treatment of belief in traditional associational psychology. Without some attention to this school one could misinterpret or overemphasize Richards' commitment to strict behaviorist psychology. Behaviorism in Richards' early career is, I believe, something like a heuristic model rather than a belief rigidly adhered to. (This assertion requires a proof that would take us beyond this introduction.) A few backward glances are therefore appropriate before returning to Richards on truth and poetry.

Richards studied the works of both the Mills at Cambridge; J. S. Mill had pondered the nature of belief in his *System of Logic* (1843) and questioned the doctrine of association as a result. Was belief only an inference drawn from experience? How could mental association account for the staggering power of belief, a conative power that an idea held over the will? Power, but toward what end? In *Emotions and the Will* (1859), which Richards also studied, Alexander Bain connected this power-to-believe with a type of instinct, with movement, and with phenomenological dimensions of the will: "Preparedness to act is the sole, the genuine, the unmistakable criterion of belief." Richards also knew the writings of the Cambridge philosopher James Ward and his student G. F. Stout. With Ward's noteworthy article on "Psychology" for the ninth edition of the *Encyclopaedia Britannica* in 1886 that subject was for the first time granted a separate entry (it was previously placed under Metaphysics). The effort of Ward and Stout went toward "saving" consciousness, toward a concept of active attention and conation, toward "end-states" and "attitudes of consciousness." Some of these topics are taken up in "Belief" and "John Watson's *Behaviorism*." Richards was sharply criticized for the adoption of the behaviorist model. As these essays may show, his early guides in psychology had long since qualified or repudiated the associational position and established in their own terms a division between the empirical and "transcendental" ego. "We know intellectually what we are as experiments," Ward said. "We may not observe consciousness, but we have it or are it (in some as yet undetermined sense)," Richards wrote in his review of Watson, "and in fact many of our observations of other things require it."

In the last half of the nineteenth century, then, belief was viewed as a major philosophical topic. It was also a widespread social question. Science and historical criticism had eroded the traditional foundations of religious belief. If historicism was the harbinger of relativism, on what new grounds could writers and artists discover, if not their own values, some standard against which their values might be measured? Arnold's personal situation illustrated the dilemma strikingly since the chief event of his youth had been the loss of Christian faith, a loss that initiated a long quest for values in poetry, criticism, and his later religious writings. The title *Literature and Dogma* presented the polarity; in the light of Arnold's conclusions it might have been more accurate to have said "Literature *or* Dogma." Arnold separated belief from what he termed extra-belief. In his redefinition of terms, belief was something like scientific acceptance; it was our conviction regarding "what can and should be known to be true." Extra-belief, taken from the German *Aberglaube*, was belief "beyond what is certain and verifiable" or "what is beyond the range of possible experience" though not less important for being so; it was hope and anticipation; it was conveyed by imaginative or mythic vision and could be wedded to moral awareness. It was belief *beyond* (Richards' recent *Beyond* employs the metaphor in a similar way in its title). Goethe was quoted in the chapter "Aberglaube Invading": "Extra-belief is the poetry of life." Arnold noted that extra-belief could be seriously misleading, especially when taken for belief; and in "Literature and Science" he admitted he did not know how the values drawn from literature (our extra-beliefs) would exercise their informing control and evaluative influence on the results of natural and social science (our beliefs). "And here again I answer that I do not know *how* they will exercise it, but that they can and will exercise it I am sure."

Richards puts the question of belief in psychological terms in order to analyze how we "translate" the communications of great writers whose beliefs, doctrines, or natural systems of thought have been otherwise superseded. What are the processes of this mental "translation," and does it help to show where to exercise and restrain any impetus toward that moral evaluation and action that Arnold claimed could occur? To deny the significance of this "translation" as a major problem or simply to aim one's critical attention toward purely formalistic matters in art would be mere acquiescence. "There is something a little ridiculous, at least, in admiring only the rhythms and 'word-harmonies' of an author who is writing about the salvation of his soul." The idea of taking up temporary belief in what is being presented, say, in Dante's heaven or Homer's gods, of pretending for the moment, then dropping the belief, is also discredited. What is covered by the higher claims of belief in major artists ought indeed to be "translated," ought in fact to sustain "permanent modifications in the structure of the mind which works of art can produce." Finally, Richards asks, how may we connect the import of these "translations" with practical experience and the evaluation of the results of the sciences?

For his own psychological starting points Richards went to William James's *Principles of Psychology* (1890), "The Will to Believe," and the later essays on pragmatism. James contrasted belief not with disbelief but with doubt. Belief and disbelief were similar in being affirmed positions; and Bain had said, belief was a "preparedness to act." Doubt is the real opposite of both belief and disbelief, because doubt is "theoretic activity," a deliberative mental state that precedes this readiness to act. Richards' argument in "Belief" is complex; he focuses on the contrast between belief and "something else" (he lists five options), and on the "readiness to act." He settles on the last option, imagination, as a contrast to belief; like James's doubt it is a state of mental activity. However, one wants to believe in certainties. With scientific beliefs one may depend on objects to which these beliefs correspond. One can test them and measure them; and, therefore, one can act upon them. With imagination and works of emotive utterance, however, beliefs are "objectless." In what ways can one test the truth-value of these beliefs, and in what manner can one act upon them?

How does one test James's definition of belief, "the readiness to act as though it were so"? How much must one rely on, believe in, the given case, before committing oneself to action? Should not commitment depend on how one expects the results of one's actions to be tested and evaluated and how precise one expects the returns of these tests to be? Very precise returns of the scientific type lead to the certainties of "verifiable belief," a category corresponding to Arnold's "belief." Here "readiness to act as though it were so" involves clearly defined junctures with actuality, "factual veridicality or consistency, a matter of logical relations," or, to go all the way back to Richards' first essay, "Art and Science," connected propositions. With philosophical, religious, and poetic beliefs, however, there are no precise junctures. Yet there is something like a strong feeling and intellectual attitude that results from emotive utterance and precedes action, moral or otherwise.

"Imaginative assent" is the term fixed to the form of belief in which the agreement with reality is a "matter of the development of thought, feeling, will, and conduct in accordance with one picture of the world or another." The truth of these emotive utterances—to return to the "decisive notion"—is tested against us and found true if it is "rare and important," when it can be "accepted and integrated into the fabric of our personality as a positive determining influence," as Richards says in "Belief": but at no point will imaginative assent entail "an act or an assertion sufficiently definite for actuality to test its truth or falsehood. Such belief, it is true, may be successful or unsuccessful and so be said to be tested by experience. But the success will be in ordering the growth of the personality or in aiding the good life." The language recalls Arnold's description of extra-belief. Richards' statement is positive, but cautious. For some, such as F. R. Leavis, it was not strong enough, did not guarantee a sufficiently stalwart or explicit moral standard as a safeguard against the all too explicit and conflicting ideologies of the thirties and forties.

Nevertheless, these statements form a principle of action in Richards' liberal and rationalist humanism. His caution, his suspicion of "beliefs" and artists' directing us to this or that specific action, does not, I believe, result from the influence of Moore's ethics, where the idea of the good was enjoyment of friends and beautiful objects, or from Walter Pater's late Victorian aestheticism. It is more than likely that it emerges from Richards' own experience, as a student being graduated at the beginning of World War I, as witness to the warfare of the twentieth-century ideologies and ruthless intolerance, as a teacher working in China when it was going through political upheaval. He once said that at Cambridge he turned from history to moral sciences because he "just couldn't bear history"; that too much of it "ought not to have happened"; that he always looked ahead, "even now" (1972).

Poetic truth, then, is tested through its "backwash effect" on us, as this truth confirms, denies, strengthens, and criticizes us. Sincerity is a kind of honesty we bring to whatever the response is doing to us; and to be sincere may be to reject what it is doing. For Richards, encountering this type of "translation" of the major writers of world literature is neither to abandon oneself to relativism nor to surrender oneself to dogmatic solutions.

I have not yet mentioned the word "beauty." After enumerating sixteen current definitions of this word (in *The Foundations of Aesthetics*, co-authored by James Wood and C. K. Ogden), Richards decided, for the sake of clarity, to avoid using it. Instead he psychologized it, defining "beauty" as *synaesthesis*, a harmonious state of thought and feeling together with an equilibrium which, while it prevented any immediate tendency toward action, did not imply a state of mental passivity or inertia: "Simultaneously, as another aspect of the same adjustment, our individuality becomes differentiated or isolated from the individualites of things around us. We become less 'mixed into' other things. As we become more ourselves they become more themselves, because we are less dependent upon the particular impulses which they each arouse in us" (*The Foundations of Aesthetics*, p. 79). We have an example of this experience described in his 1927 essay "The God of Dostoevsky." There he used "beauty" to name the complex feeling that results from contemplating Stavrogin in *The Possessed*, how one responds to the whole shaping of his development. "Stavrogin is there, not as an object lesson nor as an instance, he is there in order that we may imagine him and while imagining him, become more completely ourselves . . . We can express this change by saying that we feel in the presence of beauty. Not that Stavrogin or his suicide or his entanglements in the lives of the other characters are beautiful, far from it; but the whole thing has a combined effect upon the reader, and it is this effect which matters." Then, as a model, Richards offered the testament of Dostoevsky himself as to what matters. Late in his career Dostoevsky wrote that there was only "one cure, one refuge,—art, creative activity." "For those who are less creative," Richards wrote, "the answer is the same."

John Paul Russo

I Theory of Criticism

1 Art and Science

*His rereading of his first published utterances may well
stir in any author mixed feelings. I now scan this "Communication" with over fifty-five years of diminished confidence. But how can I now be sure what it was that young
man was so sure of? And how can I be certain that he was as
simple as he seems?*

*How would he have reacted, I wonder now, to a sugges-
tion that more may be learnt from views that are mistaken
than from those that are not? Would he have just replied
that the truth he writes of must be presupposed in any helpful use of "learn"?*

*While noting that he uses "signs," e.g., with some special
sense and not as I would now, I am nonetheless both
charmed and alarmed to find him saying several things that I
might have supposed occurred to me for the first time the
other day.*

The analogies discussed by Mr. Roger Fry (*Athenaeum*, June
6) between art and science are important both for the theory of art
and for the theory of science.[1] The problem is one which no one
need be ashamed to treat with caution. Yet it is a fair inference that
there must be some incompetence about a view of art or of science
which allows no clearer exposition of the relations between them
than that given in Mr. Fry's article. A more precise statement will
certainly run more risk of being wrong, but it will, on the other
hand, have a chance of being definitely and recognizably right.

Mr. Fry poses the question whether a theory which disre-
garded facts would have equal value for science with one which
agreed with facts. He sees no purely aesthetic reason why it should

Reprinted by permission of The Statesman & Nation Publishing Co., Ltd.,
from *The Athenaeum*, June 27, 1919, pp. 534-535.

not. The answer is, of course, dependent upon the kind of theory
and of facts which we have in mind. For instance, some of the ge-
ometries which are known quite possibly apply to given space;
others do not. But the facts which are relevant to the aesthetic value
of these theories are not facts of given space, but facts of implication, logical facts. No theory disregarding these would have any
aesthetic value. Again, generalizations proper, that is, inductions
from observed particulars, must, if they are to have aesthetic value
(whether they ever do have any or not is another matter), agree
with the particulars they cover. Hypotheses, on the other hand,
whether they agree with particular facts or not, may have value
through the inevitability of the deductions they contain, that is,
through the logical truths they embody.

The point is that the notion of truth is the decisive notion,
not only for the scientific value of theory, but for its aesthetic value
as well.[2] It is an indication of a fatal weakness in Mr. Fry's aesthetic
that it shuns this notion, the simple notion which is referred to
when we say that these remarks of mine are true or false. The reason for this avoidance is, I think, an undue nervousness lest by
making use of the truth he should be led into non-aesthetic considerations. Stupid people will of course use truth in narrow senses,
for presentational verisimilitude for instance, but so will they use
sensation, emotion, relation, and pleasure. Any aesthetic worth
considering must use truth as a main instrument. To avoid it
because in the past it has been foolishly misused is to be the sport of
reaction.

Truth (with falsity) is an attribute of propositions. Propositions are what are apprehended. They are not part of our minds, or
produced by our minds, but things to which our minds gain access.
They are not facts—for we may apprehend what is false, and then
there is no fact for us to apprehend. When a proposition is true,
there is, of course, a fact which corresponds, but still the proposition is other than the fact.[3] Nor is a proposition the same as the sensible form by which it is apprehended. A proposition is a complex
of terms in relation to one another. The terms can be called ideas
provided that no confusion is allowed between images and sensations which are in some sense "occurrences in our minds," and ideas
which are not in our minds in this sense, but things which by means
of these occurrences the mind gains access to, or thinks of.[4]

We do not, perhaps, ever apprehend propositions except by means of some sensible form, either of words or of imagery or of sensations. We need vehicles by which to approach and gain access to propositions. This is so of all propositions, those with which science as well as those with which art is most concerned. Now science is the systematic connection of propositions. It is, therefore, predominantly interested in those propositions whose connection with other propositions can be traced. The vehicles of science for this reason are composed of signs, words for the most part, arbitrarily assigned as names to defined ideas. Art, on the other hand, is interested in propositions for their own sake, not as interconnected.[5] To this is due the great difference between the ways in which art and science approach propositions, and between the propositions with which they are severally concerned. Those which are most worth contemplating for their own sake are not those whose connections we have the best hope of tracing.

The vehicles with which art approaches propositions are as a rule vastly complex systems, composed of sensations and images of all kinds *and* of the feelings and emotions provoked by and provoking these sensations and images. The whole experience which we call "contemplating a work of art" is the vehicle. Through this we apprehend a proposition. When the work of art is great the proposition is such that in no other way could we apprehend it, and our access to it is so complete that it appears perfectly self-evident and inevitable. It is this kind of knowledge, and not any more or less accidental pleasure which it may afford, which is properly called aesthetic satisfaction.

Now in science the only truths for which much aesthetic value has ever been claimed are those which belong to logic and mathematics, abstract and necessary truths. The explanation of this is to be found in the nature of scientific vehicles. Signs are perfect vehicles for abstract truths, but for no others. Thus it is not only the inevitability of these truths which gives value to their apprehension, but the accident that mathematical symbolism plays the part of the great artist in presenting them through forms by which we may gain most complete and perfect access to them.

The points of most fundamental difference between this view and Mr. Fry's are my substitution of the complete experience called "contemplating a work of art" for the "work of art" in the

narrower sense, my consequent inability to split this whole into
"work of art" and resultant pleasure or emotion, and my introduction of propositions. It is only, I hold, by reference to propositions
that any explanation can be given to the terms "inevitability" and
"unity," as applied in art.

The two theories superficially are violently opposed, yet I
am inclined to think that the real differences may not be great. I
cannot allow the language of Mr. Fry's second column, for
instance, but by a process of translation I can subscribe to the
thought.[6] Perhaps Mr. Fry may find himself in a similar position
with regard to this statement, or perhaps he may disapprove not
only of my terminology, but of the thought which I have chosen it
to convey.

2 Emotion and Art

I am amused to see what a strong taste for dryness in discourse this writer shows; he might be a shipwrecked sailor. No doubt the vogue on which Clive Bell's Art was then riding is the explanation. Neither these nor some parallel paragraphs elsewhere did anything toward checking such exuberances. I recall, however, that agreement on them was what first brought the authors of The Foundations of Aesthetics (1922) into collaboration and that we tried out, for a while, replacing "emotion" by "commotion" in discussion of the topic. Again, though, with no great outcome.

The nouns "feeling" and "emotion," the verb "to feel," the adjective "aesthetic," occur with a frequency of almost hypnotic effect in criticism and theory of art. It would be an excellent thing, then, if somebody understood what in the ordinary contexts these words refer to. It may cause surprise to hint that there can be any doubt about this. Certainly, most critics write as though they knew none, and, I suspect, most readers are too familiar with the phrases which contain them to ask what their meaning is. But a very little analysis of any assertion about works of art and emotions, especially if qualified by the term "aesthetic," will destroy this confidence.

Psychologists have, and will long have, difficulty in deciding whether feeling is a direct relation of the mind to its objects (such as, in some cases, is "thinking of"), or a quality of "thinkings of," or a quality of somatic experience causally correlated with and accompanying "thinkings of." I take this last assumption, the James-Lange view, but the points I wish to make

Reprinted by permission of The Statesman & Nation Publishing Co., Ltd., from *The Athenaeum*, July 18, 1919, pp. 630-631.

involved in art, we must deal with a problem. Are there two ways
of being a work of art, or only one? I hold that there is only one—
by being a communication of an import of a certain order. Others
hold also that there is only one way—by arousing certain specific
emotions, "aesthetic emotions," supposed to be peculiar to works
of art.[3] This view seems to me to have a small initial plausibility
which disappears completely upon analysis. For if works of art are
defined, as has been done, as just those things which do arouse
these emotions, then to say that they do so is a triviality; and if
they are not so defined, then how they come to arouse them must
be explained. For this reason it is usual to allude to works of art as
"significant." But "significant" as applied to art is either an idle
term or else comes under the more general notion of being a
vehicle, and only by being a vehicle does anything become a work
of art. There are, however, wide ranges of emotions which are
aroused by works of art and yet do not help to convey meaning.
Sometimes they interfere with the conveyance of meaning, and
then their arousal is a defect of the work of art. Sometimes they act
as a kind of bait to attract attention and to hold it through the
necessary intervals in the real performance. These may be called
irrelevant or mere emotions, no disparagement being intended.
Often they are delightful, and to be delightful is as respectable a
property as anything can possess. On the other hand, when they
are not delightful no excuse justifies their occurrence, since they do
not, as many undelightful things may do, carry meaning.

The two remaining modes in which emotion is aroused by
works of art raise no obvious problems. Emotion occurs in connection with the ease or difficulty with which we apprehend an
import. Apprehension of no matter what import, if performed with
ease, but not with too much ease, is accompanied by a lightening
and lifting emotion which may amount to joy. Bafflement, on the
other hand, in apprehending an import, which is suspected but not
grasped, may lead to distress. These effects are of interest in considering repetition and familiarity and resultant modifications of
emotion. Finally, to see any difficult thing done with success
arouses emotion. All technical triumph, if we appreciate it, does so,
whether the master is a juggler or a sonnet writer.

These are, I think, the six most important ways in which
emotions come into the contemplation of works of art. All of them

can be found in current criticism masquerading as aesthetic emotions. Is it too much to require that critics should make up their minds before writing to which of these they wish to refer, or, if to none of these, to which other case not stated here? I sometimes think that if this demand could be pressed, it would dry up for a long time our chief critical and aesthetical springs.

3 The Instruments of Criticism: Expression

This title contains my first public use of "instruments": a word which was to have a long run in my writings. I suspect that the piece took itself while being written as a sample of a treatment which might be attempted for a bookful of words: the key terms of the critical vocabulary. That this remained a dream, not an actuality, is not surprising. The first question asked [by Bonamy Dobrée and soon after this piece appeared] at the end of my first lecture in Cambridge proposed just such a compendium of clearly distinguished and cleaned-up critical terms in tidy array. Why not? A tentative answer, then as now, would be that we have not as yet the tools of analysis needed for the task. Think though of how lexicography and the art of synonymizing have advanced within living memory. Why should not men come to do as yet unthinkably better?

Criticism, which is the study of the aims and methods of literature and art in general, has not as yet turned with concentrated energy to the study of its own aims and its own methods. The omission is natural but unfortunate. Natural, because such considerations are properly the concern of the philosophers. All through, critics have had to beg, or, more often, to steal, their tools, the notions with which they work, from the workshops of philosophy. Unfortunate, because tools so acquired are easily misused. Criticism has always suffered, and suffers more than ever, from misuse of its principal instruments. Instances in even the best available criticism are not hard to find. In some cases the usage is so far sanctioned by custom that no experienced reader is in doubt as to what is meant. In these cases the usage does perform the fundamen-

Reprinted by permission of The Statesman & Nation Publishing Co., Ltd., from *The Athenaeum*, October 31, 1919, p. 1131.

tal function of speech: it does say something. But it is precisely these cases which are the most unfortunate.

Consider the following, chosen for no peculiarities, but as a typical specimen of a usage to which most critics will confess. Of a poem by Mr. Lawrence (*Athenaeum*, August 22, p. 784): "Here, we feel, is a poem which has a real reason for its existence; a compelling emotion has demanded expression, and in these twelve lines has received the poetical embodiment inevitably reserved for it."[1]

We all know what these remarks convey; something which in this case we may be eager to maintain is true and important, namely, that the poem in question is a good poem. We all can see if we will look that this is not what upon their face value they should convey. Hold them to their literal sense and they become confused mythology; the first remark combines, blurring them both, the different notions of causation and justification—a confusion not peculiar to criticism—the two, if distinguished, are supposed to go together; the speculative, the tentative, the necessarily dubious account of how the poem came to be what it is is supposed to explain why, being what it is, it is good. Most people hold that there is some connection, but to trace a connection between two things it is indispensable that you should be able to distinguish them. In the amplification which follows, this confusion is worse confounded by the occurrence of the word "expression," always a danger signal. The poem is suggested to be a kind of residuary and permanent analogue to the flood of tears which in this compound usage (where "expression of" = "result of + sign of + sympathetic arouser of") is the typical expression of emotion. The complexity of the analysis required brings out the point. No critic as such, however acute, however brilliant, however sound a *critic* he may be, is prepared to analyze out the causal, the significatory, the revelatory, and the symbolic elements contained in different proportions and degrees in the six or eight current usages of "expression." It is a tedious and not an easy task. Compare the senses in which a smile may be an expression of pleasure—noticing the total change in the causal elements included as the smile is spontaneous or calculated; a plan or a building, the expression of a purpose; a novel, the expression of life; a poem, the expression of a meaning or a truth; $a = b$, the expression of a mathematical relation. These are merely a few of the more salient steps; you may bridge the wide gap be-

tween a dog howling at the moon and Newton formulating his laws
with instances as closely graduated as you please, and all for current criticism would be cases of expression. What then can be done?
The best suggestion would seem to be that the term be banished
altogether from considered criticism, or retained only under the
heaviest suspicion. The causal elements in its meanings may be
stated in causal forms; for the other elements there are the terms "to
convey," "to suggest," "to reveal," "to present," "to mean," "to
mediate," and many others, some however tainted with the same
ambiguities. "Expression" stands for no notion which cannot be
more clearly, if less concisely, displayed by other means. But con-
ciseness is as often a vice as a virtue.

It will perhaps now be plain, in this case, why the accepted
usage of criticism is unfortunate. It is the acceptance which is most
unfortunate. For this complex bundle of notions, habitually
employed for the roughest purposes, contains many of the most
delicate and most indispensable of critical instruments. It is regret-
table that the great influence of Croce in recent years has been, in
this country at least, all in favor of this abuse. With rare exceptions
those who undergo his influence tender only a partial submission.
The Philosophy of the Spirit as a whole, as seen, for instance, in his
"Logic," leaves them unconvinced; but all the more readily they give
to the central tenet of his "Aesthetic," the tenet that "Art is Expression," independently interpreted in a fashion to which Croce would
object as vigorously as any of his opponents, an acceptance which
is disastrous in its consequences.[2] A reader of Croce has his choice.
He may—it depends upon temperament, not upon logic, because it
is a question of a choice between logics—choose to follow Croce,
but if so he ought to know what he is doing. Croce is far too careful
a philosopher for his readers to be able to pick and choose between
the parts of his doctrine. You cannot adopt his Aesthetic by itself
and handle it by the aid of a "commonsense" logic with the usual
distinctions without results abhorrent alike to Croce and to
Jevons.[3] But this is what for the most part has happened. The
critical world is filled with exoteric disciples of Croce, and their
doctrine, like most exoteric doctrine, is merely so much confusion
to be cleared away.

The further analysis of this intricate collection of relations
commonly compressed at haphazard within the term "expression"

is the most urgent of all the tasks of speculative criticism. All the chief problems, of the origins and determinants of works of art, of their functions, their methods, and their ends; the meaning for art of unity, universality, and objectivity; even the definition of the term "aesthetic" which so far, strangely enough, has received no definition which has any reference to any "aesthetic" problem—all wait upon this analysis. But so long as "expression" continues to be used in exactly the same way as the old-fashioned medical practitioner's "blunderbuss mixture" these problems will remain, so far as general criticism is concerned, unexplored, and the new powers and assurances which result from their exploration will remain unknown.

We must expect opposition to this abandonment of what is from a writer's point of view so useful a term. Whatever it may be which is to be said, the term "expression," if given a chance, will appear to say it. Actually, as is always the case with high-powered ambiguities, nothing is said. More than three meanings together form no meaning. But when the intended meaning is difficult to single out without error, we are all glad to turn on a word which like "expression" sprays out (expresses) such a wealth of meanings that the odds are great that the one we intend will be among them.

4 John Watson's Behaviorism

*When this account of Watsonian behaviorism appeared,
only a few enthusiasts—of whom that reviewer was not
one—were foreseeing what vast, dense, and tangled jungles
were to invade the then trim parks and gardens of psychology. They were a threat almost as great as the Amazon
floods of psychoanalysis—rapidly rising fifty years ago. It is
interestingly reassuring to reflect that both now seem period
movements, curious and valuable, but not now with much
influence on current designs. They are not nearly as inspir-
ing to contemporary experimental inquiries as the traditional picture they replaced, to which a notable return seems
to be under way. Nor do they offer us as much help in reflection on how Mind came about and what its business in the
cosmos may be.*

The piece was written fresh from trying (in The Meaning
of Meaning, *especially in chapter 3, "Sign-Situations," and
appendix B, and in* Principles of Literary Criticism, *chapter
11, "A Sketch for a Psychology") to fortify the old tripartite
account of the mind's doings ("thinking"-"feeling"-"trying")
with a parallel ("causes of"-"content"-"consequences") layout. What is the bond between a thought and what it is "of"?
That was the Cambridge question of 1918-22. Russell for a
time tried out an "effect theory": a thought being "of" what
it is or might be appropriate to.* The Meaning of Meaning
*made a thought be "of" its causes—in a special scrubbed-
cleaner sense of "cause". Hence the relevance of behaviorism. O. and R. remained mentalists, however, and this piece
was written to protect them from being thought to be among
Watson's converts.*

Behaviorism has not hitherto enjoyed so much success over
here as in America. This may be because our interest in systematic

Review of John B. Watson, *Behaviorism* (London: Kegan Paul, Trench,
Trubner, 1925). Reprinted from *New Criterion*, 4 (1926), 372-378.

psychology is comparatively undeveloped; or it may be because we are more familiar with materialist doctrines and therefore less easily shocked and stimulated by them. Although Watson himself is a good writer—he has force and clarity always, and, in this popular account of his system, liveliness as well; three enviable qualities—he does not please our academic minds, and his followers for the most part can only grind out the automatic springless undetachable type of sentence which is becoming an ever more wearisome affliction to those who court the sciences. For these reasons few English readers have more than a vague idea about behaviorism—the idea that it is all tiresome nonsense perhaps—or are aware what a tide has been flowing in American thought in the last few years. The vogue of behaviorism is certainly something to set against the antics of the fundamentalists. It is much to be hoped that this very vigorous and candid book will be widely read. Its crudities are so evident that they do not matter.

Like some other philosophies behaviorism contains a valuable part, and a part—the philosophical, more precisely, the ontological part—which will have to be discarded. The doctrine can be summed up briefly in two statements: (1) that psychology deals only with what can be observed; (2) that "consciousness" is a meaningless term. It is worthwhile to consider each of these statements closely.

When the behaviorist speaks of "observation" he means something which can be done by a photographic film or a spring balance just as well as by a human being. What is observed is one event, the observation of it is another; and what happens is merely that the observed event under suitable conditions is accompanied or followed shortly after by the observing event. Thus an observation is simply a causal sequence, and any event succeeding and varying with another might, on a behaviorist account, be said to observe it. But the particular observations with which the behaviorist is concerned are events in people, in human observers, which follow other events in other people or in themselves. Now it would appear at first sight that events in people and in ourselves could be divided into two kinds: those which are conscious, or are accompanied by consciousness—as when we hear a noise, have a tooth out, are frightened, lift a heavy weight, or deliberately choose between actions; and those which are not conscious, not accompanied by consciousness—as when by a series of muscular contractions we pass food through the stomach, balance ourselves, dilate the pupil, or perform a habitual involuntary gesture. This difference which has nearly always been considered very striking, unmistakable, and fundamental, is denied by strict behaviorists. And this denial is the novel point in their doctrine.

The grounds for it are simple, as simple as the denial itself. If we observe someone else, Watson points out, the only difference that we can detect between what he would claim as a conscious event in him and another which is unconscious, is that the activities in his muscles and glands and the happenings in his nervous system which accompany them are different in the two cases. *We* never observe any of this consciousness he speaks of; all we observe is changes in his behavior, including the vocal movements by which he speaks of it to us, and if he observes us *he* will never observe any consciousness in us. This is very true and the contrary view has never been held. But Watson concludes that consciousness is "a plain assumption just as unprovable, just as unapproachable, as the old concept of the soul" (*Behaviorism*, p. 5).

Compare now the case in which we observe ourselves. Let us stand before a mirror and, not to choose too violent an experiment, let us gently tweak a tuft of hair. No more than before do we observe any consciousness in the movement which we see, either in the tweaks or in the facial contractions which may follow if they grow more vigorous. Nonetheless, another series of changes is certainly taking place. Each tension of the skin is accompanied by these changes, as is each movement of the arm, and about these changes we are even more sure than about our actual movements. The problem, however, is whether these changes are known through *observation*, in the sense defined above.

If they are, we must admit that we do not yet know which events by varying with which others, are "observing" them. It is possible that conscious events only become conscious through causing other events which thus observe them—just as Watson's reactions observe an infant's reactions to a mouse—but by an inner observation. We do not yet know enough about the working of the brain to be certain that this does not happen. Yet it seems improbable that consciousness is a matter of observation in this sense. Conscious events certainly observe other events and are observed by them, i.e., they have causes and effects, but it must be doubted whether this character of being observed has anything to do with their consciousness, or whether consciousness, itself, if we allow ourselves for a moment to speak of it apart from the event to which it belongs, can be said to be observed.

The first half of behaviorism then, the contention that psychology deals only with what can be observed, excludes consciousness from its field of study, for we clearly cannot yet systematically observe it in this sense. And the behaviorists are left with a perfectly definite field for research, namely the observable responses which different situations excite and the history and interconnections of these situations and responses. Much valuable work is being done by them in this field. We shall consider some of their results later.

But the other half of behaviorism is less successful. Fortunately it is much less important. That consciousness is a meaningless term, that it "is neither a definable nor a usable concept; that it is merely another word for the 'soul' of more ancient times" (*Behaviorism*, p. 3), and that it is a pure assumption—all this does not follow from its non-observable nature. We may not observe consciousness, but we have it or are it (in some as yet undetermined sense), and in fact many of our observations of other things require it. In this respect the point of view of the behaviorist is hardly so much a point of view as a mistake.

Yet this denial is plainly not due merely to a blunder; it springs from much more interesting sources. There is, in fact, something very unsatisfactory about introspection as a scientific method. It often produces conflicting evidence which is difficult to criticize, and it requires a technique which is not strictly analogous to the other techniques of science. In physics or in physiology any able man can be trained to be a moderately good investigator, and any failings he may have (inaccuracy or clumsiness, for example) are easily detected. But in introspection the causes of discrepancies and the kind of training required to produce improvement are still very uncertain. Probably our psychological theories always exert disturbing influences. Thus men impatient of the slow task of clarifying problems, who like to see their work clear ahead of them in the form of definite questions to be answered by a definite technique, readily tend to despise introspection. This impatience rather than bad arguments is responsible for the negative side of behavior-ism. There is also the feeling that any adding in of "conscious" fac-tors which cannot be measured and do not obey the same laws as the rest of nature must play havoc with all hopes of satisfactory explanations; and this feeling is justified. An essentially physiologi-cal explanation ought not to be eked out by scraps of experience. It should remain physiology. But this is not—and here the behavior-ists made their mistake—the same thing as saying that there can be no study of consciousness or that the study may not provide valu-able indications in working out a physiological theory of behavior. In point of fact, it constantly so serves.

What is valid in the doctrine is the insistence upon external observation of behavior, as an indispensable method in psychol-ogy. But this is hardly an innovation. The more novel point is the demand that this behavior should be conceived in terms of itself and that we should exclude from our interpretations of it any but a limited number of physiological ideas. This self-imposed limitation need not be, but is, commonly confused by the behaviorist with the quite different point of the occurrence of consciousness. It is one thing to say "Let us try to describe and explain all human behavior entirely in terms of interaction between stimulus-situation and response" and quite another to say "Let us try to persuade people that they have no consciousness." The first is of real value, and likely, if it can be carried rather further, to change our views on many points, and possibly to bring out the role of consciousness in a new light. The second is merely waste of time.

The methods and conceptions so far developed by behavior-ism in its legitimate aspect are extremely simple. They derive very largely from Pavlov's conditioned reflex methods. If we sound a note just before feeding a dog we shall find after a number of repeti-tions that the note alone without any food causes a flow of saliva in him. This is known as "conditioning." We have substituted the note for the food as the stimulus to the salivation reflex. But in man reflexes often become conditioned after only one occurrence. And the situations in which human behavior takes place consist of uncountable numbers of different stimuli. Moreover, man's adjust-ment involves multitudes of responses, and the problem of strictly tracing out the process by which response depends upon situation is overwhelmingly complex. Even in Pavlov's laboratory, when the dog, a simpler animal, is shielded during the experiment in every possible way—sitting on a table in a dark soundproof room entirely separated from the experimenter who sees him only through a periscope and gives him the stimuli and measures his responses by indirect electrical means—it is still often difficult to get trustworthy results; a fly, for example, which was fluttering in a corner of the dark chamber quite away from the dog was found on one occasion to be upsetting the whole experiment. When the experimenter is not separated from the dog, accidents in his manner quite beyond his control play a hopelessly disturbing part in producing the responses obtained.

It is not very surprising, then, that the experiments of behaviorists with human beings in a more or less ordinary mixed environment should seem in comparison crude and their results doubtful. The conditions are a little better with infants, and it is here that the best work has been done. It was work which very badly needed doing, since the behavior of the very young has been for fairly obvious reasons much neglected.

One of Watson's most interesting observations is that the peculiar and recognizable response which is ordinarily known as fear—"a jump, a start, a respiratory pause followed by more rapid breathing with marked vasomotor changes" (changes in the blood flow, e.g., growing pale), sudden closure of the eye, clutching of hands, puckering of lips—is only elicited in "newborns" by two kinds of stimuli, loud noises and being suddenly left without support. But as is well known, a normal three-year old shows fear for a great number of other things. Here is a representative list from Watson: Darkness, and all rabbits, rats, dogs, fish, frogs, insects, and mechanical animal toys. Watson's thesis is that all these fears arise because at some time the appearance of a dog, for example, has coincided with either a loud noise or being knocked over (loss of support). The dog later, when it merely approaches, causes the fear, just as the note caused Pavlov's dog's mouth to water. This fear then gets transferred to other situations which the infant groups with it, and so on. Thus Albert B., eleven months old, who had an (experimentally) conditioned fear of a white rat, showed fear five days later of a rabbit, a dog, a fur coat, cotton wool, but not of bricks (*Behaviorism*, p. 128). Evidently this view has no use for "instincts" except in the sense of initial characteristic responses to characteristic situations. But these, as Watson points out, are shown by a boomerang, which when properly thrown behaves quite unlike an ordinary stick. The child is a very complicated kind of boomerang, and its instincts merely the result of its structure at birth.

Now this, it will be realized, is, if it is correct, an extremely important contribution. Watson finds in children who have not been emotionally conditioned no such fears of dogs or darkness, and if this is established, a prospect of a comparatively fearless humanity is opened up if only we can manage our nurseries aright. There is, however, the possibility that maturation may introduce complications. Even though loud noises and loss of support be the only stimuli which cause fear immediately after birth, it may be the case that later on, quite apart from conditioning, other stimuli come to have the same effect merely through the infant's growth. Maturation certainly plays some part, and some very definite responses only appear at a very late age. The specific sexual responses appearing with adolescence are an obvious instance.

The exact truth in this matter will only be discovered by further experimental research, and Watson is undoubtedly to be congratulated for the part he has played in furthering such experimentation. He has come to consider that the unlearned (unconditioned) beginnings of emotional reactions are three in number. Fear, elicited as above, Rage, elicited by hampering of bodily movements, and Love, elicited by stroking of the skin, tickling, gentle rocking, and patting. Love responses include "those popularly called 'affectionate,' 'good-natured,' 'kindly' . . . as well as the responses we see in adults between the sexes. They all have a common origin" (*Behaviorism*, p. 123).[1]

Watson further points out that since the same object (say a parent) may in one situation become a conditioned stimulus for fear, in another for rage, and in another for love, these three original groups of responses can easily become complicated through experience. Only he does not use the word "experience." To do so would be to link his labors up with those of more traditional psychologists. His extremely provoking attitude toward academic psychologists and toward psychoanalysts alike, amusing and inspiriting though it is when we realize that his work is likely to be of great assistance to them and is not in conflict with theirs, is to be regretted if it debars them, as it may, from taking due notice and advantage of it. They have already shown too often the natural tendency to reply in kind. It may be suggested that these very different views and methods are not irreconcilable. Nothing so readily gives a beginner in psychology a sense of helplessness and annoyance as the existence of violently opposed views which he more often than not suspects to be mere verbal variants. And indeed Watson's "boomerang" analogy shows that he is not far removed from the position of Koffka as regards instinct (cf. *The Growth of the Mind*, p. 106),[2] while his account of the conditioning of the love-emotion brings him very near to the important group of psychoanalysts represented by Kempf and Frink (cf. Gordon, *Personality*, chapter 12).[3] The fundamental divisions among psychologists are often less serious than they appear.

5 Belief

The first page of this reads to me now like an echo of Niels Bohr's drastic declaration (Dialectica, II, 318) quoted below in essay 12 with reference to Moore on philosophical difficulties. This is the piece that comes nearest to giving a clarifying unity to the group of essays gathered here under Theory of Criticism. It shows, moreover, what an impact life in Peking was having on its author. I think now he may have found rather easy ways out of the "imaginative assent" problem. But at that time he and the world had not had to watch what happened with Hitler. Nor had the moral apathies (exemplified by the general public acquiescence in the Vietnam wars) numbed the hopes of Western man. This decades-away slant may have been overly optimistic, but it did imply a call for action and was not so easily satisfied with insulted revulsion.

Few writers on general or abstract matters altogether escape a suspicion that there is something wrong with their whole traditional technique. They are tempted to ask themselves—not at their foggiest but at their clearest moments—whether they do really know what they mean. And the answer is not made more comforting by having it constantly brought home to their notice that, even when they *do*, other people do not. The inner history of every honest controversy is full of ghastly surprises to each and all of the disputants. Even our most trusted words, if we try to use them with precision, are found to carry meanings which ramify bewilderingly. Used vaguely they seem clear and single enough and communication seems to follow easily. It is only as we strain after increased clarity and precision, only when we try to be really careful and

Reprinted by permission of the publisher from *Symposium*, 1 (1930), 423-439.

exact in our statements, that we discover that we are not being understood. And it is then that the doubt whether we really ourselves know what we mean becomes insistent.

It may be that this effort after precision is a misuse of language, that analytic procedure beyond a certain point asks too much from it. Mr. Wells, I think, once suggested that certain distinctions we attempt to make might be really like trying to cut a molecule in two with a penknife.[1] Many people must have regretted that Mr. Wells has never applied his genius further to these matters. For it seems almost immoral to stop at this point with the mere suggestion that we can go no further. We ought at least to try to explore the limits of our field of possible discourse. Is there a point when the question "Do I know what I mean?" ceases to be applicable? Are "mean" and "know" themselves too clumsy in their meanings for the question to remain sense? If so we ought at least to try to find out when this point comes in the various subjects, if only because by the attempt itself we should learn a great deal about the workings of our minds.

But it is more likely that the difficulty of communicating through refined intellectual language is not so insurmountable, that it is due merely to an undeveloped technique. In any case, it is certain that the technique for identifying, arranging, and communicating meanings can be developed much further and until we have done what we can in this direction it is foolish to let a premature scepticism hold us back.

As an illustration of the more obvious possibilities in exploring and controlling ambiguity I have taken here the word "belief." It is central enough and important enough in many discussions to make the word worth study for its own sake. But the experiment may have a wider interest as an example of procedures which need to be applied to most of our pivotal terms—"knowledge," "expression," "thought," "mental," "love," "quality," "form," "order," and "truth"—to name a few at random.[2] The attempt, I am sure, is woefully inadequate as an illustration, but I have not tried to carry it very far. To make a proper job of it we should need first to make similar provisional surveys of the other words in the semantic and logical family to which "belief" belongs and then proceed by a comparative method. Wide comparisons alone will clear up these matters—to the extent to which they can be cleared up at present. The following notes are intended to do no more than call more attention to some types of problems too little considered.

It is certain that we do not all use the word "belief" in the same way. It is even pretty certain that we none of us use it consistently. Let me begin by separating some of the differences which make discussion of "belief" so awkward.

First come what I may call the Logico-grammatical Ambiguities: We use the word sometimes for the *object* which we believe; sometimes for the *state or act of mind* which believes that object; sometimes for the *relation* between the mind and the object it believes. "My belief" may mean "What I believe" (belief-object), or it may mean "My state or act of mind when believing" (belief-state), or it may mean "My relation to what I believe" (belief-relation). Sometimes it may mean all these together. In what follows, when I use the word "belief" without addition, I am using it in this wide and vague sense.

So we get three main sets of problems and resultant ambiguities:

1. Problems concerning *belief-objects.* For example, is what we believe a statement, a form of words, a proposition of some sort, a meaning, an act of the mind, or a state of affairs? And can we believe objects which are not capable of statement? The point is of some importance since so many of our most interesting beliefs seem to be concerned with ineffable objects, with mysteries. Can we have an object of belief which is not asserted to exist or even to be possible?

These questions are clearly not independent of the views we take as to Belief-States and Belief-Relations.

2. *Belief-states.* Here are some of the problems and ambiguities: Is the difference between a state of mind which is, or contains, a believing, and one which does not, a difference of degree? Or is this difference a question of the presence or absence of some unique component? If so, what kind of thing is the unique component? Is it, as William James at one time suggested, a certain kind of feeling, reality-feeling, like trust or familiarity, for example? Or, as he suggested too, is it a special kind of fiat of the will? Or does the difference consist, as he again suggested, not in any unique component but in a certain connection between the belief-state and action, "a readiness to act" according to the picture of things presented to the belief-state?[3]

These are only some specimens of belief-state problems. There are obviously many others.

3. *Belief-relations.* Here we come to the problem, "How direct and immediate is the mind's connection with its objects?" If we take the view that the only link between the mind and things other than its own states is through sensations—the view that all concern with other things is not immediate, but mediated by sensations which are used to stand for other things—we shall probably have to reject any suggested special belief-relation. We shall have to say that the mind is related to its object (according to one meaning of "object"; there are others, or course) in just the same way whether belief is occurring or not. Now this view that all knowledge is mediated through sensations is the view that physiology suggests to us and nearly all modern psychology assumes. But we must not forget, above all when we are considering *what people mean* by "belief," that traditional thinking has not assumed this view, but has supposed that the mind can be in direct connection with all kinds of supersensible objects. With other minds, for example, mathematical objects, and Truths.

I have had to formulate these problems rather crudely to save space. I only wanted to remind the reader that behind the logico-grammatical ambiguity of "belief"—standing as it may for belief-objects, belief-states, belief-relations—are these three sets of problems, no one of which can be handled apart from the others. The rich possibilities of ambiguity will be evident.

The separation of these three sets of problems brings up a very disturbing set of historical possibilities. It allows us to imagine three different ways in which the beliefs (in the large inclusive sense) of past ages and alien cultures may have differed. We all agree that belief-objects have often changed. We do not believe the things that the witch-trial judges believed. We perhaps do not believe those kinds of things. Perhaps the types of belief-objects have changed frequently in human history. But it is equally possible that when men in the past have said "I believe" they have been actually doing something different as well as meaning something different from any of the varied things we may be doing and meaning when we say "I believe" now. And it is possible that when the Chinese use one of their equivalents for "I believe" they may be doing and meaning something different again. Nobody can say at present just how likely such differences are. We have no technique yet for handling the question. But a shift in the meaning of belief would be of such immense importance for a historian of cultures that the very possibility is a strong argument for working toward such a technique.

Another point here is perhaps also of some importance—the special dependence of belief-problems upon the Theory of Knowledge. If we formulate these problems in the ways which come most naturally to Western philosophical language we find, each time, that the problem of cognition steps into the first place. Before we can believe something it must, we suppose, be somehow cognitively present to us. We must know it, in some sense, before we can do anything more about it. What we *feel* about it and what we *will* about it tend to seem to us later problems. *It*, whatever it is, must first, we assume, be present or before the mind in some kind of cognitive awareness. We couldn't either feel or will unless there was a cognitively apprehended *it* already present for us to feel or will about.

This assumption may easily be doubted. It is very deeply rooted in tradition and in language but experience does not always bear it out very clearly. The psychology of infancy (if one can as yet appeal to such a thing) seems to make it doubtful; so does animal psychology. So do certain morbid states of anxiety and ecstasy. And, I think, anyone who has much to do with poetry is likely to doubt it. A direction of the will and a development of feeling often seem to me in reading poetry to come *before* any sufficient cognitive apprehension of an object upon which this will and feeling are directed. However, nobody should at present be sure about anything like this. I only wish to make the suggestion that one may be unduly biased by tradition and language in the West toward giving cognition too much importance. Nearly all Western philosophers, we must remember, have been professional *thinkers*, not professional feelers or professional willers, and it would not be very surprising if men whose business it was to know things, or to try to know them, should tend to make knowing more important than it need be made. Knowing retains, of course, another importance as our best means of control.

The point is not new but it comes up with special insistence when we try to give precision to our notions of belief.

Passing now to some other ambiguities, here are two different ways in which we can explore or classify uses of the word "belief":

A. With regard to the field of discourse in which it is used. For example, we can divide beliefs into everyday beliefs, scientific beliefs, mathematical beliefs, religious beliefs, philosophical beliefs, poetic beliefs, and so on. The sense in which I believe that my watch is a little fast or that I am in China is probably not the same as the sense in which I believe that some stars are millions of light years distant, and this again is probably not the same as the sense in which I might believe in the multiplication table, or in the Resurrection of the Body, or in Plato's Doctrine of Ideas, or in Milton's view that the Fall of Eve and Adam was due to their triviality of mind and their too intermittent interest in philosophy.

The difficulties of this kind of classification are obvious. The fields merge into one another and inside each we have to make distinctions quite as important as those that divide the fields. For example, what might be called Scientific Beliefs seem to be a very mixed lot, varying in ways other than in degree only. Also no one knows at present how much philosophy is lingering in science, how much in mathematics.

This way of approach is chiefly useful because it again forces us to recognize how much the word changes its meaning from context to context and from mind to mind.

B. But this change becomes still more evident if we try another method and examine some uses of the word "belief" by considering the words which are used in opposition to it. Thus we have:

1. Belief as contrasted with knowledge, the rational acceptance of established fact. E.g., "What used to be questions of belief are now matters of common knowledge."

2. Belief as contrasted with mere opinion. E.g., "I've been told he used to do that, and, what's more, I believe it." "You may prove it to me as much as you like but I don't (won't) believe it."

3. Belief as contrasted with superstition. E.g., "It's not belief: it's only superstition."

4. Belief as contrasted with doubt. "I try to believe it, but I can't."

5. Belief as contrasted with imagination.

All the first three uses, in their very different ways, seem to be concerned with the grounds of belief.

In (1) when the grounds become complete and sufficient the acceptance ceases to be called belief.

In (2) unless the grounds are sufficient (are more than hearsay and sometimes more than logic based on observed fact) the word "belief" is rejected.

In (3) insufficient grounds may be the reason for rejecting the use of the word but often the nature of the belief-object also comes in. People sometimes call other people's beliefs "superstition" just because they don't approve of what they believe. Often too an objection to the character of the belief-state (greed or desire too much present) is responsible for the use of the word "superstition" in place of "belief." The belief-superstition antithesis is perhaps more often emotive than intellectual. It has been used for all sorts of purposes by all sorts of people with corresponding changes in the sense of "belief."

The same applies to the belief-doubt antithesis (4). Those to whom doubt is a virtue and those to whom it is a weakness will not be using "belief," either in the same sense (if by "sense" we understand the intellectual content) or with the same total meaning (if we include in the total meaning all the varied functions of the word).

The belief-imagination opposition (5) works on a different principle from these others. When people contrast belief with mere imagination, the opposition is often between the mere presence of an object to the mind, and the questioning (doubting and disbelieving as well as believing) which the mind can exercise upon its objects. This, at the moment, to me, is the most interesting of all oppositions. Certainly one of the most important tasks which a theory of knowledge would have to tackle would be a demarcation of the fields in which this questioning-doubting-disbelieving-believing activity is relevant from those in which it is not. Since the general problem has arisen for me out of a definite literary problem I can perhaps best start from the literary problem. It is this: There are many great poems which seem to have sprung from and to embody beliefs. Can we understand them without ourselves accepting and holding these beliefs? The presence of the belief in the poet seems to have been a condition of the poem. Is its presence in the reader equally a condition for successful reading—for full understanding?

Either answer, yes or no, to this question brings in great difficulties. If we say yes, then clearly we can understand very little poetry—only the poetry in which we can find our own beliefs. But we do seem to appreciate poetry containing beliefs that are quite unacceptable to us. On the other hand, if we answer no, it becomes very hard to say what our appreciation is, whether without believing the beliefs we are really submitting enough to the poet, and whether we ought to say we are understanding him. This negative view easily turns into a barren aestheticism.

Doubtless, in fact, much of our appreciation of the literature of other ages is of a shallow kind. But we ought not to acquiesce in this unless we must. There is something a little ridiculous, at least, in admiring only the rhythms and "word harmonies" of an author who is writing about the salvation of his soul. It is like admiring the "form" or the tassels of a Chinese executioner's sword without recognizing the object for what it is. We may agree that we should escape from such arty superficialism if we can.

There seem indeed to be several ways out for those who want to use them. One is by practicing temporary belief. We might take up the beliefs in the poem for the time being and drop them as soon as we had finished with it. This seems a very discreditable resource, and I am not recommending it. Certainly there is something covered by the term "belief" which is immensely important and not to be played with. It will be better to try to frame some definitions with which to ask whether we do not (or, rather, should not) believe the poem's beliefs in one sense and refrain from believing them in another and so escape the literary dilemma.

It is not very difficult to think of several pairs of meanings which might do this for us. On the other hand I have found it very difficult indeed to get anyone to accept and use the pair of meanings I suggest, and I am personally inclined to think that the fusion (or confusion) of this pair of meanings into one is an essential feature in the structure and mode of operation of the traditional Western mind.

Here are the two meanings. I can put them best perhaps in terms of James's "readiness to act as though it were so" theory of belief. If we define belief as "readiness to act as though it were so—or in accordance with the picture of things we have before us" we obviously have to consider what we mean by "act" very carefully. Action may be specific or very general—ranging from such general action as leading the good life to such specific action as is involved in catching or missing a train. Again, action may be overt and observable, or hidden. Compare such overt action as is shown by a physicist when he adjusts his apparatus and looks to see whether a particular spot appears inside a particular square on his photographic plate with the hidden action which is taking place when someone makes a moral or aesthetic decision. Thirdly, the picture of things that we have before us may very narrowly and closely determine our action or only control it in a most remote and indirect general way. Compare the very definite control that chemical theory has over the chemist's actions in his laboratory with the indefinite influence which a moral or religious outlook exercises upon conduct in general. In which connection the importance of ritual as giving a definite set of actions determined by the view may be remarked upon.

I think we can agree that there is room inside James's definition for very different kinds of belief. But there is yet one other difference between actions in their connection with the views that prompt them, and this difference is still more important for my purpose. It is the difference in the degree to which success or failure in the action can affect the view which prompts it.

For example, if I have the view that my train leaves at three minutes to three and actually it leaves at two minutes to two, the failure of my action in trying to catch it at once changes my view. In contrast to this, philosophical and religious beliefs do not and, I think, cannot come into this kind of close testing contact with what actually happens. They do not entail precise and specific consequences and therefore cannot be themselves upset by the failure of their consequences to correspond with actuality.

What I suggest is that this difference in the form of action prompted by a view and in the backwash effect on the view of success and failure in the action is enough to give us two quite distinct meanings of "belief." Whether they are introspectively distinguishable is another matter. As I have defined them they would appear not to be, but many of our meanings, though indistinguishable, are really different, as their consequences show. "Readiness to act as though it were so" will in the case of everyday and scientific beliefs entail fairly clearly defined *junctures* with actualities which are in no sense within our sphere of control. "Readiness to act as though it were so" in the case of philosophical and religious beliefs will involve no such junctures—it will be a matter of the development of thought, feeling, will, and conduct in accordance with one picture of the world or another. But at no point will there be entailed an act or an assertion sufficiently definite for actuality to test its truth or falsehood. Such belief, it is true, may be successful or unsuccessful and so be said to be tested by experience. But the success will be in ordering the growth of the personality or in aiding the good life. It will not be success in meeting definite situations and failure to order the personality will not discredit the view in the way that failure to correspond with a definite situation disproves an everyday or scientific belief.

By distinguishing these two kinds of belief—let me call them *verifiable belief* and *imaginative assent*—I think it is possible to clear up the literary dilemma. If the kind of belief the poet puts into poetry and we must receive from it is verifiable belief, then clearly we can understand very little poetry. On the other hand, if it is imaginative assent that we are talking about, *that* is quite clearly asked for and indeed part and parcel of the understanding of good poetry. And there is in practice nothing to prevent our giving this imaginative assent to all kinds of different views. Only imaginative assent is needed, or, as a rule, possible in reading the poem, and the difficulty in giving it in the cases we are considering seems to come from our habit of treating it as though it were verifiable belief. We have secondary derived attitudes toward verifiable beliefs and we take them up with regard to imaginative assents also. Hence, I think, these difficulties; but of course there are many other difficulties in understanding poetry.

The distinction if it is valid appears to have wide bearing and drastic consequences. Imaginative assents, unlike verifiable beliefs, are not subject to the laws of thought. We can easily hold two or more mutually incompatible views together in imaginative assent if their incompatibility is merely logical. I think it is relevant to remark here how often religions and philosophies present us with self-contradictions as their central secrets. Imaginative assents are not ordered logically—they have another principle of order based on the compatibilities of movements of the will and the feelings and the desires. This order it is the business of serious poets to explore and follow.* But we know, I should say, hardly anything about it as yet in terms of theory; though we know a good deal in terms of practice.

If they are not subject to the laws of thought, it seems doubtful whether they can be said to be either true or false—in the sense in which "true" and "false" apply to verifiable beliefs. A verifiable belief is shown to be false by failure at its juncture with actuality. An imaginative assent cannot be shown to be false in this way. Suppose we define "true" and "false" for verifiable belief as correspondence or non-correspondence with actuality; shall we be able to apply this sense to imaginative assents? The question is very difficult. We do no doubt often feel that the views to which we give imaginative assent or dissent are true or false in this sense, that the picture does represent or misrepresent something which really is so or otherwise. We say to ourselves, "Although I can't prove or disprove this view of the universe or of man in a scientific way, yet it must really be a view, right or wrong, about something, not just an imaginative picture of nothing." And so traditionally these views have nearly always been asserted or denied.

And yet if we look closely at what actually happens at the juncture of a verifiable belief with actuality and consider the kind of correspondence that occurs there, I think we shall grow very doubtful indeed whether to use the word "correspondence" in connection with unverifiable assents is more than an unjustifiable metaphor.

We must remember that in an ordinary or scientific belief at its juncture with reality only a small part of it is actually verified. It nearly always contains a great deal of imaginative material, scaffolding, metaphysics, theoretical constructions, and interpretations which are not tested and are not involved in the correspondence. Physicists seem to be coming to a remarkable agreement upon this point—that what is actually established or able to be established is only a small part of the whole picture they use in thinking over

---

*I use "poet" here in an unusual sense. I mean a man who endeavors to develop his vision of life and utter it with the resources of literature.

their problems. And many of them are prepared to admit that the rest of their world picture is not a picture of anything but only a piece of intellectual machinery.

It seems to me very likely that nearly all the rest of our views, metaphysical, philosophical, ethical, psychological (apart from those parts of psychology which are neurological observations under another name) will have to be treated in the same way, as machinery. Not as intellectual machinery only—useful in ordering our observations—but as the indispensable imaginary means of ordering the rest of our lives.

Against this proposal to regard our philosophical, religious, and psychological views as not views at all, not pictures of anything, there is a strong habitual resistance. To many people, and to everybody sometimes, the suggestion will seem nonsense. This is that fusion (or confusion) of a pair of meanings I spoke of earlier as perhaps an essential feature of our traditional mentality. Perhaps I am giving you an instance of it myself here, in raising the question "Do imaginative assents correspond with reality?" Perhaps to say that they do and to say that they do not are equally nonsense, since by the nature of the case the juncture with actuality by which we define correspondence does not occur.

An ancient mystery so closely linked with all the sanctions of our lives is not, I know, to be reduced to a game of definition dodging. And I am not pretending to have solved the problem of belief above but only to have offered some suggestions toward finding out what it is.

People in the past have spent an enormous amount of the best human energy discussing what we should believe and why and when. But very little attention, comparatively, has been given to the questions "What are we doing when we believe?" and "What do we mean by belief?" The reason is, I suggest, that thinkers traditionally have not sufficiently considered language. They have used it but not examined it. With this instance of "belief" I have wished to suggest that the proper technique for discussing all such subjects must pay much more attention to the theory of meanings. We have not developed the means for controlling our instruments nearly as far as we need to. Even with such an important word as "belief" the range of its ambiguities in different contexts has not been plotted. And the same is true of all the key words in philosophy and in the psychological and social sciences. We have not worked out a plan of their possible meanings and until we do so the progress of these subjects will go on being backward. At present it is becoming increasingly difficult for anyone, who is not linguistically naive, to hold any philosophical position—not because of objections to it but because he cannot be certain what it is. I have sketched, in the paragraphs above, what may look like a philosophic position, but I don't hold it. I have had to use in sketching it too many words whose meanings I am not clear about. The cure for this sad predicament is, I am sure, in devoting to the comparative study of ranges of meanings the energy we now give to reconstructing and redestroying philosophical systems, or to following, as best we can through the fog of ambiguities, the history of these changes. And there is this finally to be added. We might as well gain through this comparative study of meanings so much control over the actual workings of our minds that our traditional psychology, theory of knowledge, logic, and methodology would look silly. Language, after all, *with its ambiguities* gives the closest imprint of our minds that will ever be available to us. We have been using it long enough *incuriously*, as primitive man used his sticks and stones, his plants and animals: it is time for us to study it with the care that the geologists and biologists have given to their material. There is good reason to think that the results might be equally surprising.

6 Between Truth and Truth

This essay has done for me now three things. It has brought back the admiration and regard I have felt for J. M. Murry ever since I wrote the first three items of this collection for him while he was editing the Athenaeum. *Second, it has reported my position on the key problem before I had—with* Interpretation in Teaching *and* The Philosophy of Rhetoric—*my severest sustained bout of study of it. Third, it has made me reread "Ode on a Grecian Urn" and compare what I wrote of it in* Mencius on the Mind *as an offshoot of this essay with what I tried to say much later in various lecture and television presentations printed for the first time in the essay "Beauty and Truth."*

Mr. Middleton Murry's lucid *Note* in the October *Symposium* seems to call for some further remarks.[1] He is certainly right in pointing to the expression "Beauty is Truth, Truth Beauty" as a revealing test of the different ways in which men will use words in their *readings* of poetry. It is tempting to take these readings as a test of their *theories* of poetic language, its difference from prose; but to do this we should, I think, have to forget that our theories are derived from our experience with poetry, and ought not to interfere with it while we are reading. Nor can solitary acts of interpretation be fairly taken as indicating our theories. A man may have an admirable theory of poetry, and yet fail to act up to it. And conversely a poor theorist may be a very fine reader.

Nonetheless our general theories of language do influence our reading. Especially when they are unconscious—forgotten or implicit assumptions rather than explicit provisional hypotheses.

Reprinted by permission of the publisher from *Symposium*, 2 (1931), 226-241.

Indeed one of the reasons for trying to drag the theory of meaning into the daylight of discussion is that it may help to free us from the spell of unconscious assumptions about it which are actually an impediment to interpretation. Interpretation both of poetry and of prose.

Prose rather than poetry, indeed, most needs discussion and improved interpretation now. For, as a rule, we leave our minds freer with poetry, if we read it at all. Only when the poetry has a novel technique, or there is a sudden change in method, as in this case so well described by Mr. Murry, are we shocked into a more deliberate and arbitrary interpretation which lets our unconscious assumptions come in embarrassingly to our rescue. But with prose of an argumentative kind we are always trying to "grasp" the author's ideas and grasp them firmly enough to put them safely where they belong in our mental schemas. And if, through ambiguity in his language, they elude our grasp, or call for two or more mental hands, we do not, as with poetry, count this an added richness, we complain about it, publicly, and privately take note of the equivocation to use it later as a weapon in discussion.

The fact that the prose of discussion, with the habit of thought behind it, is grounded, if not in an instinct, at least upon a tradition of combativeness is extremely important. Poetry is based upon suggestion, perhaps, but prose upon coertion. The difference is hidden where we cover them both, as primers of composition do, with the blanket term "persuasion." But persuasiveness as a literary merit in argumentative prose is happily beginning to be regarded with suspicion; perhaps through the example of scientific prose which, at its best, is eminently unpersuasive. It is a survival from rhetoric, from the mentality of Roman pleaders and from later ages in which controversy was political in spirit, or theological in the sense of presupposing a revelation. Our task in this age is to understand, not to combat, and as we realize this the temper and technique of criticism is changed. But to break away from this argumentative tradition is difficult. I write in a country (China) which well supplies an allegory, for there are still plenty of War Lords in the Republic of Letters.

These remarks are not apropos of Mr. Murry, they rather concern rival possibilities in ways of discussing what he says. Indeed, on a topic which rarely gives any writer the pleasure of feeling that he has been understood and so is being replied to, Mr. Murry's criticism of my assertions about pseudo-statements has been most welcome and sustaining. On the other hand, such is the difference between his use of language and that toward which I strive that a major assault upon his positions as, to me, he enunciates them, is not easy to avoid. The cannon, in fact, are itching to go off and are kept in check only by a belief that his real positions are not those he seems to hold but in fact at many points not easily distinguishable from my own.

The pivot of the opposition between our doctrines is, I am confident, in our attitude to words in prose. In Mr. Murry's prose, his feeling toward what he is writing of and his sense of how his readers have felt toward it and should feel, are factors of great importance. As important perhaps as, if not more important than, his sense of the structure of the idea, or thought, he is conveying. To me, so far as my conscious intention can ensure it, the structure of the thought is all-important. I have no resources comparable with his for conveying feeling, and find the job of following and controlling the implications of the thought more by itself than my verbal means can achieve. In this neglect of feeling on my part, I find some of the causes of misunderstanding between us.

Mr. Murry has himself pointed out a good example. In choosing the term "pseudo-statement" I was certainly not intending any contemptuous nuance. I took it on the analogy of pseudonym or pseudoscope or pseudopod—for use as a mere neutral technicality, to stand for a form of words which looks like a statement but should not be taken as one. It should not be taken as one because, if it is, the most important point about statements, their truth or falsity (in the sense of their correspondence or non-correspondence with what they are of) becomes relevant to the state of mind which ensues on contemplating them. Taken as a statement it may be true or it may be false; it is not necessarily false although in fact it is likely to be so.

Here, and I think attention to a felt derogatory flavor in "pseudo" has contributed, is one point of misunderstanding between Mr. Murry and myself. For me a pseudo-statement may perfectly well be true; but, for him, I had implied that it was equivalent to a false statement. For me the interesting opposition was between uses of words whose truth or falsity (in the correspondence sense) is (or should be) irrelevant to their effect, and uses of words where truth and falsity are relevant. For him my opposition turned into one between true and false statements. Rejecting my antithesis, he seems to me to put very nearly in its place a certain antithesis between statements taken literally and taken "metaphorically." Very nearly in its place, in the sense of serving many of the same purposes—those of enabling us to use statements, *without believing them*, as "descriptions" or "expressions" of "conditions of the organism," otherwise not able to be "described" or "expressed."

But the meanings of these words need very close and careful attention. I must come back to them shortly. First let me try to state what I understand Mr. Murry to say as to the "metaphorical" use of statements. I must ask his pardon, if, in changing his formulations at certain points, I misrepresent him. Certain "statements" (of which "Ripeness is all" and "God is Love" are examples) may be taken in either of two ways: literally, in which case the question of their truth or falsity comes up, or metaphorically, in which case they are neither true nor false. When taken literally they are considered in isolation, their component words are treated as names of objects and their meaning is an arrangement of these objects in conformity with the syntax of the statement. When taken "metaphorically," they are "reinstated in the total statement of which they are part." I take this to mean that they are used (with a different kind of meaning) by the contemplating mind as a necessary and indispensable part of the meaning-structure through which a certain condition of the mind can (alone?) be attained. I am not sure however whether I understand Mr. Murry here. Perhaps in such a formulation I am making the "metaphoric" statement too much "a magical talisman by which emotions and attitudes can be efficaciously organised"—something Mr. Murry expressly insists it is *not*. I confess that this magical description does seem to me to fit the facts of poetry rather well, if we clear the sneer out of it by taking it literally and making use of what we now know about magic. It is not a description, however, which fits the feelings we have toward such "metaphoric" statements and this I take it was Mr. Murry's meaning in setting it aside as a description.

His formulation of the relation of the subsidiary statements —which may be untrue—to the total statement, which is "in a very real and practical sense 'true,' " is the point that I find obscurest. I have an impression that it is here that our different uses of language most come between us. To me the words "total statement" as he uses them seem rather to evoke a feeling of respect for what the metaphoric subsidiary statement, in its full context, *does*, rather than to inform us of what this is. I genuinely share the respect, but am anxious to inquire into what it does—in other words, in just what sense is it (the metaphoric statement) a statement? and what is it a statement about?

For Mr. Murry's view of this question we have to consider his examples. He takes John Clare's description of the primrose

> With its crimp and curdled leaf
> And its little brimming eye,

as well as three lines of Catullus and a passage from Meister Eckhart.[2] Each of these are total statements, as I understand him, in the sense that they accurately describe something: the John Clare lines, an object; the other two, experiences. "All objects and all experiences are unique. When their uniqueness is adequately communicated, then, no matter what unverifiable subsidiary statements are incorporated into the language by which they are communicated, the total statement is in a very real and practical sense 'true.'" "When we understand the statement in its totality, we have no difficulty in accepting it for true." These quotations I take to mean that to be a "total statement" is to communicate adequately the uniqueness of an object or experience; and further that such "total statements" are in all cases "true" in some sense, and that this "truth," once we have fully understood the statement, is recognized without further investigation.

Three points in this give me hesitation. "Uniqueness" is the first. I wonder whether Mr. Murry means anything more by the uniqueness of anything than the relevant characteristics of it? Uniqueness in a strict sense means, I suppose, the characters which distinguish a thing from all other things. In this sense it is often the least important or interesting characters of a thing which make it unique—for example those that distinguish one pin from another, and sometimes those that distinguish one man from another. Certainly the great utterances ("Ripeness is all") which Mr. Murry has in mind seem often to describe what all men or all primroses have in common rather than the uniqueness of any one of them or of any sub-variety. But this is probably an unimportant verbal point which need not stand between us; it would be foolish to drag the minor logical squabbles between Oxford and Cambridge of twenty years ago into a discussion with wider issues.

More relevant is a difficulty due to the ambiguity of "description" and "communication." I cannot quite satisfy myself in which sense he is using them. Which sense it is makes, for me, an enormous difference—the difference in fact between being able to agree substantially or not. Two alternatives, and not more I think, are before us, two main senses of "describe" and "communicate." With one of them what Mr. Murry is saying would be fairly simple and entirely acceptable. With the other—which, unfortunately for me, his language elsewhere suggests—it would be an extremely abstruse, unverifiable speculation. The first sense is that in which a form of words describes or communicates the state of mind or experience of the speaker; the second is that in which it describes or communicates some state of affairs or fact which the speaker is thinking of or knowing (something in all but one case, that of introspection, *other than* the experience which is his thinking of it or knowing it). Put briefly and crudely the difference is this. Are we, when we interpret "a total statement," interpreting no further than the speaker's experience, or are we going further to something *else* which he is telling us about? Our implicit language assumptions as well as many of the subtlest ambiguities in the psychological vocabulary constantly tempt us to suppose that the second is the case and that we are going further. My chief contention in this whole discussion is that ordinarily with poetry we are not. To take an extreme instance, when a man says "I'm damned!" he may be saying that eternal judgment has gone against him or showing that he is surprised or annoyed. In such an instance we don't confuse the two types of interpretation, but in reading poetry we meet with examples where the two modes of utterance are so mixed and interdependent that there is real danger of misunderstanding.

Let us see now just what Mr. Murry says about this. Of Clare's lines he says: "His is surely an accurate description; but accurate with an accuracy unknown to and unachievable by science." He does not say explicitly whether he takes it as a descrip-

tion of an object (the primrose) or of the experience of seeing one.*
Since his other examples are all experiences, it might well be that it
is as of an object that he intends us to consider it. However, since
he expressly, and truly, says that the two problems—accurate¹
description of objects and accurate description of experiences—are
only two aspects of a single problem, we need not perhaps linger
with the distinction. It seems to me not likely that there will be
widespread disagreement with the view that the description applies
to the experience of seeing or imagining a primrose rather than to
actual primroses. The characters in the description are introduced
in the process of imaginative apprehension. It is a description of
this experience in the sense that the words, thanks to our past experience, cause in us a certain condition of mind, the experience.
They communicate and so describe this experience and it is by
doing so that they are valuable. On the other hand they appear,
taken literally, to describe the physical primrose and to communicate facts about it. I should say that the only fact about the primrose that they communicate is that it can produce this experience in
certain people who look at it. And I am not in very much doubt
that Mr. Murry would say just the same. He is, indeed, so specific
in his *Note* on this point—that it is the experience, a condition of the
organism, that is communicated and described—that I should seem
to myself to be merely reiterating his points were it not for other
passages, notably those in which he speaks of "truth"—which
brings me to a third point at which I hesitate.

The doubt still turns on the ambiguity of "describe." It may
mean here "convey," or it may mean "tell us about." If these "statements" are taken as describing only, in the sense of conveying experience, then to say that they are true and that they are accepted
for true without difficulty once they are understood (in Mr. Murry's

---

*"Object" is Mr. Murry's word. I would prefer to avoid it here; and it may be
well to insist that the distinction I am using is not a metaphysical distinction. It
is prior to metaphysics and would have to be respected and preserved by any
adequate metaphysics. It is the distinction between the presented primrose as a
"sensed or imagined object" and the inferred or constructed common or
gardener's primrose. As a "sensed or imagined" primrose it is, of course,
common to many people thanks partly to Clare, but it has a different standing.
It does not, in any ordinary sense, weigh anything for example.

sense of "understanding") seems not to add to the view. That such a statement instigates the experience and guides us adequately to it— so that it is this experience and not another that we have—is just, I think, what saying that it is "true" means here. We may mean further things, of course, adding what I should call "emotive uses of 'truth' "—that the experience is rare and desirable, important to us, that it meets deep needs in our nature. That it is to be accepted and integrated into the fabric of our personality as a positive determining influence (accepted for "true"?), not merely undergone as a stupid person's remarks may be, which exert thereforward only a negative determination if any. But this "adequacy as a guide to the experience concerned" is, I think, the only non-emotive use of "truth" which comes in here, if we are not talking about anything which the experience *tells us* about something else.

It may be suggested that the statement not only guides us to the experience concerned but also tells us about it and so can tell us truth or falsehood about it. This suggestion brings us, I believe, to the crux of the whole discussion. Do poetic and metaphoric statements really tell us anything about the experiences they convey to us? I admit freely that they certainly seem to. Clare's lines do seem not only to reinstate in us an experience of looking at a primrose but to tell us something about the experience—for example, that it is like, in some respect though not in others, looking at curds. By explicating a metaphor we can often excogitate in its place a statement (true or false) which is unquestionably about the experience that the metaphoric statement conveyed. And it is possible that, if we were sufficiently discriminating and acute, we could always, for each metaphoric expression in poetry, excogitate an analytic statement saying—in terms of the distinguishable operations of the mind—how the expression worked, what parts of the conveyed experience were being compared with other experiences, and so on. Such an analytic statement would clearly be psychology, and my personal belief is that one of the best hopes for psychology in the future lies in this kind of work. But—here is the point—the metaphoric expression does not say what the analytic statement thus arrived at says. The metaphoric expression gives a part of the material from which the analytic statement is excogitated, but it does not contain the statement. And it does not make the statement.

This, at least, seems clear to me—though I do not see how, at present, it could be *proved*—that such metaphoric expressions as Mr. Murry and I have in view do not *state* anything about the nature or structure of the experiences they convey, and that the sense in which they "describe" them is quite a different one from that in which an analytic statement excogitated from them might be a true or false "description" of the experience. There are of course other metaphoric expressions, belonging, I should say, to science, not to poetry (Mencius' "The will is the director of passion-nature" is an example),[3] which do state something metaphorically about the mind, but this is another use of "metaphor" altogether. Even the passage Mr. Murry quotes from Meister Eckhart is, to me, a "description" of a condition of the human organism in the first sense—when understood the description *conveys* it—not in the second sense. It does not state anything true or false about this condition. An excogitated analytic statement, such as psychology might attempt, of the nature of this condition would give us, as Mr. Murry says, "no help at all in our effort to understand" it. ("Understand" it in the sense of in some degree undergoing it.) As Mr. Murry points out, "We must have actually experienced, in full or in part, a similar condition of the organism." But the psychologist's account (description) of a mental condition we *can* understand, in his very different sense of "understanding," without having experienced the condition. Otherwise where would the alienist be?

How far Mr. Murry would agree to these distinctions or how far he could allow them and yet say what he wishes to say I am uncertain. In my view they do not restrict us but rather give us liberty in our use of pseudo-statements. I am not so pessimistic in my conclusions as he suggests. For when I say that innumerable pseudo-statements about the soul for example are gone irrecoverably I do not mean that they can no longer be used. I mean only that they are gone irrecoverably as items of knowledge in the sense in which the chemical constitution of water for example, or the circulation of the blood, are items of knowledge. Formerly they were by many regarded as items of knowledge in this sense and the experiences which ensued were very often due to their being so regarded. Our problem is that so many minds have ceased to take them as items of knowledge and are thereby cut off from the experiences. The attempt to get back to these experiences by trying to regard the defunct "items of knowledge" as more than indispensable imaginative fictions is what I have been trying to discourage.

I agree with Mr. Murry that disbelief in the existence of an object does not make a mention of it (or a statement about it) lose its meaning. I should say however that it certainly changed it. Its logical meaning is perhaps not changed, but we are not discussing "logical meanings" here, and total meanings—including our feelings and attitudes as well as our ideas—are, I think Mr. Murry will agree, certainly altered as we believe or disbelieve that their object exists.

Indeed this very fact is at the bottom of our joint preoccupation with this topic. It is the fact that for so many people disproof of what I call a "pseudo-statement" (and Mr. Murry calls a "metaphorical" or "subsidiary" statement) does imply deprivation or rejection of what I should call "the required experience" (and Mr. Murry the "total statement"), it is this fact with its lamentable and unnecessary waste which causes us to write about it. We are both concerned to remove a very dangerous obstacle to what we severally regard as fine organization of the mind. Our differences may be in formulation more than in anything else. For we seem to agree that what are most important are certain conditions of the organism. Mr. Murry prefers to describe those conditions, if I read him aright, in a way which makes them appear to be some form of knowledge (I am not certain whether he still holds to this). I am concerned rather to insist that any sense in which they are knowledge is not to be confused with certain other senses of knowledge— those in which science gives knowledge. If it is agreed that in these senses they are not knowledge and do not know anything my point is here met. I should add that this negative description of them is not, in my view, derogatory to them. My motive is to preserve them from bogus and unnecessary conflicts.

A few remarks upon readings of "Beauty is Truth, Truth Beauty" *in its context in Keats's poem* may help out these abstract distinctions. I find myself agreeing with all Mr. Murry's admirable analysis of the poem and with, I believe, very much of his attempt to shadow forth in discursive form the experience which the enigmatic words utter. My doubts concern the division between statements and pseudo-statements (the literal and the metaphoric) in

Mr. Murry's prose. For example (p. 479), if pressed, I do not believe
that "the innocent vision of the child" does really behold existence
"under the aspect of eternity." The child, I should say as a psychologist, is typically Keats's Dreamer, he entirely "submits the shows
of things to the desires of the mind."[4] But I am not sure that Mr.
Murry himself would wish us to understand what he says so literally, and the point is only worth making because so many readers
do take a "necessarily metaphorical expression" such as "the realm
of pure Being which the pure Spirit contemplates" very literally
indeed. When they do so they are, in my view, in more danger if
they accept what they then understand by it than if they reject it.

The different readings of "Beauty is Truth, Truth Beauty,"
cited by Mr. Murry, illustrate the central point very finely. Both
Dr. Bridges and Sir Arthur Quiller-Couch take it, I think, as a
statement (or literally)—with different interpretations both of
"Truth" and "Beauty," however. Both terms have so many senses,
vague and precise (quite apart from metaphoric uses), that this is
not surprising. Some of them would certainly make the line an
extremely bad one. Certainly it would be so if it were what Mr.
Humbert Wolfe has recently called it, "a plain statement of one part
of a very simple poetic faith—that in fact beauty must be true or
everything is false and inversely that truth must be beautiful or
everything is ugly."[5] Keats was not playing here with any such
"faiths." I doubt if any interpretation of it as a statement would
make it a good line, but so many are possible—perhaps (allowing
for different theories of Beauty and of Truth, different interpretations of "is," and intensive and extensive readings of the proposition) as many as twenty open to Keats and many more open to a
present-day philosopher—that confidence would be unwise. The
mere fact of the ambiguity is not, of course, in the least against the
line. I do not know whether Mr. Empson in his remarkable studies
of ambiguity in poetry has touched upon this passage.[6] I hope he
has or will—for it would be hard to beat as a meeting point of possible senses. As a statement—however it is taken—it will be as
something *somebody* (Keats or the ideal speaker of the poem) says,
not as something the Grecian urn says. Mr. Murry remarks most
pertinently that it is constantly forgotten that the urn is speaking.
But this is a pivotal point for a satisfactory interpretation. What an
urn can "say" is not and cannot, in such a context, be the same kind

of thing that a speaker says. The sense of "says" is different, the word has undergone an immense metaphoric shift. What the urn does is to induce a certain condition of mind; it does not formulate a philosophic doctrine however vague or uneducated or however transcendental and profound. This, to me, with the first two lines and the repetition in the last stanza of "silent," is the textual objection to any reading of the questionable words as a statement. I am not sure that Mr. Murry's own interpretation quite escapes this objection. I am afraid that many who read his pages will take from them a belief that Keats, *in the poem*, is giving them a philosophic message about life.

My own feeling is that Keats was quite aware of the effect of this shift in the sense of "say" and was using it; that he was not putting a philosophy into the mouth of the urn, but giving expression to the condition that the imagined urn, as he imagined it, led him into. An expression not in terms of thought but in terms reflecting his own inner acceptances and choice between conditions. Introspectively he can remark, "I can never feel certain of any truth but from a clear perception of its beauty." Some conditions he felt immediately to be what he needed—those that gave him a clear perception of the beauty of whatever it was induced them. Using "Truth," in the poem, as it is so often used, for "what is to be accepted, held in mind, sought for" ("That is sooth, accept it!") and "Beauty" for "the source of the condition," we could make the equivalence asserted in the poem come to a philosophic pronouncement that "aesthetic experience is its own sanction." But for the reasons given above, *in the context of the poem*, I take it to reflect simply the acceptance of the condition, whenever and however it comes, as an ordering experience with indefinite powers over the sequent experiences of life.

7 *Max Eastman's* The Literary Mind: Its Place in an Age of Science

Science and poetry again, but in another spirit from the last: a lightweight rather than a deep-fraught encounter. Eastman and I had our fun, but the issues on which I sparred with him here are nonetheless momentous.

Mr. Eastman is a controversialist and as pretty a hand at this rather out-of-date game as any now writing in English. His chief victims are Professor Irving Babbitt and Mr. T. S. Eliot, with whom he makes a kind of sport that should infuriate the faithful and exhilarate the others.[1] But what a pleasure it is to read a man who so evidently enjoys what he is doing, a writer with a swift feline grace of movement and at least the appearance of a punch! Whether the figures that go down again and again so pat before him are really the men known by their names is a question that need not disturb our enjoyment of the show; for it is Mr. Eastman who is here on exhibition.

This is what "Professor Irving Babbitt" faces:

> He has no plan. He is blandly indifferent to the propriety of his suggesting a plan. Having pointed out that a multitude of men are being "mechanised in order that the captain of industry may . . . live in a state of psychic unrestraint", having warned us that "a leading class that has become Epicurean and self-indulgent is lost", and having assured us that thanks to the inadequacy of our leaders, "both progressive and conservative", we are "moving through an orgy of humanitarian legalism towards a decadent imperialism", and that moreover "the whole elaborate

Review of Max Eastman, *The Literary Mind: Its Place in an Age of Science* (New York and London: Charles Scribner's Sons, 1931). Reprinted from *Criterion*, 12 (1932), 150-155.

structure that has been reared by the industrial revolution is in danger of collapse", he leaves the job right there, and wanders off vociferating about Confucius and the "inner life"—the "superiority", in fact, "of inner over outer action". It seems to me that anybody who cared about the state of affairs Professor Babbitt depicts so eloquently, would want to analyse the process by which those miserable leaders got into their positions, and think up some scheme for getting some better ones in.[2]

It seems almost proper that the most illustrious phantom-thrasher of our time should be so treated!

And here is the medicine for "T. S. Eliot" and the "Neo-classics":

> And since they are waging the same struggle as the humanists, they show of course the same home-sickness for feudalism, the same antagonism to the masses of mankind and to those interested in their destiny. It was no accident that in expressing his polite scorn for the early efforts of psychology and sociology, T. S. Eliot should have tossed in among them the movement for social emancipation. "Social emancipation crawled abroad" was the phrase in which he expressed his feeling. And it is no accident that in advocating a revival of "intellect" and a "control of the emotions by Reason", he should deliver the essential force of his attack against Bernard Shaw and H. G. Wells and Bertrand Russell.[3]

Minor champions fare no better: "It is perhaps unfair to base an argument upon Mr. Munson, for he is a kind of specially privileged infant-of-letters."[4] "Suppose that Miss Sitwell knew a little something about the senses and the brain! It sounds ludicrous, but when you consider that these are the subjects about which she is writing, it is not perhaps an altogether preposterous suggestion."[5] "Not knowing what you are talking about is no mere accidental default, however, in most of these neo-classic writers. It is the substance of their faith."[6] Nobody after all this can go away saying he has not had his $2.50 worth.

Controversy is largely an exercise in adroit misunderstanding. Mr. Eastman starts here, I am afraid, with large natural advantages which he has not omitted to cultivate. He comes forward as the champion of Science, and beguiles us in a short part I with an account of the scepticism of the scientist and a protest against the "desire to get somewhere and sit down" that leads to premature unscientific conclusions.[7] This is admirable, but it makes a queer prelude to the red-hot certainties that follow. And to sprinkle these later pages with remarks about "the cool scepticism in which scientific knowledge hangs suspended" hardly makes matters better.[8] "I perhaps owe my apologies to the New Humanists," says Mr. Eastman, "for so vigorously jumping on them after they are dead . . . Besides, I am not really jumping on them but attempting to explain them."[9] It is the last thing he is really attempting to do. Mr. Eastman is not a man of science; he is as much a man-of-letters, and suffers as much from "the literary mind" as any of his opponents. And the Science he appeals to, disowns and demolishes him along with them. For to pretend to "explain" any *individual's* motives and actions in this present age is to be—not a scientist—but a politician. Mr. Eastman is in fact an ardent politician—sadly divided in his loyalties to the Revolution and to a Science which he invokes distantly without practicing its discipline. Those who share his politics, and who think that exact inquiry and the attack on economico-social privileges can be combined, will regret his book as a tactical mistake bringing in an awkward confusion of the issues.

A scientific criticism would point out, I think, that Mr. Eastman—along with Professor Babbitt and Mr. Eliot—is untrained in the technique of interpretation. It would add, with prudent haste, that this is not really their fault since the proper training has not yet been provided. But the general conditions it must fulfill are pretty clear. To be a good interpreter you must not only know how you are using your words yourself, but be able to imagine how the other man has been using his. In brief, you must *understand* before you argue. Such interpretative freedom requires the scientific spirit, but it needs moreover a systematic exercised acquaintance with the possibilities of meaning and a conscious technique of questioning. When the right training is provided, our three champions here will be seen to be each journeying through and battling with his own set of mirages. Criticism becomes "scientific" as we learn to compare these mirages and arrange them in a common framework. And this effort, whenever it is made, is science. But, as Mr. Eastman shows very clearly himself, it is easy to describe quite other efforts, political for example, in very similar terms.

Meanwhile, in default of a scientific critical technique, we have to do the best we can, undismayed by the reflection that serious efforts toward it will make us almost unreadable. Here Mr. Eastman's general thesis is very much sounder than his practice. The argument of his book, which gives it a certain importance at this juncture, is that the matters which criticism has to discuss are becoming the subject of technical treatment in psychology. As such they are being taken out of the scope of the literary man (who naturally resents and resists this progressive pilfering from his province). I have no doubt that Mr. Eastman is in the main right about this, and in thinking that it explains a good deal that has been happening in literature. But he exaggerates the positive attainments of psychology, as literary men often do through reading chiefly the more enthusiastic of the psychologists.[10] The important results hitherto are certain destructions. There is also the beginning of the provision of a set of alternative hypotheses, but these are still a very long way from being worked up into the kinds of ideas that anyone could use *directly* in criticism. So Mr. Eastman, though right in the main, is somewhat anticipating matters in suggesting that the critics' concerns can be handed over to psychologists. It will be some time before the chemist can replace the wine taster and chemistry is much further advanced than psychology. On the other hand many literary men do undoubtedly feel nervous in talking about these feelings, emotions, senses, and such. They have lost their naive traditional certainty, and suspect that there is something in some psychology book that they ought to know. This is probably an illusion, but its effect on literature is not less. The subject is evidently an important one, and Mr. Eastman deserves credit for drawing attention to it.

His best pages are those in which he traces the increasing interferences of science with poetry. But he is not content—I suppose no one who is seriously interested in poetry can be content—to let poetry lapse as an obsolete and superseded human activity. So he comes, from an interesting description of his own difficulties as a poet (p. 242), to "find a way of escape from this dividedness"—to the problem "of bringing truth back into poetic literature." But the way of escape he finds leads him, as far as I can see, either nowhere or straight back into his difficulties. To see how this happens we must look rather closely into his various conceptions of poetry and science.

To begin with poetry: "Pure poetry is the pure effort to heighten consciousness" (p. 170), "to convey the quality of an experience" (p. 169), "Poetry *is* the attempt to make words suggest the given-in-experience" (p. 175). The poet "communicates to us a kind of experience not elsewhere accessible, and which we like to touch" (p. 149). As to how he does so, he "must arouse a reaction and yet impede it, creating a tension in our nervous systems sufficient and rightly calculated to make us completely aware that we are living something—and no matter what" (p. 205). The last four words are sufficiently heroic, but they give Mr. Eastman's definition away in a fatal fashion. A torture chamber would do much better than a library as a place in which to submit ourselves to art. If "heightened consciousness" is all we are to ask for, what is wrong with lumbago? The crux of the whole matter only comes when we ask "Why do we like to touch some sorts of experience and not others?" To answer it we have to apply some theory of values—an endeavor upon which Mr. Eastman pours some of his brightest scorn. And once we begin to consider the comparative values of experiences our whole conception of poetry is forced to change. Mr. Eastman, it seems to me, has still to begin his investigation of this branch of the subject. Instead, he stops with the epilogue to Pater's *The Renaissance*. No doubt we should "burn always" with a "hard gem-like flame"; but the theoretical problem is, "What is its difference from a soft and smoky one?" The answer to which is inevitably in terms of that order or disorder among "impulses" (or however else you care to describe the elementary processes on which consciousness depends) that Mr. Eastman so objects to our bringing into an account of poetry.

His fullest discussion both of poetry and science is in the form of a twenty-page small-print *Note* on my mistakes, which prevents my comment from being as impersonal as I could desire. Mr. Eastman says that I have caused him much "heavy labor," "tiring to the mind," and finds in this an evidence of my "fundamental error of trying to cut off the organization and control of practical activity from science and bring it over into poetry." I am sorry, for it is clear to me that Mr. Eastman has not understood what I was trying to cut off or what bring over. He seems to have mistaken my attempt at a microscopic analysis for a very perverse piece of macroscopic misdescription of common observations, and is at cross-purposes with me almost throughout. After saying this, I must trouble the reader with some examples. They might be many, but shall be two—enough only to show that Mr. Eastman has not imagined the position I was trying to expound and is again fighting with a dummy. "How can poetic words help us to order, consolidate and control our experience?" he asks.

"Tiger, tiger, burning bright . . .

"Can anyone control the tiger by confusing him with a campfire?" Amusing! But not more beside the point than many of Mr. Eastman's most confident refutations. I had said nothing about poetry controlling the thing it refers to. I had remarked that a poet (Blake will do as well as another) in writing his poem is organizing (ordering, consolidating, and controlling) an imaginative experience. Mr. Eastman says something of the kind himself—every critic from time to time must—but he will not let me say it since thereby I give a practical utility to poetry.

Again, I am shown up by Mr. Eastman through my remark on metaphor. What he does (p. 306) is to confuse what I had called the four prime language functions: Sense, Feeling, Tone, Intention (I sometimes have called them "uses," as a less repellent word than function) with the "use" of a word *literally* or *metaphorically*—as "low," for example, is in normal literal use a spatial epithet, but in "low temperatures," it is used metaphorically. By crossing these two quite different subject matters Mr. Eastman makes up a remarkable muddle. But it is his muddle, not mine. I take no responsibility for any part of it, since Mr. Eastman insists on identifying Sense with Science and Feeling with Poetry directly against my insistence that all four functions are present in most utterances and preeminently in poetry.

Mr. Eastman's misunderstandings of the distinctions by which Mr. Ogden and I try to divide science from poetry in *The Meaning of Meaning* are equally complete. He seems to think that we would disagree with an operational doctrine of physics of the Bridgman type (suitably limited since physics is plainly about *more* than just what the physicist does) and that we would deny the utility of science and its historic dependence upon practical needs.[11] But the strange misconceptions must not detain me here. What matters is that the gap in Mr. Eastman's view of poetry at the point when *Value* has to be considered is paralleled by a gap in his account of Science at the point when *Truth* should come in. And it is lack of reflection upon these matters that makes his final rehabilitation of "the realm of literary truth" so lame a sequel to the spirited skirmishes of the earlier sections. "I think everybody who has passed through the ceremonies of initiation and been led up to the inmost altar of the New Humanism has had an involuntary giggle escape him when he found out what it was all about" (p. 42). Alas! the same giggle threatens us when we discover that for Mr. Eastman the hope of the new "truth-speaking poetry" is in Sir James Jeans and in "the tendency of men of letters to lend their pens to the agreeable communication of scientific knowledge."[12]

8 Multiple Definition

This was truly an experimental paper. That it failed, entirely, to elicit any coherent response from the audiences to which it was addressed need not imply that the fault lay with the paper, or with the proposals it presented. There can be many other interpretations of this outcome. However, I am not, as yet, ready to opine as to why an imaginatively exciting possibility of developing a truly useful help to great and pressing planetary needs, suddenly, after most encouraging initial trials, became taboo: something otherwise open and exploring minds have not cared to look into. Why and how such things happen is a matter of deeper and more general import than can appear through any instance. The reign of fashion in philosophy and in morals is notorious. When will it be adequately investigated?

The purpose of this paper is to invite discussion of a type of analysis which has, I believe, a number of novel features. We shall be agreed, I hope, that a chief task of philosophy is analysis and that this is because the words we use in philosophizing have many meanings not the same for different users, and that, further, the very words we use in giving our analyses are apt themselves to have—being more abstract, and being used with a more ambitious intention of precision—more troublesome ambiguities than any others.

Every word in every philosopher's abstract vocabulary has, I take it, a number of different senses to mislead his readers (and, alas, too often, himself). A remedy for this would seem to be to have more words; and to put "one word, one sense; one sense, one

Reprinted by permission from *Proceedings of the Aristotelian Society*, 34 (1933-34), 31-50. The paper was read before a meeting of the society in London on November 27, 1933.

word" before us as a slogan. But, as we all know, the new words tend to take over the ambiguities of the old, and the result is only more words which need still more careful watching.

Another remedy, and I hope a more hopeful one, would be to have fewer words, and it is as an experiment in vocabulary restriction that what follows has been drawn up. The advantage of a minimum philosophic word-list—for use in analysis—would be that we should be forced to attend as closely as possible to the ambiguities of each word in it. A strictly minimum word-list would be a measure of our power to keep in mind the ranges of different senses which each word would, for our philosophical purposes, carry.

The word-list I am using below is clearly very far from being a minimum list—it is perhaps about halfway toward one. It is used here as a step toward a minimum word-list which would let me say anything which any philosopher would wish to say in a way which would have a fair chance of being understood not only by trained philosophers but by all reflective persons—including persons (Chinese, for example) not of the European linguistic and intellectual tradition. A further condition was that what was written in it was to seem quite like normal English. It is in fact the word-list of Basic English, and as such is governed by many purposes which are not of philosophic interest.[1] Its philosophic interest is that it aims to be a language, a system of words, with which any thought of any kind can be expressed so as to be distinguishable by ordinary untrained intelligence from any other thought with which it is likely to be confounded—a system with which any two thoughts which we have a wish to separate may be separated.

This you will agree is a grandiose aim and I do not pretend that this word-list, as worked out at present, entirely fulfills it. The words essential to it are between two and three hundred. A number of them, and these the most important, have (as in ordinary English) a variety of senses. The problem is to find ways of distinguishing between these senses with the aid of the other words in the list. Naturally enough the fact that different words often have (in a given context) the same sense and the same range of senses soon becomes very evident. It would have been possible to cross out a number of words on this ground, but the effect would have been to make my specimen discourse more monotonous than seemed desirable at this stage. That was one of the philosophically irrelevant considerations alluded to above.

This list then is certainly redundant. The doubt will rather be, I think, whether it is *sufficient*—whether all philosophic ideas are capable of being displayed in terms of the multiple senses of so small a list of words, and whether these multiple senses can be reciprocally controlled within the system with sufficient refinement for philosophical purposes. I do not want to put any limits to the senses of the word "philosophical" here that are narrower than those usually observed. We might find, however, that some kinds of philosophical views went into a restricted language much more easily than others and this might be an interesting confirmation of our opinions—whatever these were—of certain philosophical aims and methods.

In stepping over into this limited language (from now on I make use of no word not in my word-list without straightaway giving an account of its sense) three other ways in which such tests might be of interest may be noted. They may give us a way of learning more about our use of words in everyday talk, writing, and reading: a way of teaching those who are starting serious reasoning to put questions about the senses of their words; and a way of making a new sort of comparison between different views and of controlling these comparisons by putting them into a system.

The opinions which come now are put forward not only for purposes of argument but for comparison with other statements of like views made with an unlimited word-list.

The best thing will be to get agreement, if I am able, to a general question about divisions between the senses of words. This is the most important point of all. It is not hard to make clear, but it is very hard to keep in mind, and till we are able to do this all the time troubles of every sort will get in our way at every turn. It is this:

When we take a word and give it a sense, we are free; we are able, for the purpose in hand, to give it any sense which for the purpose in hand will be of use. The sense we give it first may in fact not be of use. We may not be able—keeping to that sense—to say something which we have a desire to say. If so, then we have to make a new attempt; we go back and give a different sense to the word. But when we first give a sense to a word we are not limited in any way. We may give any sense which seems of value so long as there is not serious danger of other men taking it in other senses; that is, if only we are able to make clear which sense *we* are giving it.

Words have not got—by natural design as it were—senses of which they are the owners. They are instruments by which men give direction to thoughts,* nothing more; though the conditions under which we are able to make them do this are limited. But—and here the trouble comes in—when we give a fixed sense to a word we have at the same time made it possible to say some things with it, and not possible to say other things, which we will probably have a strong desire to say later on. We are not able to see, at first, what we will be able to say with the word so fixed, and what we will not be able to say with it. We have to let the test of experience give us the answer to this secret. A time may come and probably will come when we have a strong desire to say something with the word which the sense we have given to it will not let us say. Then we may come to the decision that the first sense we gave to the word was not the right one, that we made an error in using the word so. But here we have to take great care. There are two important and very different ways in which we may be said to have "made an error" and in which the sense we gave may be said to have been "not the right sense":

1). The sense we gave may not have been the sense of most use for the purpose in hand. In this way we frequently make errors and the senses we give to words are frequently not the right ones. We may make an error in this way without ever making any false statements.

2). But there is another way of making errors. When we make a false statement, we are in error—but in a quite different way. In taking a word and giving it a sense we are not in error in this way—till, having given the word this sense, we make some false statement with the word. Till we do this we may be unwise in our use of the word but we are not saying anything which is not true.

---

*And feelings, and desires and acts, in addition. But here we have in view only the use of words for the control of thoughts in the narrow sense in which thoughts are separate from other processes in the mind. (See 1.2.)

The great danger, and the cause of most of our trouble with words in arguments, is that we do not keep these two ways of "making errors" clearly separate in our minds. When we see that we are unable to say what it is necessary for us to say without a change in the sense of a word, the feeling may come strongly that somehow in giving that sense to the word we were making a false statement. It seems to us as if there was something which was the true owner of the word and that in giving the word to another thing (that is, in giving another sense to the word) we were taking it away from its true owner and falsely making some other thing seem to be different from what it is. Bishop Butler's saying that "Every thing is what it is and not another thing," or some thought to the same effect, may come into our mind, and give us the feeling that we have done wrong.[2] We have, by the effect of teaching and, it seems possible, by birth, a strong impulse to take words to be the names of things—one thing, one name: one name, one thing—and go on to the idea that, if we were only able to see enough, the true answer to the question "What is ——?" (What is Art, the Mind, Existence, Value, Science, Belief? etc.) would become clear to us. But these "questions" have no answers—in the form in which we most frequently put them. Some of them are not questions at all; others are questions which have to be put in the form "What is this word '——' being used for in this connection?" Putting them in the short form "What is ——?" gives us a quite wrong idea of the sort of answer which is possible, and the first great step to a better control of thought is to see why this is so.

An example may make the position clearer. We have, say, the word "Poetry." There are a great number of interesting statements we are able to make in connection with the word "Poetry." We may say that Poetry is a way of putting words together so as to be the cause of a special sort of effect; or that it is a way of putting words together which comes from a special sort of act or event or experience in the mind of the man who puts them together; or that it is a way of putting words together in verses—that is, such that (with the right instruments) tests may be made which make clear that some quality of the sounds or motion of the words comes back time after time in a regular way; or that it is a way of putting words together in which it seems that there was a regular order (rhythm) of sounds or motions in the writer of them; or that in a complete reaction to them some regular order of sounds or motions will come into the mind in connection with which they will take their places (these give two other senses to the word "verse"), or we may say that Poetry is words put together in such a way that when sense and feeling are given to them in reading the motion and sound seem to be in special agreement with the sense.

We may go on for a long time saying things of this sort with the word "Poetry." We may say that it is beautiful and high thoughts in delicate and right language, or that it is the coming back into the quiet mind of strong feeling, or that it is an important amusement, or that it is a sort of teaching which is full of pleasure, or that it is the breath and higher being of knowledge, or that it is the look on the face of science. (Some of them may seem strange, but three of them are the opinions of Wordsworth; the others are from Shelley, Sir Philip Sidney, and T. S. Eliot.)[3]

If we make a comparison between these sayings, we will see that the word "is" is not the same in all of them. In the first group it will seem natural to put the sign = in the place of "is," in the second this will not seem so natural. This change is most important. To make use of a special word from logic, the first group are naturally taken as *definitions*—that is, as attempts to give an account of a sense of the word "Poetry." The second group are more naturally taken as statements—that is to say we take them as if the word "Poetry" had some other sense given it before and as if we are now saying something about the things of which the word (in this before-fixed sense) is the name. It is clear that only the second group, taken as statements, are able to be true or false. The first group (as definitions) do no more than give a sense to the word "Poetry"; they do not go on to say anything about the things of which the word "Poetry" in this way becomes a name—and because they do not say anything it is happily not possible for them to be wrong. But, in most arguments, men give their chief attention—not to making open and public the senses which may be best used—but to the attempt to say the right thing about a nothing whose form and qualities are changed with every statement made about it. When a man says, with much weight upon the "is," that "poetry *is* ——" he is probably giving us a definition and then it would be better if he did not become so heated.

A strange light on all this—that it is strange is the strangest thing of all—comes with thought on how the senses of our words are given to us. "Poetry" for example. We have knowledge of it first, let us say, in connection with certain verses. Which of the qualities of the verses (so far as we may then see them separately) do we first take as the sense of "Poetry"? And which later, when the other sorts of things named poetry come before us? Is there any need to be surprised if, after years of this sort of thing, we have no clear, fixed, and complete sense for "Poetry" in our mind; if the best we do, when we make use of the word, is to give with it a mass of mixed, broken senses one of which will seem the most important at one time, another at another (as acting definitions) changing with the different statements in which the word is used? For purposes of amusement, for attacking one another's opinions in a general way, for stitching together slow minutes in company, such play with unnoted senses is of value, without doubt. But not for serious discussion.

Let us take the most important words, in the theory of the comparison of senses and in the work of taking statements to bits for the purpose of comparison, and make lists of their chief senses. We will give numbers to these senses, so that we may put a finger on them, without trouble, when in the process of discussion it becomes necessary to give them separate attention. We will be able to see—together and on one page—the chief senses which may be coming into use at this point in the discussion. We will then see not only which tricks and twists we will have to keep in mind, but— and this is more important—the other possible theories.

The first reaction of most readers to numbers (12.112, 3.24, and so on) in pages put before them is normally one of fear mixed with disgust. It is hoped, however, that here the great help which such numbering gives in keeping different things separate will make you more kind to them.

I give in my account only some of the reasons for making the divisions where I do. This apparatus is a machine for separating the senses of other words when it is necessary to do so. The test of the value of our divisions is the amount of help they give us. It is important to keep in view this fact that we are not here putting on paper something which is given to us, so much as making a machine—a machine for controlling thought which will let us do some things and keep us from doing other things. It is a good machine if it is of use to us; any changes which will make it of more use to us will make it better. They are not able to be tested in any other way than this.

On the other hand, if it is to be of use, it is necessary to keep some of the divisions in the places in which our minds normally put them. The attempt to make a machine like this is, in fact, a way (and the best way) to the discovery of how our minds do their work. But, as we will see, our minds do their work in a number of different ways. They put the chief divisions, upon which all the others are dependent, in a number of different places for different purposes. So a number of different machines, different "philosophies," different "logics," are possible and necessary. Very little of the theory of the connections between these possible machines has been worked out and the history of thought is still waiting for such a theory.

The most important words in this machine are:

Theory of Knowledge	*Theory of Connections*	*Theory of Instruments*
Thought 1	Cause	Property
Thing 2	Effect	Is
Fiction 3	Force	General
Fact 4	Law	Special
Knowledge 5	Part	Quality
Belief 6	System	Relation
True 7	Change	Necessary
Sense 8	Same	Possible
		Probable
		Sort
		Degree

With accounts of the chief senses of these key words before us on paper in clear lists, the worst troubles of all discussion will in a short time be seen to give the best chances for new discoveries. They will no longer be, as they are now, causes of unfertile doubt and complex errors. The lists we make here will at first not be complete and clear enough to give us every sense which is needed. But even lists which are not complete will let us see much which we do not now naturally see without them. Even a bad attempt will be much better than no attempt at all.

We will take the word "thought" first—and let us not be

troubled if at first we seem not to be saying anything new or important. All men have knowledge about most of these things from their
early years, from the first steps in their learning. We are only putting this knowledge into order.

Thought

1.1. (*In the widest sense*) *any event in the mind*. In this sense all the
history of a mind is made up of thoughts; but for most purposes we
have to make divisions between thoughts and feelings, for example,
or between thoughts and desires. Feelings and desires are equally
events in the mind. So take as a narrower sense for "thought":

1.2. *An event in the mind which puts something before the mind.*
Some writers say, or take as said, that the thing which is put, by
thought, before the mind is a picture, or that, if it is not a picture, it
is something which is like a picture in being a copy of something
which is not before the mind (or in the mind) in this sense. These
things which, on this theory, are before (in) the mind are frequently
named "images." For example, when we have a thought of a tree,
we will be said to have an image (or picture) of a tree before the
mind: and when we have a thought of a noise, we have an image (a
copy) of the noise before us, and so on. This theory of images may
be wrong. A great number of persons say that they do not ever
have images, and persons who sometimes have images say that
they are able to have thoughts without having any images. Even
those who make use of images in their thought say that their images
are sometimes not at all like the things they are having thoughts of.
So it is wise not to make our account of thoughts dependent on any
theory of images but to say that what is before the mind in thought
is in some way the thing which the thought is about and not only
some picture or other copy of it in the mind. It will be clear that, if
we say this, the word "before" is not being used in the same way in
which it is used when we say "This book is before my eyes." We
take "before" here in "before the mind" in a special sense (not quite
like any other use of it) as the name of the relation which thoughts
have to the things they are thoughts about.

What is important is that thoughts (in this sense, 1.2) put the
mind into a special connection with things. A thought is *of* or *about*
something and so it may be true (7.1) or false. A feeling or desire is
not about something *in the same way* (when we are not, as we fre-

quently are, giving to the words "feeling" or "desire" a sense which makes them the same as thoughts in this sense). It will be noted that we may equally say that a thought is *of* something or *about* it. In most places the two are not different. We may, however, make them different—as we will see in connection with the word "thing" (2.2)—and this gives us sometimes a feeling that they are different in some way in other places where, in fact, their sense is the same.

A division in this sense of thought is of much use:

1.21. *A thought may be of something as true, as being so;* or it may (1.22) *be only of something, without the question "Is the something so or not?" coming up at all.* In other words a thought may be, in addition, a belief (6.2 or 6.3), or it may be only a thought. When we are not deeply interested, or needing to do anything, then our thoughts are frequently without this addition. This division is important when we come to questions about the limits of knowledge, and the different senses of "true," "belief," "fiction," "possible," and so on.

1.3. A division which is sometimes important comes up with "thought" (and a great number of other words). A thought may be *an event in the history of a mind* (1.2) or it may (1.5) be *a group of general properties which that event has and other events may have.* For example, we say "Newton's best thoughts took place in Cambridge" and "Newton's thought about space was changed by Einstein." In the second of these we are not saying that Einstein did anything to the events in Newton's history. We are saying that in place of thoughts (such as Newton had) of one sort Einstein made use of thoughts of another sort.

In sense 1.2 a thought is one event with a fixed place and time; in sense 1.3 a thought is a general property which thoughts (1.2) may have. If they have it, we say that they are the same thought, and by a fiction (3.2) we take them to be one thing (2.4).

We may now go on from "thoughts" to "things."

Thing
2.1 The word with the most general sense possible. We have to say "Every thing is a thing" because we have no more general word with which to give an account of them. In this sense, to say about anything that it is a thing is not to say anything about it. If it is then it is a thing. So "thing," in this sense, is almost without sense. It has

less sense than any other word. Like "is," "being," and "property" it is an instrument which is of use only in putting the senses of other words together. Minds, events, processes, qualities, properties, numbers, relations, time, points, spaces, changes, rates of change, fictions, doubts, smells, destructions—all things we have or make names for—are, in this sense, things.

2.2 *In a narrower sense only those things* (2.1) *are things about which other things are said.* This sense is sometimes a little hard to see. The division is between words used as names of substances and words used as names of properties. But these two words "substance" and "property" are almost as hard as "thing" to make clear in their different senses. Our best way of getting the question straight will be to give some examples. It is hard only because it is so very simple.

When we say "Grass is green," "grass" is the name of a thing (in this sense) but "green" is not. Grass here is a substance—we are saying something about it. Green here is a property—a property of grass; it is something we are saying about grass. If we say "Green is pleasing to the eyes," now green has become a substance—we are saying something about it. The division, as I put it here, between things (in this sense) and what are not things is a question only of how we are using our words. It is not a division in the things (2.1) we have thoughts of, but only in the order in which our thoughts are put into language. For this reason it may seem unimportant, but for some questions it is very necessary to be clear about it.

It is with this division that a thought *of* something and a thought *about* it may be made to seem different. A thought may be *of* grass when nothing more is said, but *about* grass when it is a thought that grass is green.

In logic the discussion of this question makes use of the word "abstract." An abstract thought (Latin "taken from") is of a property taken from the substance which has the property; or of a substance taken from the properties which it has. It is probably not possible to have a thought of a substance without any properties but it frequently seems possible to have thoughts of properties—for example, green—without any thought of anything which is green. So we may get the idea that green is something which may have existence by itself without anything which is green. But what we see is a green space. Green, like other properties, only comes to us joined to other things—not by itself—but we do not necessarily take note of the other things it is joined to.

2.3 *A thing is a body.* In this much narrower sense only bodies are things, bodies being what we are able to see or to have knowledge of by touch, smell, hearing, or other forms of observation through the senses (8.2). Earth, grass, bread, bits of iron, and anything which has the same sort of existence as these, are things in this sense.

2.4 *A thing is anything which has existence for some time.* Most bodies have existence for some time and so are things in this sense, in addition. But we take, as having existence for some time, some things which are not bodies—our minds, for example, nations, laughs, digestion, events, chains of events, acts, and processes. The important point is that things in this sense keep the same (or seem to be the same) long enough for us to go with them in thought from one condition to another. We are able to say of them that they are now this and then that, now here, for example, and then there, now red and then green, now quick and then slow. If, for example, a mind does not keep in some ways the same from year to year, it is not possible to give a history of it. Our tendency to make up histories, to give accounts which seem to be about one thing and its changes, and not only about the way in which different things take one another's places, or different events come one after another, is responsible for our wide use of this sense of "thing." The question "Is a mind one thing, in fact?" (in this sense of "thing")—that is to say, "Does it keep the same?"—is possibly not one to which we will ever be able to give an answer. The question may only be about the way in which our thoughts make an attempt to give order to events. So a thing (in this sense) may be only a trick of our thoughts to make their work simple. The question comes up very clearly in connection with the new ideas in science. Is an electron a thing in this sense, for example, or are the waves with which men of science give an account of the motion of light? And how about the points of which space has been said to be made? Or how about nations when they go through a change of organization or government? Or ideas when we have seen that they are not wise but foolish? Are they the same things before and after?

With this we come to:

Fiction
3.1 A story not put forward as fact (4.1: See *Belief*).
3.2 A thought (1.2) used as if there was a thing (2.4) in agreement with it when there is in fact (4.2) no such thing.

Fact
4.1. Anything which is so.
4.11. That which makes a thought false when it is false.
4.2. Anything which is (has been, will be).
4.21. Anything complex which is.
4.22 Anything which may be.
4.3 Our only way of putting a thought to the test is by comparison with other thoughts, and by having other thoughts about them. To get at facts we have to have thoughts about them. This seems right, but it may not be true of those facts which are our histories as we go through them. These events in our minds, some say, may be got at straight without any need for us to have thoughts about them. (Bergson is a representative of this sort of view.)[4] But generally it is true that the test of a thought is another thought. If this is so, then the question "Is X a fact?" (4.1) or "Is the statement 'X' true?" becomes a question not about the agreement of a thought with a fact but about the agreement of a number of thoughts with one another.

This gives us 4.3, a fact is *that which a thought which is in agreement with the rest of true thoughts* (7.2) *is of*. And, if we take "what the thought is of" as changed here into a fiction, the question "Is a thought true?" becomes equally a question about the agreement of thoughts with one another, not about the agreement of thought with things. This view goes with the view that all things are thoughts (which has the name "Idealism" in the history of thought). But there is no need to take this last view even if we take the first, that thought has to be tested by thought. The two may be taken separately, though they have been made by some writers to seem dependent upon one another.
4.4. That which is in agreement with a general thought.

From "fact" is it a natural step to:

Knowledge
5.001. That of which we have knowledge.
5.002. Those processes (thoughts 1.2) by which we have knowledge.
5.1. A reaction to something.
5.101. That of which we have knowledge—the causes of our reaction.
5.102. Those processes in us by which we have knowledge.
5.11 Our reaction taken without further reaction to it.
5.12. Our reaction to this reaction.
5.13. Reaction without any events between it and the causes of it.
5.2. An event in the mind, part of the history of a mind, a bit of experience.
5.3. A special relation between the mind (or some event in the mind) and things.
5.5. What is said by an authority not able to make errors.

This puts the questions of "belief" and "true" before us:

Belief
6.1. A thought taken to be true without being tested.
6.11. A thought taken to be true which is not able to be tested.
6.2. A thought we take as a guide in our acts or feelings.
6.21. A feeling, desire, impulse, tendency in the mind as a guide in our acts or feelings.
6.3. A thought we are certain is true.
6.4. A special feeling which is the cause of our being certain.

True
7.001. A statement is true when the thought using it is true.
7.1. A thought is true when it is in agreement with what it is about.
7.2. . . . in agreement with all other thoughts in comparison with which it may be taken.
7.21. . . . in comparison with which it is possible to take it.
7.22. . . . in comparison with which it is wise to take it.
7.3. A thought (feeling, desire, etc.) which we have a need to take as a guide in our acts is frequently said to be true.

7.4. A thought which comes with a feeling like the feelings which come with true (7.1, 7.2) thoughts is frequently said to be true.

And now we come to the senses of "sense":

Sense

8.1. A general property of a thought by which what the thought is about is fixed.

8.2. Seeing, hearing, touching, smelling, tasting—the five senses— and any other way of getting knowledge which is like them.

8.3. A use of "sense" which is nearer to the one we are making is that in which *persons who are wise are said to have sense,* that is, to have *good* sense.

Good sense is, at least in part, a power to keep our thoughts, the senses of our words, in the right places. So there is a connection between the control of the senses of words and good sense. One who is not able to keep the senses of his words in order is said to be "out of his senses." In this sense, who among us is in them?

The reader may be waiting to put a question which has been in his mind from the start. What is this "agreement" on which almost everything in this apparatus of divisions seems to be dependent? It came at the start in the account given of our purpose; it came again in the senses of "thought," "fiction," "fact," "knowledge," "true," "sense," and in the senses of "of" and "about." It comes, but not so openly, in the chief senses of "cause" and "law." It is at the back of any discussion of "change," "same," "property," "general," "necessary," "possible," and "probable." No other word seems so important, but no special discussion of it has been attempted till now in these pages.

We have seen, with "true," with "sense," with "fact," with "knowledge," and we would see again with "property," "general," and "sort," that the same questions may be put again and again in different words. A way, a form, a sort, a group, a property are all ways (sorts, forms, groups, properties) of things; and a thing may be a law, and a law again a way. The words with which discussion goes on are more in number—though every word has its group of senses—than the senses they are used to put in order. And at more than one place the trouble and danger to thought which come from our way of taking an answered question as a new one might have been pointed out. Is this question "What is agreement?" only the other questions "What is a sort?" "What is a way of being the same?" "What is a general property?" "How are thoughts true?" "What is knowledge?" and "What is a cause?" put in another form? As questions—as forms of words to which, when senses for them have been fixed, answers may be given—these are, or may be made, clearly different. But the fact (4.2) about which we put them seems to be *one* fact—a very complex fact, of which a number of views, of parts of it, may be taken. The part which may not be clear—for which a separate account of the senses of "agreement" might be a help—is covered by senses of the words "general," "property," and "cause." It is possible, and not hard, to give a list of them by using these words. But then someone might say "Ah! you are saying what agreement is by using 'cause' and 'general,' and you said what cause and general are by using 'agreement'! You are moving in a circle and your account of these things is only a trick!" If, on the other hand, I took some new words, say *X* and *Y*, with which to give an account of the agreement which has been used in talking about knowledge, then someone would say "Ah! he has given no account of *X* and *Y*, the senses upon which everything in his system is dependent; so it is not complete and has no base!" These two protests would equally be signs that the purpose of these pages has not been rightly taken. As was said at the start, this apparatus of senses is to be tested by the help it gives us in putting our thoughts in order, in letting us say what we have a need to say and keeping us from saying other things which will get in the way of our purposes. If it is a help, that help is its base. What the purposes are for which the machine may be a help is only made clear by the range of its uses. We are able to give an account of a purpose only by saying in detail what it is a purpose *to do*. A purpose, in this sense, is not something different from the way in which it may be worked out.

What is important is to see that the senses of words may be taken in groups, and that if the form of one group of senses becomes clear to us, the form of other groups of senses, which we may not ever have put in connection with them, may become clear at the same time. This gives us new chances for the control of our thought and for taking over the knowledge we have of one field into other fields. As Coleridge said, "that only is learning which comes again as power."[5] And to see how any sense is in relation to any other is to get a sort of learning which comes again as power.

9 Meaning and Change of Meaning

This review hoped to highlight what was, from its origi-
native hour [see item 27, p. 255], the prime aim of The Meaning of Meaning. *Ogden and I were even then too realistic to*
suppose that the philosophic problems of meaning could be
finally "solved"—as though they were but puzzles. We were
inclined to hoot at such notions and preferred to quote the
Seigneur de Seingalt: "Je vous permets de traiter de fou tout
homme qui viendra vous dire qu'il a fait une nouvelle dé-
couverte en métaphysique." But with the optimism of youth
we did imagine that a sufficient exposure of men's chancy
behavior with "meaning" and similar words might in some
measure amend their conduct. Sad to say, we were early
able to perceive that, even when possessed of what we took
to be better views of meaning, people went on entirely as
before. We knew, of course, how much more there is and
must be to a muddle-free use of words than any protective
theory. Nonetheless, we found ourselves recurrently sur-
prised that our exhibit of type-specimen absurdities had
little effect even on those who enjoyed it.
The very high merits of Stern's book reinforced an invita-
tion to explore what seemed a distressing, if anticipatable,
shiftiness in the use there of "referent," the kingpin of the
whole venture. I am glad its reviewer noted "It is not odd—
whatever the cynic may aver—that the study of meaning
should, more than other studies, give rise to mutual mis-
understanding among its students." May he have avoided
them himself!

The system (if we may call it such) of human studies shows a
number of unfortunate cracks, or gaps. There is a bad one between
logic and psychology, another between logic and ethics, another all

Review of Gustaf Stern, *Meaning and Change of Meaning, Göteborgs Hög-
skolas Arsskrift,* 38 (1932). Reprinted by permission of the Orthological Institute from *Psyche,* 13 (1933), 185-196.

round epistemology; but the most embarrassing and obstructive of all is that between this group as a whole and semasiology (or the study of linguistic meanings, the inquiry into how words are used). [1] It is true that at times an exceptional logician will daringly wonder if perhaps the aim of logic (and philosophy) is to provide the methods by which the meanings of words may be defined—but there the matter usually ends; he will not thenceforth proceed anymore as though it were so. For the detail, and it is from study of the detail that advances must come, the detail of how words mean, how they change their meanings, how they combine and separate them, is another subject needing another training. And on the other side of the gap, the philologist—though he too sometimes suspects that his subject is ultimately capable of swallowing up philosophy, has learned by grim experience that logic and psychology—not to mention epistemology—are awkward things to play with. So he keeps away from the intellectual buzz-saws; and, as both philology and philosophy grow ever more and more technical, the gap between them, if anything, widens.

The honor due to Dr. Stern, then, for throwing a bridge across this gap, is the greater; his book will be extremely welcome to all who realize how dangerous the gap is and who hope that in time, before long perhaps, means may be found to close it. Dr. Stern combines very exceptional qualifications. He has the philologist's training and width of scholarship—with the caution and love of thoroughness (which so often seems excessive to the outsider) that only such a training can give. He combines with this a lively, very intelligent, critical interest in psychology (and remarkably wide reading, especially in experimental work), and a capacity to take care of himself amid its pitfalls which would be distinguished in a specialist. And he here devotes 400 large pages of closely constructed, coolly argued, richly instanced, clearly displayed thinking (in admirable English), to the question: How are we to treat the meanings of words systematically so as to examine their history and the modes of changes that take place? I propose to divide my review into two parts: giving first a short inadequate summary of his decisions, and second a more detailed examination of some of them.

After stressing the need for a comprehensive theory and the dangers of remaining too long contented with Wundt, he goes on to two questions preliminary to the first great problem—the definition of meaning.[2] "One of them is the functions of speech, which are intimately involved in the definition of meaning, as well as in the whole problem of sense-change. The other is a general theory of signs." These occupy chapter II. His account of the speech functions I reserve for later discussion; the theory of signs is similar to that outlined in *The Meaning of Meaning*.

Three factors must be jointly considered in attempting a definition of meaning. "The fact that words and meanings are secondary conditioned phenomena, has been neglected by most philologists writing on semantic theory, and also by earlier psychologists. They handle words and meanings as primary, independent entities, a view that leads them into various mistakes." Not only words and subjective apprehension must be considered, but objective reference also. Word, meaning, and referent; all three are involved in a definition of verbal meaning. The definition that results is: "The meaning of a word—in actual speech—is identical with those elements of a user's (speaker's or hearer's) subjective apprehension of the referent denoted by a word, which he apprehends as expressed by it." Some considerations as to Stern's use of the word "referent" I postpone. Meaning, so defined, is then subjected to close analysis —from the psychological point of view first: as regards cognitive and emotive ingredients; the imagery and "imageless thought" problem; central and peripheral elements, and kinds of vagueness —an extremely important matter to lexicologists. Secondly from a logical standpoint: actual meaning in speech and the lexical meanings of the isolated word; general and particular meaning; specialized and referential meanings (e.g., "Be a man!" "All men are mortal"); tied and contingent meanings (e.g., "dog," "yesterday"); the problems of relations, word and phrase, autosemantic and synsemantic meanings (complete and dependent meanings, e.g., "boy," "the boy's"). Chapter IV closes with a criticism of Paul and a useful note on Gomperz' analysis.[3] The next two chapters deal with the production and the comprehension of speech, chiefly on the basis of experimental and clinical studies. Throughout very full references are given.

The author then comes to his general theory of sense changes and so to the main subject of the book. "I define change of meaning as the habitual modification, among a comparatively large number of speakers, of the traditional semantic range of the word, which results from the use of the word (1) to denote one or more referents which it has not previously denoted, or (2) to express a novel manner of apprehending one or more of its referents."[4] He thus distinguishes from *change* of meaning, both fluctuations: i.e., occasional modifications by individuals as opposed to "habitual modifications of the semantic range of a word among a comparatively large group of speakers" ("Semantic range" is the totality of meanings a word can express—as opposed to "referential range," the totality of the referents it can be used for), and occasional specialization, e.g., "This is a *book*, not a collection of scribblings."

The classification of sense changes follows. The author began his work with an empirical sorting of historical instances, mainly with regard to the psychic processes involved. He then turned the matter round to consider whether systematic theory would justify the divisions thus arrived at. They are:

1. *Substitution.* Changes due to external, non-linguistic factors, e.g., "ship"-"airship," language only registering a change due to factors outside it.

2. *Analogy.* The change following by analogy a change in the meaning of some other word, e.g., "fast," adjective from "firm" to "quick" following the adverb "fast."

3. *Shortening.* A part of a compound expression takes over the meaning of the whole with omission of the other part, e.g., "private" for "private soldier."

4. *Nomination.* The intentional naming of a referent, new or old, with a name that has not previously been used for it. Subclasses are: intentional naming with a new invented word; intentional transfer (non-figurative); figures of speech (causes more or less emotive).

5. *(Regular) transfer.* Unintentional transfers, based on some similarity between the original (primary) referent of the word and the new (secondary) referent. E.g., "leaf" (of tree), "leaf" (of paper).

6. *Permutation.* Unintentional change in which the subjective apprehension of a detail—denoted by a single word—in a larger total changes and the changed apprehension (the changed notion) is substituted for the previous meaning of the word—e.g., "counting his beads" (prayers), "counting his beads" (balls of a

rosary); "boon" (what is asked), "boon" (what is graciously given); the two notions must be *functional synonyms* with the *phrase* meaning.

7. *Adequation.* Unintentional sense change consisting in a shift of attention from one characteristic of the *word* referent to another. E.g., "horn" (of an animal used as musical instrument), "horn" (instrument of a certain kind).

Thus summarily presented this classification may easily seem—to a reader whose interest is not deeply engaged—trivial or pedantic. It is only when we pass from a distant schematic view to a close comparison and a speculative endeavor to analyze and interpret instances, which occupies the rest of the book, that the important possibilities of such work appear. It was not a part of Dr. Stern's purpose to point these out, and his work may, for this reason, not receive for a time the attention it deserves. It is quite likely, for example, that my reader may say "A philologist applying psychology to his special field, high time too! Careful and well-informed? Excellent!"—and leave it at that. But if Dr. Stern has here shown how to make modern psychology at last begin to clarify semantics he has, at the same time, begun to show something else, of very much more interest to us all—how, namely, to make the study of language tell us—what it alone, perhaps, can tell us—about ourselves. Again and again in his patient, lucid, cautious analyses, an attentive reader will feel that a method is coming into sight by which the record that the history of language holds can provide a quite new type of evidence to psychology. "It has often been assumed that a word could be transferred to denote a referent standing to its primary referent in practically any relation. In my opinion, the material at present available shows that this is improbable. When the relation between the primary and the actual referent is not one of similarity, the shift is not so simple, and can occur only through the mediation of a peculiar verbal context, as described in the next chapter (permutation), or in the form of an adequation."[5] We can, it is true, as a *fluctuation,* and with the aid of a special verbal context devised for that purpose, intentionally shift the sense of a word along any relation we take as holding between the referents. We do in dialectical gymnastics and debate endlessly so shift them. (Just as in artificial conditions we can get creatures to do all kinds of things they do not do "in Nature.") But

Dr. Stern's observation, if it proves correct, gives us at least a glimpse of what may be some of the normal forms of mental operation under normal social conditions as opposed to temporary special group conditions. (All psychologists belong as such to special groups which is one of their main difficulties.) To use a figure, the history of language, if we could work it out a little further, would begin to give us geologic evidence by which to check what we get from introspection and other work done under comparatively arbitrary and changeable conditions.

   Toward all this Dr. Stern has made a notable contribution. I am anxious to stress the debt which all seriously interested in these matters will owe him, before going on to discuss points at which a worker on the other side of the philology-philosophy gap may have a fancy that his treatment can be improved. One cannot tinker with a kettle which has not yet been made. To have put forward a clear statement on these matters is to have shifted the whole thing, for everybody concerned, to a new level of accessibility and control. To work with this book is to realize its rare lucidity, order, and design (its cross-reference system is very well handled) as well as the author's discretion in avoiding the traditional vapidities and his good manners in a subject in which wrangling is almost traditional.

   To turn now to the points at which difficulties seem to me to arise in Dr. Stern's general theory and classification. The most important concerns the terrible problem of how to use the word "referent." I suspect—though it is excessively hard to be clear-minded, for any length of time, about it, or to find formulations which will keep the matter clear—that the working of some of the divisions in the classification depends upon a systematic equivocation (let us hope it is a case of functional synonymity) of the word "referent." Consider the following problem:

   Dr. Stern distinguishes "three main types of substitution, according to the origin of the change. The origin may be a factual change of the referent, or a change in our knowledge of the referent, or a change in our emotive attitude towards the referent" (p. 194). The first two types raise the problem. In the first the referent is subjected to a factual change, due to progress or modifications of technique, habits, etc. Among his examples Dr. Stern gives: "ship," the referential range extending in course of time to include steam-, motor-, air-ships . . . ; "telegraph," "artillery," "Deutschland" (not the same as it was last year!), "meaning" (whenever it is redefined), proper names (their referents changing as the owners grow up—one might say, hourly), and he adds, "the meaning of ethical, aesthetic, religious, philosophical and other scientific terms are in a constant flux. I shall only quote the words *religion, God, sacrifice, holy,* and so on, which together with their equivalents in other languages, have had their meanings greatly modified by the introduction of Christianity" (p. 197).

As instances of the second type—"when the referent in reality remains unchanged, but our knowledge of it changes"—he gives, among others "electricity" and "atom."

The paradox involved if we have to say that Augustine changed God but Clerk Maxwell did not change electricity, or Rutherford the atom, is fairly startling. I thought at first that the choice of these examples was merely a slip on the part of the author (easily excused by anyone accustomed to the tricks of the word "meaning"). But further reflection shows, I think, that the paradox springs from an ambiguity in the use of the word "referent" which is difficult to avoid, especially if we use it in connection with isolated words or phrases. Dr. Stern excellently explains on an earlier page the difference between actual and lexical meaning and points out that he is concerned only with actual meanings, that is, with words in actual speech, not with words as they appear in a dictionary, for example. With an isolated word, "two of the three determining factors of meaning are left vague: we do not apprehend definitely the objective reference, and we do not know under what aspect the referent is to be apprehended—the subjective apprehension is vague. It is only the third determining factor, the traditional range, that is, or at least may be, definitely known."[6] In spite of which, we are inevitably, in any large-scale survey, forced to take words in isolation, supplying vaguely, and in imagination only, the contexts necessary to give them actual meaning.

This accounts for part, though only for a minor part, of the difficulty. As we supply different contexts for "God" and for "atom" in this example, we can easily get actual meanings for them which will let us place changes in their meanings in either of Dr. Stern's types of substitution—change of the referent and change of the notion of it. But the worst part of the difficulty still remains. It is this:

When we ask about any two instances (or collections of instances) of the use of a word, whether the referent is or is not the same, we cannot answer unless we have means of finding out what the referent is on each occasion. And—with the sense of "referent" that Mr. Ogden and I proposed in *The Meaning of Meaning,* a sense Dr. Stern adopts and uses in a great number of places in this book—it is not easy to do this except in the case of words which are being used in statements which are true. To put the matter simply —when a man is talking about something which *happened* we can sometimes inquire about the something in order to find out more about what he is talking about. But when he is talking about something which did not happen . . . how are we to start identifying it? This is like the old problem whether phoenixes must, in some sense, *be* if we can mention them. The way out, I still think, is to recognize that "the sense in which a false reference may be said to have a referent must be quite other than that in which a true reference has a referent" (*The Meaning of Meaning,* 1st ed., p. 158; later eds., p. 66). A false reference, on that view, is a complex of true references each referring to its referent but together, as a complex, giving them an arrangement with which fact does not tally. There will thus be a referent (the fact) for true references (notions of "real" things) in a sense in which false references (notions of fictions, substitute shorthand symbols, etc.) lack one. For some purposes of epistemology and logic, this plan seems to work well, but clearly it is inconvenient (and sometimes worse than this) for some of the purposes of the semasiologist or the lexicographer.

A man who is tracing the history of sense changes does not want to have to stop to ask, Was this a case of sense or nonsense? at every step. The point is irrelevant to him. What he needs is a sense for the *referent* in which he can compare what a word was *taken to refer to* on various occasions. And his evidence for this will not come from investigations in the special sciences (physics, theology, psychology, history, etc.) that inquire into the actual facts in the various fields about which all men, without special knowledge, discourse; it will come from the contexts of the remarks which will show what these remarks were taken by their speakers and hearers to be about.

This, indeed, is, I think, the sense of "the referent" that Dr. Stern really uses on most occasions. But sometimes, apart from this section on Substitution, he uses the other sense: "When the referent is a material object, it can evidently not coincide with meaning, which is a psychic entity" (p. 33). And, in general, whenever he is distinguishing between the referent and a subjective apprehension of it, the referent is likely to be used in the other "epistemological" sense and difficulty arises. My phrase above, "what a word is taken to refer to," is obviously equivocal. (Rapid *fluctuations by permutation* can, I think, be detected as it goes from sentence to sentence. It would be interesting to know whether Dr. Stern would allow this description. Perhaps varying psychic stress on "what" or on "taken" introduces a further factor that would disqualify it as an example of permutation.) Let me try to make plainer what the "referent," in this sense, would be.

1. For true and false references indifferently and alike, it would be that which seems to be before the mind—to which for true references something corresponds and for false references nothing corresponds.

2. I put "seems to be before the mind" because of the well-known dangers of this all but unavoidable metaphor, and to give myself the occasion to remark that such a description is not an analysis to be taken as a serious attempt to say literally what is happening.

3. It seems wisest—for semasiological purposes—to treat "what seems to be before the mind" as a fiction introduced to allow us to keep to our usual syntax in discussing what an idea (a meaning) is *of* and a reference *to.*

4. The referent (as such a fiction) varies with the reference. In this sense to talk about two different references to the same referent would be nonsense. (Evidently with the other sense, in which I can refer in two different ways to my pen, it is not nonsense.)

5. As a function of the reference it would still be quite distinct from what Dr. Stern calls "the subjective apprehension" or "meaning which is a psychic entity." It would still act—in its capacity as the correlative of fact for *true* references—as the indispensable third factor in a functional account of the use of referential language.

The use of "referent" in this sense (it is not in any way novel, of course, being only one of the traditional senses of "object" renamed) may be shown, perhaps, most easily in a translation of a paragraph from Dr. Stern.

"When anyone speaks of relativity, the meaning of the

word, according to the definition that will be given below, is the speaker's subjective apprehension of the concept of relativity (i.e., of the referent), and it is clear that such apprehension will vary widely for different individuals, as well as for the same individual on different occasions. But the trans-subjective concept of relativity remains untouched by these variations. I therefore make a strict distinction between the concept of relativity as referent, and the various individual ways of apprehending this referent as meanings" (p. 33). Translated this becomes:

"When anyone speaks of relativity, the meaning of the word, according to the definition given above, is the speaker's reference to what he takes to be relativity (i.e., to a fiction which would seem to be before his mind as what he supposed relativity to be, if he stopped to reflect upon what he was talking about, a fiction that is a function of his reference) and it is clear that such references will vary for different individuals, as well as for the same individual on different occasions. But that with which his *referent* (i.e., what would seem to be before . . . etc.) would have to correspond if his reference was true remains untouched by these variations. I therefore make a sharp distinction between the set of operations with which Einstein and others have been so successful and the various individual ways of referring to what individuals have taken to be relativity." It will be evident, I hope, that this shift in the sense of "referent" is by no means drastic in its effects. In fact, the change in the definition only makes a difference at certain points —notably in the discussion of substitution and adequation. I return then to these. A substitution is a sense change, Dr. Stern says, due to external, nonlinguistic reasons—the cause lying "altogether outside language and the speech activity." I do not think closer analysis will support this. In the case of "ship," "The new referents were apprehended as belonging to the category of ships." No doubt the invention of the Zeppelin (but the imaginative exploits of folklore and of Jules Verne gave a meaning to "air-ship" and "flying-ship" long before) may be said to be in a remote sense the cause or the occasion for the change, but the process of change itself does lie in the speech activity, and can be traced therein. I suggest that, apart from the misleading effect of the opposition between the referent (old sense) and the subjective apprehension of it, Dr. Stern would have found in regular transfer the explanation of most cases of substitution. When "leaf" (tree) takes the sense of "leaf" (of paper) was there not an "external, non-linguistic cause" in the introduction of paper? Dr. Stern does not for that reason class it as a substitution. If we treat, as I suggest we must, words like "air-ship" just as we treat, for example, "glass-ship," or "stone-ship," and say that for semasiological purposes the coming into actual being of Zeppelins no more interferes with the referent than the going out of use of triremes changes the meaning of trireme, then the whole class of substitutions as a separate category of sense changes, I think, vanishes and we shall treat each case that was formerly a *substitution* as an example of one of the other classes—usually perhaps of regular transfer.

The same redefinition of referent also disposes, I believe, of the paradox about "God" and "atom." As the references using those words change, so, with the new definition, the referent changes too, and the question, in each case, whether this referent corresponds to a fact will be left to the appropriate authority, as outside the concern of the semasiologist, *as such*, who will, however, in consultation with the specialist, be responsible for deciding when a change of referent has occurred and how it has changed. But the danger that he may forget that to have referential function, to correspond or not, is essential to the referent—and that, as Dr. Stern admirably insists, meaning is not merely mental content—must be borne in mind.

With such a change in the sense of the word "referent," the theoretical arrangement of Dr. Stern's Seven Classes would, at points, be modified; only a detailed working over of instances could show how much.[7] Probably the changes would be slighter and fewer than at first sight appears. His distinction between objective reference and subjective apprehension would essentially remain as a distinction between the referent (new sense) and those aspects of it (may we say) which are being used in a given meaning. To settle whether or not a referent (as opposed to the choice of its aspects) has changed—which is so often the prime point of difficulty (e.g., does "love" change its referent in post-Freudian usage; or does "thought" for a behaviorist?)—we must, as before, consider whether the states of affairs with which the referent must correspond if the reference is true are the same or not. And it will do no harm if we more realize how far we are from being able to answer such questions with justifiable confidence. Are we saying new things about the same old things, or are we talking about quite new things?—that, put simply, is, as a rule, the urgent question.

My chief other point of difficulty with Dr. Stern's Seven Classes concerns his use of the distinction between "intentional" and "unintentional" processes. He is himself extremely frank about the difficulties of this distinction. He applies it only to Nominations and Transfers (Classes IV and V) and I connect with this my feeling that his treatment of these types of change is less illuminating and instructive than his discussion of the others. The author seems to be led to use it through a reluctant conviction that "the ultimate causes of speech change, the functions of speech, cannot be utilized as a basis of classification." His reason is that "any one of them may lead to any type of sense-change." This reason is, I hope, insufficient. Though we cannot at present align types of sense change with interventions of the speech functions in any *simple* manner, yet this must surely be one main direction in which to work. As Dr. Stern says, "most sense-changes are the result of the striving of speakers to adjust speech yet more closely to the functions which it has to perform."[8] One possible principle of classification, then, will attempt to show sense changes as examples of this striving, arranged according to the mode of combination and precedence of the speech functions that in the given instance are adjusting themselves. Another principle would be Formal merely, concerned with comparatively demonstrable types of change at the service, indifferently, of any combination of speech functions. Dr. Stern's classification is, I think, a combination of both—Formal in places, as in giving a separate class to Shortenings; Functional elsewhere, as when he divides figures of speech from intentional transfers (non-figurative) as having emotive, not cognitive causes (p. 293). And the distinction between intentional and unintentional processes seems to introduce yet a third principle of classification. These bogglings on my part display chiefly the fact that the purposes for which Dr. Stern has devised his Classification are not the same as those that a psychologist would be pursuing. A systematic arrangement of linguistic materials, which have already to a large degree grouped themselves by felt similarities, is not the same as an arrangement planned to throw light on mental process. It must be added that Dr. Stern's arrangement will greatly help the psychologist in his different task.

I can point my difficulty by an instance or two. Dr. Stern's classification seems to exclude purely cognitive figures of speech (p. 283)—dividing them into regular unintentional transfers, e.g., "leg" (of a table) on the one side, and, on the other, into emotive figures—thus turning an emotive function which may so far as I can see be only catalytic (to use a word here which seems to be a case of a cognitive figure of speech) into the prime agent of the change.

Again, in discussing Keats's "Thou still unravished bride of quietness" Dr. Stern appeals to a wish in the poet "not only to present the topic to the listener in an objectively correct way, but also to make the hearer take up a definite attitude towards it, to perceive it in a certain colour, and so on." For him, "unravished" and "bride" are intentional emotive transfers—the proof of the intentionality being in the user's effort to express his thoughts in a special *form*. This seems to me not to come nearly close enough to the matter. For surely the emotive effects of the words are mediated through quite definite, though subtle, cognitive transfers. Moreover, the doubt that Dr. Stern mentions as to whether this may not be all unintentional (a choice not conditioned by an aforeseen intention but made in the course and as a part of a forming intention) is very troublesome. On p. 285 he really takes "intentional" so widely (to include under it the whole mass of metaphors, popular or poetical) that the distinction in effect breaks down. I feel that he would have done better, for some purposes, to use instead a distinction he touches on elsewhere in this connection (p. 291): that between cases where the verbal context guides the transfer as here, and cases, e.g., "leg" of a chair (regular transfer), where no guiding verbal context of equivalent power is required.

The attempt to classify sense changes by the speech functions which cause them requires as a preliminary a more thorough analysis of the speech functions and of their interrelations in specific instances. This brings me to the last point at which Dr. Stern's analysis leaves me unhappy. His constitutive speech functions—the communicative, the expressive, the symbolic, and the effective or purposive—overlap or include one another awkwardly. The author is well aware of this and struggles manfully with the difficulty. No treatment of the speech functions that I know of has yet succeeded in straightening the tangle out. Either Intention (the effective function) or Communication turns into a more general function including the others or acting through them. The trouble, if we knew better what we wanted the functions *for*, would not, I think, be insuperable.

Dr. Stern gives the *word* three constitutive functions only—communicative, symbolic, and expressive—for him the effective function (intention) comes in only with *speech*, with the complete utterance. But in a book which deals only with actual not lexical meanings the restriction does not come in. As part of an utterance the word must take on its effective function. Whether all these four functions are essential, necessarily present in all use of speech, is also doubtful. Swearing often seems to drop the symbolic function and mathematics the expressive function. Similarly most literary use of speech adds functions not universally present—namely the expression of the speaker's attitude to how he is saying what he is saying, how well or ill, easily or not, etc., also of his attitude to his thought, etc., as such, his confidence, or lack of confidence, etc., that he has really thought of what he wanted to think of. By translation into the symbolic function (i.e., explicit statement) these attitudes bring into use words like: "perhaps," "more or less," "roughly," "as it were," "so to speak," "unless I am deceived," "unmistakably," and so forth. To distinguish these from attitudes toward referent or toward interlocutor is often surprisingly easy in literary analysis. I mention them here because Dr. Stern seems to have been puzzled (footnote, p. 21) by a fifth function, fifth component of the general function of communication, listed in *The Meaning of Meaning*. I should be inclined now to regard it as a group of functions normally present in a complete utterance. He also seems to doubt whether there are non-communicative uses of speech—which doubt Piaget's account of much of the speech of young children might allay.[9]

These notes upon a few points where differences of opinion, or of tactics, call for much further discussion, will not, I hope, give the impression that Dr. Stern's admirable work has been taken as merely an excuse for more wrangling about definitions. It is not odd—whatever the cynic may aver—that the study of meaning should, more than other studies, give rise to mutual misunderstanding among its students. Attempts at fine measurements show best the imperfections of our instruments and the inexactitude of our methods. Dr. Stern has made a memorable advance toward the closing of that gap between philosophy and philology which has been the chief source of futile miscomprehension in these matters. Misunderstandings in future have a better chance than before of becoming what they should be—instructive examples for analysis and comparison. Everyone who realizes how much invaluable material for psychology awaits us in language, properly studied, will welcome this book and join in making its contribution as widely recognized as possible.

10 Emotive Language Still

This ends as a sermon evidently. On a rereading, twenty-five years later, I find it eloquent and edifying. If so, I know now, better, I think, than I did earlier, that for this very reason there are tough-minded persons who must scorn and hate both the preaching and the preacher.

The close is a sketch of themes studied in detail and at length in Beyond, *of which a reviewer writes: "The traits Professor Richards deplores in human beings—hatred, admiration for power, and the instinct to requite injury— are more deep-seated than mere choice of reading matter can account for." He might have recalled how deeply cultures are shaped by their sacred books, which is what* Beyond *was about. And to speak of instinct here is to beg the key question. He goes on: "Hatred and a desire for revenge are the only wholesome human responses to such a crime [described by Ivan Karamazov], and they are inextricably connected with the impulse to protect the weak and innocent, which is basic to justice." We all know how readily we feel so and how virtuous such feelings can seem to us. Nevertheless, they are symptoms of the disease we most need to learn more about and treat more successfully if man is to survive the destructive powers that the sciences have given him.*

What does our language do?[1] In putting out now a list of its various jobs, it is important not to take their names as doing more, at first, than suggest. They will only too soon crystallize into a summary of doctrine. Every sentence we use in describing and differentiating these functions is, inevitably, a focus for their transactions. We should therefore try to keep our account of them free and fluid and non-technical for as long as we can.

Reprinted by permission of Yale University Press from *Yale Review*, 39 (1949), 108-118.

The following six jobs—as I imagine them—are all in some measure in progress simultaneously, and interdependently, whenever we use language: Indicating, Characterizing, Realizing, Appraising, Influencing, Structuring. These names *indicate*, more or less sufficiently, which the jobs are.

INDICATING words point to what is being talked about. Indicating corresponds to the question: WHICH?

CHARACTERIZING corresponds to the question: WHAT? We say something about what is indicated.

REALIZING puts the something *more* or *less* actually, vividly, and presently before us. This function would often be said to be "representational," "intuitive," and "symbolic." Language has many means of raising or lowering the degree of *realizing* it induces.

APPRAISING ranks the something—ups or downs it as desirable or not. This function corresponds to the question: GOOD or BAD?

INFLUENCING promotes or discourages some way of dealing with something. It sways us toward or from some sort of action.

STRUCTURING, or organizing, looks after the cooperations of the parts of the utterance in forwarding all the above jobs—simultaneous and interdependent as I have suggested they are. This is the foreman's or the administrator's work. For larger utterances it is the statesman's care. It is the governing of what is being done—departmentally as it were—by the five subordinates; and has to do with ordering and, ideally, selecting the HOW as well as the WHAT of their doings.

In using such a list of jobs, we have above all to resist a temptation: to separate them and suppose they concern different sorts of words and sentences. All the jobs belong in common to every utterance. We cannot as a rule say of a particular English word that it is *indicating* merely or *characterizing* merely or *realizing* merely or *appraising* or *influencing* merely or *structuring* only. Sometimes we can. "There," "this," "that" may be, most often, merely indicating words; and, at the other limit, the words "and" and "only" may be merely structuring words which do no more than organize. But almost all our words and phrases commonly exercise a simultaneous multiplicity of functions. In particular they will often both *characterize* and *appraise*, jointly *realize* and *influence;* they will be descriptive and emotive together, at once referential and influential.

This is an important point, I think. So many people have gone around calling this or that word or phrase "merely emotive." What they thought they were doing then with the word "emotive," they themselves best know. I would like to make very clear, however, that, in the only uses of this word "emotive" I have had any use for, it names functions of language which are only separable by abstraction from the rest. For me, it names the appraising and influencing components, if any, in the total work of an utterance. My title "Emotive Language Still" is thus an occasion to urge that language does not usefully sort into distinct kinds, emotive and referential. But it *has,* in almost every utterance, different jobs to do together, and one contrast between these jobs may usefully be indicated by the pairs of words "emotive"-"descriptive"; "influential"-"referential."

For example, what I have just been doing, and will go on doing, is *influencing* you, if I can, to look with disfavor on one sort of use for the word "emotive" and with favor on another. And I am trying to do this in part by *characterizing* the jobs of language, describing how it works; but in part I am influencing you by other means.

This influencing job, I suggest, is two-fold. It may be done indirectly: through things and situations I get you to think of, and statements, true or false, which I get you to believe. But it may also be done more directly: through a more direct action of words upon you due to their conjunction with situations in the past.

But, you will say, it is through their conjunctions with situations in the past that words mean things and make statements: make us think of this or that in one way or another. Granted. That is reference. But there is a more massive, a more concrete mode of action, by which words do not necessarily make us think of situations—of this or of that. In this other mode of action the abstractive process which yields references—thoughts of this or that—need not occur. What are awakened are feelings, attitudes, impulses to action which were on the move in those past situations with which the emotive words were conjoined. These more direct and concrete modes of influence, these urgings this way and that, are, I have suggested, a matrix out of which referential language forever develops —in the race and in the child. Furthermore, these powers more directly exerted through language—these underground influences from our pasts upon our futures—make up a no small part of the guiding and shaping means by which we damn or save ourselves.

What we have now to consider is how we do this, and first, what a phrase like "damn or save ourselves" may be: how referential, how emotive.

Note first: there is no question here of deciding how this phrase is used but only of exploring its possible uses. It can be, usually will be, both referential and emotive. As referential it may carry very wide ranges of views indeed. If you get people to say in other language what this phrase, in such a context, may mean, the scatter of interpretations is nearly limitless. Here are a few: "fail to solve, or solve, our problems"; "get into trouble or out of it"; "deserve misery or happiness"; "lose or return to our true selves." You can supply others without end.

Now consider what I'm calling the emotive meanings. We cannot, of course, *paraphrase* these as we can the referential interpretations. That in fact seems to be one operational test for distinguishing between emotive and referential ingredients in meaning. I do not know whether a purely referential language is anything but a theoretical fiction. But I think such a language would offer no resistance to paraphrase. Other words, rightly chosen, could do the same work. Mathematical language aspires and approximates to this condition. But the rest of language, in the measure in which it is directly emotive, resists paraphrase. Other words won't do the same work. The emotive influence comes, in part, straight from prior occurrences of the words, with other words, in former situations—not through the sorting, combining, dividing processes of abstractive thinking.

For this reason the scatter of emotive meaning for a given phrase, "save or damn," say, seems likely to be greater even than for referential meaning. Thought is a way of economizing in experience, of making our limited overlap of common experience support the greatest area of communication. Emotive ingredients, as I am defining them, are much more dependent—if you and I are to share them—on the occurrence in our pasts of the emotive words in similar situations. Consider what certain sorts of sermons, or the reading of the *Divine Comedy*, for example, can do to the words "damn" and "save."

But these direct emotive ingredients are important—in the

conduct of our language and our lives—far less for their own sakes than for their part in the indescribably complex structures they enter—frequently with decisive effect, tipping these fabulous balances for good as well as for evil.

I would stress this power for good. Since the term "emotive" got about and began to make its rather insinuatingly prosperous way in the world, too many people, I think, have used it disparagingly as a partial substitute for "sentimental." It has been as though they were afraid of all meanings which are not wholly and starkly referential, as though they felt themselves at the mercy of such meanings. And so this poor word "emotive"—which originally professed to be as technical and referential as the word "referential" itself—has picked up a peculiar emotive savor of its own somewhat similar to that of the word "hooey"! People who feel a bit more able to cope with language should remember, however, that emotive ingredients of meaning are, after all, responsible for most of the work done by the language of poetry and religion. If language which was predominantly emotive served Hitler, it also served Homer, Hosea, and Jesus.

This brings us to what I may call the politics of the United Language Functions. The parallels which suggest themselves with the politics of the United Nations will not, I believe, need pressing. Nor will the fact that a state of war exists among the language functions. Let us look at two rival schemes, two disputing principles of structuring or organization. We may call them the patterns of Science and Poetry. Each proposes its own hierarchy of control and raises a standard to which those of the appropriate inclination may repair.

SCIENCE	POETRY
INDICATE CHARACTERIZE	APPRAISE INFLUENCE
Realize	INDICATE
	CHARACTERIZE
APPRAISE	
INFLUENCE	*REALIZE*

Wordsworth once described poetry as the impassioned look upon the face of science.[2] We may perhaps regard the two patterns above as the two countenances with which these great rival organizations of our doings with language envisage their nonetheless common world. We may approach them as we please; label them "left" or "right" and pick our villain—exclaiming, if we will, "Look here, upon this picture and on this," with any desired amount of Hamlet's indignation at apostasy and defection.

For the referential hierarchy of control, Indication and Characterization are the overlords. They determine whatever Appraising or Influencing are allowed to be at work. Realization tends to be passed over as a suspect function likely to be only Appraisal and Influence covertly intervening to distort pure reference.

Truth, accordingly, for this hierarchy of control, has to do with *verification*—which will be a technique for testing the agreement of each part of the growing system of references (Indications and Characterizations) with the rest of that system. Appraising tends to be limited to approval of action in accord with such truth and to disapproval of action not in accord. And Influence, while allowed to assist—through Definitions—in the ordering of the body of referential truth, is supposed to get its force and authority solely from that body.

Now consider the emotive schema, that right-wing, reactionary, counter-revolutionary program for a hierarchy of control.

Here Appraisal and Influence are the overlords. Our appraising of something and our urge to influence others to pursue or eschew that something; these rule the selection: (1) of the things to be thought of (Indicating) and (2) of how they are to be thought of (Characterizing). All this with a view to the fullest Realization: the expansion and enriching of awareness. And Realization in turn is sought as a means to growth and self-regulation of the Appraisal and the Influence.

And what will Truth and Falsity be for this hierarchy of control? They will have to do with two things: (1) the inner order of the Appraising and Influencing—their justice in the Platonic sense, we can call it, if their components and co-inmates keep to their roles, mind their business, are true to themselves and thereby to their colleagues, superior and inferior; (2) the loyalty of the Indications and Characterizations, how these keep to their Troth—their mutual promises and agreement when chosen.

Notice how *agreement* turns up in the accounts of both scientific and poetic truth, but with what different though analogous senses: as *factual veridicality* or *consistency*, a matter of logical relationships, in science; and as *undertaking* or *engagement of the will* in poetry. Science is true as a correct account is true; poetry as a "true lover" is true. Mixed senses are frequent, as we all know; promises and predictions are often hand in hand. Nonetheless, Falsity for poetry is very far indeed from being mere failure to fulfill expectation. I think we will have to let the poet, *the* poet, tell us how far.

> Tir'd with all these, for restful death I cry
> As to behold desert a beggar born,
> And needy nothing, trimm'd in jollity,
> And purest faith unhappily forsworn,
> And gilded honour shamefully misplac'd,
> And maiden virtue rudely strumpeted,
> And right perfection wrongfully disgrac'd,
> And strength by limping sway disabled,
> And art made tongue-tied by authority,
> And folly—doctor-like—controlling skill,
> And simple truth miscall'd simplicity,
> And captive good attending captain ill:
>   Tir'd with all these, from these would I be gone,
>   Save that, to die, I leave my love alone.[3]

Leave her *alone* in a world of which all this is *true*.

And true, for poetry, in a sense beyond the survey of sociology.

That remark is unfair to sociology—unfair in fashion typical of the relations between too many of the subjects. In considering these attempted definitions of Truth for science and Troth for poetry —as so often when we are using one set of words to clear up another —the elucidation, if any, may be reciprocal, be reflected back and back again; not go one way only. In using words like "loyalty," "faith," "justice," "duty," "responsibility" to throw light on the inner order and accord of the parts *in* poetry and their troth *to* it, I seem to see some gain in luminosity result for these words themselves. If they help us to explore what the structure of poetry may be (and that with most people still is the structure of their world), may not that in return suggest things about the structure of a social order? Is not *that* in many ways itself a poem in which as social beings we participate? And might not a self-critical literary criticism by studying the language functions have something to offer to students of societies made up not of words but of men? So, in another way, if Von Neumann is right, theory of games and economics can assist one another.[4] There is nothing to be lost through friendly communion between these fields.

"Responsibility" is one of these words. I suppose there are several responsibilities appropriate to each of the language functions, and another appropriate to the system they jointly make up. The word "responsible" has a way of straddling all levels, and its straddles are, I think, not uninstructive.

Compare:

He was responsible for the safety of the mine.

The spark was responsible for the explosion.

We are responsible, however, for the conduct of our language as a whole, for all the cooperations and the mutual frustrations among its functions and, as the supreme command, for deciding between rival plans for bringing in better order.

This question of the overall politics of the to-be-United Language Functions is by no means so simple and aboveboard as we ordinarily seem to suppose. Just about the time when the First World War was breaking out, two ladies were discussing the serious situation in the Balkans. "Don't you worry, my dear," said one. "It will be all right. There won't be war. The Powers will intervene!" It was hard for her to realize that it was the Powers themselves—the Great Nations—who were coming to grips with one another, *themselves* and not through any Balkan puppets or protégés, at last. Similarly, we are slow to realize, after so many alarms and preliminary, or rehearsal, conflicts—between fiction and fact, vitalism and mechanism, geology and Genesis, religion and history, the heart and the head, ideals and actuals of all sorts—that the great showdown between the Powers has at last arrived and that the language functions themselves are vitally, desperately, self-preservingly interested in any serious discussion of their relations one to another.

To which of them, for example, does the distinction of the Troth of Poetry from the Truth of Science belong? Both Poetry and Science, I fancy, will repudiate it. When this happens, I do not believe the distinction itself should be hurt or discredited. But what is *its* authority? What, in brief, governs the language of language theory? What *am* I talking, or perhaps rather, what *should* I be talking now?

With this we approach the great, decisive, unsettled, and

unsettling question of a constitution for the United Studies—a question which falls under my Function 6, that of Structuring, or governing the operations of the other functions. This should be a pacific topic, but it is the point where all the pressures converge, where every interest has to fight for its future. There is accordingly more warfare than peacemaking in these negotiations. In his sagacious and mild book upon these matters—one of the few books which discuss them—Mr. C. L. Stevenson remarks that "Language about language must share some of the complexities of all language." "Share," indeed! "Complexities," forsooth! I would say that it must represent all the conflicts in language. It is a perpetual meeting of Secretaries of State! It is not surprising therefore that hard words are sometimes to be heard in this discussion. When *Ethics and Language* appeared, we were told that to publish it in wartime was an insult to the fighting man and tantamount to an attempt to subvert the armed forces.[5] It held, so reviewers said, that "Germany is wrong" means no more than a dog's growling! It was tempting to reply that this comment itself was not a bad specimen of philosophic growling. Yapping, perhaps, would be an apter word.

As you may notice, I am not altogether resisting the temptation to reply in kind. This is the great frailty of man, which gives us all cause now to tremble. In the Western intellectual tradition we are taught to be combative in discussion. Mental brawling is no disgrace. The ethics of the duelist or even of the gangster are acceptable to lovers of wisdom. We feel it no shame to dispute and are proud to be trenchant in debate. We admire attacks even when unprovoked, and have not yet dreamt of any need for an intellectual police to guard self-governing topics from aggression. "Dialectic" itself, to which Plato may have meant to assign that role, has nearly always been a fighting word and a technique of overcoming. And in the province of persuasion the military metaphors which sustain even the literature of lovingkindness and pacific aspiration are the most familiar things in our culture: "Wherefore, take unto you the whole armour of God, that ye may be able to withstand in the evil day, and having done all, to stand. Stand therefore, having your loins girt about with truth, and having on the breastplate of righteousness . . . And take the helmet of salvation and the sword of the Spirit, which is the word of God" (Ephesians 6:13-17).

The Prince of Peace Himself accepts this image: "I came not to send peace but a sword,"[6] and the greatest poetry in that ceaseless revolution echoes and echoes with these warlike figures.

> Bring me my bow of burning gold!
>   Bring me my arrows of desire!
> Bring me my spear! Oh clouds unfold!
>   Bring me my chariot of fire!
>
> I will not cease from mental fight,
>   Nor shall my sword sleep in my hand,
> Till we have built Jerusalem
>   In England's green and pleasant land.[7]

Only poetry—such poetry, changing all to its own ends— can take the harm out of these images. In the current routine of argument and discussion the harm is not diminished. We have not learnt yet how to think except in patterns of conflict and opposition and mutual strife. We have not realized that charity could rule the doings of our ideas with one another, or considered that there may be a connection between our taste for wordy warfare and the world's danger. Perhaps we will not save ourselves, but continue to damn ourselves, until we learn that it is the duty not of men only but of our poor words, our ideas and desires too, to understand one another, be merciful, and to pity and love one another.

This brief essay takes leave of you with what is, it thinks, a representative specimen of emotive language. What a full declaration by the United Studies would be like, whether it would be a statement or a prayer or neither, is another matter. "The deeper implications are merely indicated."

11 Semantics

I consider this the most tightly packed and comprehensive of my compositions in would-be strict expository prose. It contrasts in this respect with the preceding sermon. And yet the two belong together and attempt to cooperate—as closely as our two eyes and our two hands. When we come to understand better how these last cooperations control one another, we may, it seems likely, "see" better how saying the same thing in different ways can be of such essential service to understanding. We may learn too to "handle" utterances better.

That reviewer of Beyond *whose remarks on hatred I quoted above had his animadversions on my little metasemantic markers (specialized quotation marks). He found "something uncommonly spareable about a writer who dockets his words with marks that denote (among other things) 'Query: what meaning?' How should the reader know, if he does not?" It is well to be reminded that people can suppose they are never rightly in doubt what a word or phrase in a particular setting will, may, and should be saying.*

Recorded uses of the word "semantics" and conceptions of the nature and scope of the subject are both remarkably various.* Coined in 1883 by Michel Bréal as a name for "the science of significations" (a) and, more narrowly two years later, for "the history of changes in the meanings of words" (a1), it soon developed into "the doctrine of the principles that underlie the processes of the development of the meanings of words" (b) and then into "a thorough study of the relation between linguistic form and meaning" (c) "based on psychological [and anthropological] considerations" (for

Unpublished essay, written in 1969.

*The definitions are quoted from Allen Walker Read, "An Account of the Word 'Semantics,' " *Word*, 4, no. 2 (August 1948), 78-97. (a) Michel Bréal, example, the Eskimo word for both "thought" and "outside" is the same because Eskimos conceive thought to take place outside the head) (*c1*); thence into attempts to correct "all the ontological morass in philosophy" (*c2*). It could be stretched further and "when rightly understood, embraces the entire domain of both grammar and lexicography" (*d*) or be contracted to become, as "the rules of correspondence between symbol systems and experience," the instrument of the logical positivist revolt against idealism (*e*). Further, the term was expanded in "general semantics" to cover all reactions mediated by meanings (*f*), formalized in *Foundations of the Theory of Signs* (1938) to label one of three components (semantics, syntactics, pragmatics) (*g*), and popularized to replace such words as "suasive," "emotive," "propagandist," "verbal," or "meaningful." These varied applications of the term itself, now used most generally to mean "the study of the roles of meanings in communication," exemplify the problems faced by semanticists. As here sketched, materials toward a dictionary article are assembled. A fuller treatment should distinguish and relate not only the positions indicated so far but many others.

It is apparent that *a1* points to a relatively unambitious field for scholarship; that reflection on how *a1* proceeds leads to the high designs indicated in *b*; that *c* and *c1* commit themselves to types of answer to *b*; that *c2* has a reformist intent, as in their very different

---

Semantics: Studies in the Science of Meaning, trans. Mrs. Henry Cust (London, 1900); (*a1*) Arsène Darmesteter, *La vie des mots: etudiée dans leur significations*, 5th ed. (Paris, 1895); (*b*) Charles R. Lanman, "Reflected Meanings: A Point in Semantics," *Transactions of the American Philological Association*, 26, app. 11 (1895); (*c*) Bronislaw Malinowski, "Classificatory Particles in the Language of the Kiriwina," *Bulletin of the School of Oriental Studies of the London Institute*, 1, pt. 4 (1920); (*c1*) Bronislaw Malinowski, "The Problem of Meaning in Primitive Languages," in C. K. Ogden and I. A. Richards, *The Meaning of Meaning: A Study of the Influence of Language upon Thought and of the Science of Symbolism* (London: Kegan Paul, Trench, Trubner, 1923); (*c2*) ibid.; (*d*) Alan H. Gardiner, *The Theory of Speech and Language* (Oxford: Clarendon Press, 1932); (*e*) "En vertu des règles de correspondance de nos systèmes de symboles aux expériences vécues qu'ils symbolisent," Louis Rougier, "Allocution d'ouverture de congrés," *Actualitiés scientifiques et industrielles* (Paris, 1936), 388, 8; (*f*) Alfred Korzybski, "A Non-aristotelian System," in *Science and Sanity: An Introduction to Non-aristotelian Systems and General Semantics* (Lakeville, Conn.: Institute of General Semantics, 1933); (*g*) Charles Morris, *Foundations of the Theory of Signs, International Encyclopedia of Unified Science*, I, no. 2 (Chicago: University of Chicago Press, 1938), and *Signs, Language and Behavior* (New York: Prentice- Hall, 1946).

ways have *e* and *f*. These last (*e* and *f*) propose to find remedies for what they take to be malpractices in philosophy and verbal behavior. In contrast *d* and *g* relate to more clearly communicative concerns: how grammars and dictionaries should be constructed; what sentences can be about; how words work together; and what words can do for people—all this within more inclusive conceptions of societies and cultures. They aim further to assist all studies whatsoever to use their means of communication more efficiently with less loss from avoidable confusion and obstruction (chief sources of which are mistakings of definitions serviceable to one purpose for those useful to another).

Semantics is thus a study which should be peculiarly self-critical and scrupulous as to its own conduct. Probably semantics should, at least, make no claims to regulate or supervise other studies. It might well be defined as the science of miscomprehensions. Its service to other endeavors is to make what it discovers more available.

For its own purposes semantics needs an account: (I) of the sorts of work sentences can do, the diverse meanings they can simultaneously carry; (II) of how these meanings can be encoded by a speaker and decoded by a hearer; (III) of how these transactions between would-be communicators can break down and of how breakdowns can be remedied.

We can represent the sorts of work sentences can do and show something of their interrelations by means of a simple diagram.

1. Points to, selects. . . .
2. Says something about, sorts. . . .
3. Comes alive to, wakes up to, presents. . . .
4. Cares about. . . .
5. Would change or keep as it is. . . .
6. Manages, directs, runs, administers itself. . . .
7. Seeks, pursues, tries, endeavours to be or to do. . . .

1. Selecting
2. Characterizing
3. Presenting
4. Valuing
5. Adjusting
6. Managing
7. Purposing

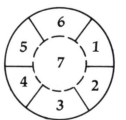

Figure 1

In figure 1 the speaker is (1) *selecting* something to be thought (talked) of; he is (2) *saying* something about it; he is (3) *presenting* this (1 + 2) in a certain way—vividly or plainly, excitingly or quieteningly, close up or remotely; he is (4) *valuing* what is presented, giving it more or less, plus or minus on some value scale; he is (5) trying, with all this, to *adjust a situation* or get someone (maybe himself) adjusted to it; he is also throughout (6) *managing* all this so that (1), (2), (3), (4), and (5) do not interfere too much with one another; and (7) he is doing all this under the direction of some *purpose* or *purposes*. If we apply this diagram and description to a few sample sentences—including this last long sentence—we will find that we can usually *see* fairly clearly what the sentence is doing under each of the seven heads, though it is harder to *say* what is being done, and harder with most poetry than with most prose. Not all sentences do all these things at once, but many do. And any sentence may fail in any or all of these aspects of its task.

One broad distinction, not affecting the previous classification, that might be made between sentences is that between *cognitive* statements, which convey either true or false information (scientific statements, eyewitness reports, and similarly descriptive communications are good examples), and *affective* statements, which express emotions and attitudes (most poems and political speeches exemplify this type).

With the aid of a pair of diagrams, we may now consider encoding and decoding. Encoding means a replacement of signs belonging to one system by signs belonging to a different system. Mental images, which cannot be transmitted, can be replaced by words, which can be transmitted. The character of the transmission process settles what it can handle as signal. The transmission is the directional emission of the signal (sound waves or configurations on a surface) to be reconverted on reception by ear or eye into words, capable of participating in the interplay of meanings presented schematically in figure 1. A sentence as a mere stream of sound or as a visual presentation is a thing of a far simpler order than the same sentence when understood or misunderstood.

Figure 2 is the communications engineer's picture, good enough for his purposes. Figure 3 is on the way to becoming a picture good enough for our purposes here. The contrast between the two should help us to reflect on what we know about what we do in communication.

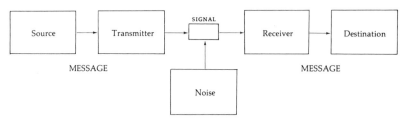

Figure 2

The engineer does not care about the meanings of the messages he transmits with his signals. But for semantics they are all-important. What is the speaker trying to say? What is the hearer trying to understand? These are the semantic problems. Figure 3 accordingly opens up Source and Destination to suggest that what we find to say comes to us, perhaps out of the distant past, from our situation as speakers, and that what we understand as hearers comes again out of our past and leads on into our developing situation. For semantics, situations are recurrents, going back and back and forward and forward.

The arrows in figure 3 suggest the cyclic complexity of the selection process by which we compose what we hope to $^?$say$^?$. (Special question marks around "say" or any other word are a device to indicate that the word, as used here, needs to be questioned as to its meaning—the work it is doing here—in this sentence.)[1] And $^?$say$^?$ here includes "be understood as meaning by a hearer who has gone through a suitable DV (development)." At this point

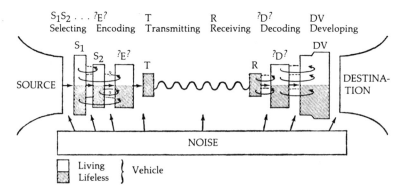

Figure 3

we may well remind ourselves through figure 1 of the intricacy of our meanings and through figures 2 and 3 of how easily noise may interfere with intended communication.

The problems of encoding and decoding are exemplified by the use of the word "code" itself. "Code" has a wide spectrum of uses in which we can note the combination, in various ways and degrees, of different senses. On one side we have the Morse code; on the other, codes of conduct. With the Morse code, a formulated and unambiguous rule governs how letters may be represented by dots and dashes. With legal, social, and moral codes, there is no such simple, applicable one-to-one rule. What we may or may not do is in a high degree governed, but immensely intricate questions of interpretation enter into the application of any rules that may be proposed. With Morse we have two sets of signs equally definite and observable. With moral rules no such distinct sets of signs are operating.

In between these extremes we have language or, rather, a wide range of various types of language use. With the Morse code we have an inventory for a hardware store, a set of names which have a well-defined and largely one-to-one correspondence with items in the store. Any competent person can point out which names label what. With moral codes we have poetry, in which no one, however skilled and experienced, can say exactly what any phrase is doing, though to see in some way just *that* is the aim of the study of poetry. In between the technical list and lyrical poetry we have the varying bands of business uses, social chat, lovers' tactics, administrative and political strategy, teaching and preaching, as well as the specialized languages of mathematics and of the physical, the social, the behavioral, the aesthetic, the mental and moral sciences, philosophy, and semantics itself—defined as "the study of the roles of meanings in communication."

For each of these bands of language use, the kinds of meanings employed, their organization, and the types of work they are engaged in are likely to be different. A similar distinction governs the use of the word "code" appropriate within each band. To distinguish and relate the various uses, both in principle and in detail, is the business of semantics. Further, it has the still more exacting question to answer: How can we minimize the danger of miscomprehensions due to such wide differences in the meanings of words, such as "code," that play such key roles in communication? ("Code," it may be noted, has here been selected as a typical specimen of a key word which—within and between subjects—can generate endless miscomprehensions.)

Unfortunately, although the working principles of separate disciplines are generally self-consistent, that is, consistent within the discipline, they tend to be contradictory between disciplines. The communications engineer confines himself to those transformations from message to signal and back again which can be controlled by mathematical or physical rules. For his purposes message and signal must not be confused; they are two different sets of signs, messages having semantic aspects (including why they are sent) which are not his business. But, if we move from engineering into psycholinguistics, defined by its founders as "that one of the disciplines studying communication which is most directly concerned with the processes of decoding and encoding,"[2] we find that when A talks to B, his postures, actions, etc., may all be considered part of the message; the engineer's distinction between message and signal, which makes things so relatively easy for him, is here given up. On the other hand, in microlinguistics, or linguistics proper, the structure of messages (the signals in the channel connecting communicators) is treated independently of the characteristics of either speakers or hearers. When a phrase like "learning to decode the environment" is used, there is no need felt to note or be concerned with the metaphor employed. But in contrast again, if we move on to poetic theory, we find the transformation of $S_1 S_2 \ldots$ into $?E?$ (the selection of words for the intended meanings in a poem) and of what R receives (mere sounds or black marks on a white field) into $?D?$ and DV (the findings of meanings for the words heard or read), being supposed to be the same sort of event as the transformations of $?E?$, via T, into the signal (sound waves or patterns on paper) which is sent to R. When such extremely different types of occurrence (as different almost as any can be) are lumped together under words as undifferentiating as "code," it is not surprising that Message at Destination so often fails to have due accord with Message at Source.

As we have just seen, semantics, or at least awareness of semantic problems, can reasonably account for miscomprehensions. However, it has also the duty of prescribing remedies. This takes us back to the "reformist intent" of *c1, e,* and *f.* Many students have attempted to trace human ills to misconduct in language. In most cases the reformers are by no means clear as to just what it is they are against, so that the positive sides of their positions are more likely to be useful than the negative. For example, it is certainly well to stress that the meaning of an utterance derives from the situations, the controlling contexts, past and present, through which its parts have come to be used (*c1*); that we must distinguish between language used about things in the real world, or "object language," and language used about language, or "meta-language" (*e*); that any devices which will increase and clarify our consciousness of how we are thinking are useful (*f*); and that comparing different ways of saying what we call ⁷the same thing⁷ can show us much about what each utterance is doing with it.

The diversity and the uncertainty of the positions in semantics may be due to the undeniable importance of its theme. What everyone chiefly wants to know about any utterance is what it says. How may ⁷What is said⁷—even with, to take extreme instances, ⁷the same words⁷ and in what may seem almost identical contexts—differ from instance to instance? What apparatus have we for comparing such differences? It would seem that we must somehow already know more than a little about all this even to ask these necessary questions. Much of this "immediate knowledge" is at work in the comparings, known as syntax, by which the grammarian builds up his system of rules for the cooperations of words. The grammarian's comparisons are largely conscious and explicit. They develop from the largely unconscious, implicit comparings through which the child first learns to talk. The subtle and exact "know-how" we so early attain as to which sorts of words require and exclude which, and as to such problems as word order and inflection, is what the grammarian tries to translate into rules. In terms of figure 1 school grammar is a reflection of (6) in a (1-2) form; but (6) and (1-2) have very different work to do, though teaching may mistake them. Both have been called structures of "syntactic or linguistic" meaning, and are often contrasted by theorists of language with "referential" and "pragmatic" meaning. It has sometimes been declared that such linguistic meaning is the only sort of meaning linguistics need be concerned with, but this seems shortsighted. It risks disregarding the connections that hold between such an abstract study and the concrete performances of communication.

As many sentences in this article have demonstrated, we have to recognize the extreme and peculiar ambiguity of the language in which semantic matters are discussed. Among the devices semantics may well develop for discussing its own distinctions less confusedly, in addition to the aforementioned dual question marks, are signs such as $\equiv$ for "equivalent to," superscripts (^{W}word^W $\equiv$ that speech act, sound, or written mark), subscripts ($_m$meaning$_m$ $\equiv$ adjustment that an utterance is aiming at), abbreviations, such as "e.g.," "etc." In the case of "etc.," the aim would be to provide a compact pervasive reminder that all utterances are inevitably incomplete and partial. Along such lines much improvement in the notations through which semantics conducts its business may be expected. Consider the value of differences in spelling for similar vocables, e.g., "There, there! Their meanings: they're clearer here than when we hear them." There may well be similar gains to be made through refinements in the mutual control of eye and ear in the management of meanings. Then, at least, the formulation of semantic problems could be clarified: E.g., $^?$what is said$^?$ serves equally well to point to ^{W}the words uttered^W or to what those words $_m$mean$_m$. And ^{W}meaning^W in turn can point equally to a speaker's thoughts, intentions, etc., or what those thoughts, etc., are of. (In terms of figure 1 what they point to (1), would question (2), would promote or oppose (4, 5) etc.)

Semantics necessarily uses language about language; indeed much of it must be language about language about language.[3] Though speech cannot manage it, in written language necessary distinctions can be indicated and kept in order. In a fashion familiar in mathematics and as suggested in the preceding paragraph, notational and typographical devices can take care of much that has as yet only been handled through contentious and confusing debate. Such devices have been consciously adopted in the presentation of this article. As semantics develops such improved techniques of communication for its own purposes, its devices will probably be found of service in other fields, much as mathematics serves engineering. Advances in mental and moral communications comparable to those which have recently occurred in physical communications are not only possible but probable. Technological advances make semantic developments urgent.

Two further probable developments in semantics should be mentioned. Current increases in the scope and power of data processing are likely to stimulate new types of inquiry into the oppositions and mutual requirements among meanings. Computerized dictionaries and other such aids to the control of language use are imminent. The other development would be in techniques of instruction in the handling of meanings. Here again the computer may have an important part to play by showing the learner, in a designed sequence, the other situations and sentences which can best help him to see what a sentence in a given situation is saying. We develop our abilities to discern meanings through comparison. The computer is our best means for discovering and for controlling the comparisons which will be most fruitful.

12 Complementarities

That same reviewer of Beyond *complains: "He never tires of telling us that Niels Bohr's Complementarity Principle . . . should be taken over from physics and used in the humanities. That seems to preclude rejecting any view as simply 'wrong.' " Not a bit. People interested in and duly concerned with complementarities have not been that silly. Though derivatives from mutually exclusive setups may jointly contribute, mistakes, of all sizes, remain as possible as ever. The particular mistake of this reviewer, I should add, is frequent and accounts for more than a little of the confusions about and resistances to complementarity studies. Attempts to warn against it are also frequent. If no view could be rejected as wrong, none could be accepted as right. "Simply" (as here used) raises other questions and might accordingly be written as ?simply?. How corrupting partisan attitudes are!*

Long ago, sixty years ago (in 1912-15 and again in 1918-19), Alec and Marjorie Mace and I made up the most part of G. E. Moore's audience at Cambridge, and in 1915 we three were all who took the Moral Sciences Tripos. It was not really surprising that Moore's regular lecture audiences were small. He was not in the least like Owen Glendower. Still

> To trace Moore in the tedious ways of art
> And hold him pace in deep experiment

Lecture delivered at Birkbeck College, University of London, on June 28, 1972, in honor of the late C. A. Mace, professor of psychology at the college from 1944 to 1961. Reprinted by permission from I. A. Richards, *Complementarities* (London: Birkbeck College, 1972).

was never any light undertaking.[1] He was not like any other lecturer I have heard or heard of. He made you sure that what was going on mattered enormously—without your necessarily having even a dim idea as to what it could be that was going on. We were, in truth, undergoing an extraordinarily powerful influence, not one that I would suppose Moore could for a moment conceive. He was not at all interested in that. He was interested in the problem in hand: more interested in it than, I think, I have ever seen anyone interested in anything. Some of this, to use Alec Mace's phrase, "rubbed off" on us.

It is reasonable, is it not, to expect that a deep influence may take years—even decades—before producing its full effect. And the effect produced may often be very unlike what might be thought likely. As we listened to Moore we were noting—I, at least, was— his immense difficulty in believing that any other philosopher could possibly be *meaning what he said.* And we, on the other side of the communications barrier—"barrier" is the right word—were having reciprocal trouble. There, with Moore's example before us, we couldn't believe that anyone could *say what he meant.*[2] This, you know, is a very old trouble. Socrates, you recall, asked the poets (and others) what they meant. And they could not tell him. Maybe there are ways of asking "What does this mean?" which destroy the possibility of answering. They interfere with the meanings under investigation. And this, I take it, is the main point in a complementarity doctrine as it comes to us from atomic physics, to which I will very shortly be returning.

Another thing we were learning from Moore was for how long a time a problem can be worried. In his "A Reply to My Critics," he says, "I cannot possibly discuss any single one of [their questions] as fully as it deserves."[3] He certainly expanded our notion of how much discussion a question can deserve. For example, he could take a single sentence from James Ward's *Encyclopedia Britannica* article on psychology and stay with it for three weeks lecturing on: What on earth could Ward possibly have meant by saying that "the *standpoint* of *psychology* is *individual*" —underlining the key words perhaps seventy times, gown flying, chalk dust rising in clouds, his intonations coruscating with apostrophes, and come out by the same door as in he went, looking up to heaven and shaking his head in despair.

Now as to "Complementarities," I chose my title because I wanted to keep as close as I could to topics I thought Alec Mace would be interested in and on which I would most like to have had his comments. On the many occasions through the last few decades when I have found myself in more than usual accord with something he wrote or said, I have had one of those vague "Ha! Here's a clue!" feelings we all know so well. In time I came to label these feelings with Niels Bohr's term "complementarity," and to wonder too whether these agreements and affinities I felt with Alec's thinking might not in part stem from some reaction we had in common to what we had jointly undergone from Moore.

Rereading, for this occasion, the very winning pages of *C. A. Mace: A Symposium*, so well edited by Vida Carver, I have been struck by the way the contributors recur and recur to his "attempts to reconcile conflicting viewpoints . . . his search for a harmony that lies behind appearances"; his "stress on the structure of the situation as governing the behaviour of the individuals in it"; his "ability to look without blanching at the full implications of *different* ways of thought"; his insistence that we should "extend the boundaries of a problem and see it in a wider setting." And again, to his concern for contradictions, for dialectic oppositions: "From the juxtaposition of apparently incompatible ideas he would suddenly strike off a new flame."[4] And in rereading his own pages it has been easy to note the same concern for the expansion of frames of consideration, as in his brilliantly lucid survey— in "Some Trends in the Philosophy of Mind"—of the history of psychology in terms of "categorical distinctions," pointing out in so salutary a way that there are *both* "categorical blunders," mistakings of one category for another (a fact, say, for an event) and *also* "categorical revolutions": switching from one set of categories to another.[5] And again there is, in his whole treatment of "How We Know Material Things Exist" the same reference to the fullest possible, the most inclusive frame or situation into which we can put our account.

All this made me feel that complementarity might be the right topic for this occasion.

A few words now on Niels Bohr's way of describing the great lesson (as he puts it) that the exigencies of atomic physics (the investigation of the simplest of all systems) could teach psychologists—and perhaps even philosophers—people investigating immeasurably more complex systems.

The lesson, he says, is conveyed through "the opportunities offered us for . . . the examination and refinement of our conceptual tools." May I stress that for him concepts are tools: things with and through which we do things.

"When new discoveries have led to the recognition of an essential limitation of concepts hitherto considered as indispensable, we are rewarded by a wider view and a greater power to correlate."[6]

Does there not seem a sort of poetic justice about this? That, when we have brought ourselves, somehow at last, to acknowledge an inadequacy in our conceivings we should be *rewarded,* not penalized; that the outcome should be a gain, not a loss of power. It has its resemblance to the Sermon on the Mount, or to Isabella on that Representative Man, Angelo:

> man, proud man,
> Drest in a little brief authority,
> Most ignorant of what he's most assured—
> His glassy essence . . .[7]

It is like Shakespeare to make ignorance and assurance thus vary together. And to hint so that the last thing we may know is that whereby we know.

Here is Niels Bohr on that: "An analysis of the very concept of explanation would begin and end with a renunciation as to our explaining our own conscious activity."[8] Bohr's key idea is of the "mutual exclusiveness" of various sources of understanding. Typically, and most instructively, in atomic physics, as between wave and quantum conceptions of the transmission of energy. It is important, however, to recognize that extension of the complementarity principle from atomic physics to other and incomparably more complex fields of inquiry is not a matter of finding "more or less vague analogies" in them of what has made itself so manifest in physics. It is a question of recognizing in the more complex investigations the same mutual exclusions among intelligential procedures which the relative simplicity of atomic transactions has brought out so unmistakably. Bohr insists on this: we are not looking for vague analogies but finding through analysis the very same dependence of the outcome on the means used in the inquiry. His favorite examples are from psychology and linguistics. In psychology "the mental content is invariably altered when the attention is concentrated upon any one feature of it." And he notes that it is "impossible in psychical experience to distinguish between the phenomena themselves and their conscious perception."[9] We may be reminded of Alec Mace's remark that a microscope is a bad instrument with which to find one's way about a town.

The complementarity principle may be divided into two components: an instrumental component and a complemental component. Here are separated statements of these:

> The properties of the instruments or apparatus employed enter into . . . belong with and confine the scope of the investigation. (*Speculative Instruments*, p. 114)[10]

> Two seemingly incompatible conceptions can each represent an aspect of the truth . . . They may serve in turn to represent the facts without ever entering into direct conflict. (Louis de Broglie, *Dialectica*, II, 326)[11]

The first is from a book of mine whose title, I believe, comes from Coleridge, though I admit that I have failed of late to find it.

The most important of our instruments, I would like to stress, are our *concepts*. Anyway our *methods* of thought, our intelligential procedures, are to be counted as the chief of "the instruments or apparatus employed."

On conceptions, may I suggest that a conception (or a concept) ought to bring to our mind its parents. There is an *intellectual genetics* that is very relevant to this whole topic. Where do we get our ideas, our methods, our procedures from? How much—we have been wondering—were Alec Mace's procedures descended from, say, G. E. Moore's? How far can this notion of "descent from" cover "reaction against" as well?

Here is Bohr's most striking linguistic example: "Our task can only be to aim at communicating experiences and views to others by means of language, in which the practical use of every word stands in a complementary relation to attempts of its strict definition" (Niels Bohr, *Dialectica*, II, 318).[12] I hope to illustrate this with the following diagnosis which Moore gives of philosophi-

cal difficulties: "It appears to me that in Ethics, as in all other philosophical studies, the difficulties and disagreements, of which its
history is full, are mainly due to a very simple cause: namely to the
attempt to answer questions, without first discovering precisely
what question it is which you desire to answer" (*Principia Ethica,*
p. vii).[13] Taking that as an example of "the practical use" of words,
does it not seem highly reasonable? But make real "attempts at the
strict definition" of the key words in it: *question, answer,* and *precisely.* What happens then? And just what is *discovering* here?
How do we do it? What is the relation of a *question* to its *answer?*
Can more than one *answer* be equally useful? If one *answer* is right,
must all others be wrong? If we press such questions and note how
much a question can change as we study it, and how often finding
better questions is the best way to progress, we will come to wonder whether this diagnosis of difficulties as "mainly due to a very
simple cause" is as much to the point as it may have seemed. And
yet when you have felt that doubt sharply enough, can you not get
back to the former, the first original viewpoint from which we can
think we do know enough about questions and answers to agree
that this *is* what philosophers *are* always attempting and that this *is*
"the very simple cause" of their difficulties. Or will you want to
say, instead, the *"not* so simple cause"?

I suggest that we practice this switching from the one
position to the other for a while—from the practical use of words to
the attempts at their strict definition, and then back again. After
which we may consider whether this alternation does not make us
"more knowing," to quote Coleridge, as to how language works. A
psychologist, such as Alec Mace, may, moreover, I think, properly
regard a question as an imbalance, a vicissitude in homeostasis,
useful and necessary, and take an answer to be something restoring
equilibrium. And, if so, may there not be many ways of doing that?

You will have noticed perhaps what an important role the
metaphor of a *point of view* and the metaphor of *seeing* (= *discovering*) has been taking?[14] Let me offer you now what I believe is
a simpler and a more instructive TYPE SPECIMEN of a complementarity situation. It is so simple (seemingly) that I am alarmed. Can it
really be the type specimen of complementarity I think it is?

I found myself deep in it when I first tried hard (as a philo-

sophic exercise) to recall what my earliest memory is. It turned out
to be my first conscious inquiry into a problem. It was this: what I
saw through one eye wasn't the same at all as what I saw through
the other eye. I suppose I may have been quite small at the time:
perhaps in a cot. Anyway what was puzzling me were the varying
appearances of the undulations of linen surfaces: the waves, crests,
slopes, hollows, troughs, peaks in the bedclothes as I lay gazing at
them first with one eye then with the other, then with both at once.

To experiment with this (without going to bed, much less
back into a cot) crumple up a handkerchief, hold it about a foot
away, identify a peak among its crumples, and then compare carefully how its ridges look as you alternately shut one eye or the
other. Try drawing the two landscapes. Notice, further, that not
only the two forms differ, but the colors of their slopes are different—if one eye is exposed to a light, to the sun, or to a lesser illumi-
nant and the other eye is in the shade. I am reminded of how pertinently Alec Mace used this very case in discussing "How we know
material things exist." The two main criteria for a complementarity
situation are (1): that the experimental setups should be *mutually
exclusive* and (2): that the separate *outcomes* should support,
complement one another.[15]

That is my type specimen of a complementarity situation. It
is a *two-points-of-view* combination. But we should remember that
most complementarity situations should be attempting to combine
many more points of view. And, commonly, to combine many
visual points of view with components which are not visual at all:
for example, I regard my right thumbnail. In so doing, I twist my
head and my hand about combining countless visual points of view
with rotational reports from my neck, arm and wrist joints, etc.;
also my knowledge of what it would feel like if I rubbed it with my
left forefinger. Also of what it would feel like if I were to trim it a
bit smoother. Also with what Mrs. X-Quisit might think if she saw
it at her dinner table. Also, perhaps with the thought that "Nature
is red in tooth and claw" and with thoughts of what its ancestors
may have had to do.

These are complementarity situations from the routine of
perception. Into them enter—for possible resolution—innumerable
resultants, initially incompatible and discrepant, from apprehen-
sive processes of all levels and orders. Their super-resultant is
"What I see as my thumbnail."

Remember, this itself is but a *thumbnail sketch* of something having far greater semantic complexities—which I am asking you to compare (contrast, if you like) with Moore's "very simple cause" of philosophic disagreements.

Incidentally, the phrase "thumbnail sketch" itself offers in miniature what I take to be a complementarity situation. The OED gives "of the size of a thumbnail"—something you might write or draw *on* a thumbnail. Another definition might be "something you might write or draw *with* a thumbnail, scratching it so in a surface." These are mutually exclusive situations. Together they yield a useful meaning: "short, rough description or depiction."

The complementarity principle can seem to outrage logic, to destroy some much-prized intellectual virtues: rigor, consistency, and such. On the other hand it can seem to be the most peace-bringing liberation ever, comparable with that of Yeats's early poem "The Rose of Peace."

> And God would bid His warfare cease,
> Saying all things were well;
> And softly make a rosy peace,
> A peace of Heaven with Hell.[16]

However, here is Bohr being, I think, more subversive than he knew. "Words like 'thoughts' and 'sentiments', equally indispensable to illustrate the diversity of psychical experience, pertain to mutually exclusive situations characterized by a different drawing of the line of separation between subject and object" (*Dialectica*, II, 318). That line can be, as we know, a truly momentous affair, a way of raising all the greater problems of our being. I wonder whether Marjorie Mace recalls an occasion at the Moral Sciences Club in those old days when a Welsh visitor asked us: "What happens when a Subject becomes an Object and yet remains a Subject?"

Nobody thought then of quoting Hegel or Bradley on Hegel as answer to this. (Moore had made Bradley and Hegel unmentionables in the Cambridge of those days. How fashionable intellectuals commonly are!)

> The individual who knows is here wrongly isolated, and then, because of that, is confronted with a mere alien Universe. And the individual, as so isolated, I agree, could do

nothing, for indeed he is nothing. My real personal self which orders my world is in truth inseparably one with the Universe. Behind me the absolute reality works through and in union with myself, and the world which confronts me is at the bottom one thing in substance and in power with this reality. There *is* a world of appearance and there *is* a sensuous curtain, and to seek to deny the presence of this or to identify it with reality is mistaken. But for the truth I come back always to that doctrine of Hegel, that 'there is nothing behind the curtain other than that which is in front of it.' (F. H. Bradley, *Essays on Truth and Reality*, p. 218)[17]

Alec Mace's interest in Hegel has been remarked on by many.

Another aspect of this overall complementarity situation may be pointed to in terms of the limits of metaphor:

You know that all your creeds and definitions are merely metaphors, attempts to use human language for a purpose for which it was never made. Your concepts are, by the nature of things, inadequate; the truth is not in you but beyond you, a thing not conquered but still to be pursued. Something like this, I take it, was the character of the Olympian Religion in the higher minds of later Greece. Its gods could awaken man's worship and strengthen his higher aspirations; but at heart they knew themselves to be only metaphors. As the most beautiful image carved by man was not the god, but only a symbol, to help towards conceiving the god; so the god himself, when conceived, was not the reality but only a symbol towards conceiving the reality. (Gilbert Murray, *Five Stages of Greek Religion*)[18]

For "the god" can we not substitute pretty well anything: "my right thumbnail," for example?

What we may suppose we are seeing, thinking of, meaning, then, is not *it* but merely *our way, our means, of trying to see, think of, mean IT.*

Merely metaphors?

Some time ago—forty years, to be exact—I tried to help the discussion of metaphors by introducing two new technical terms: "Tenor" and "Vehicle."[19] They were chiefly a means of describing the extreme and necessary complexity of what happens in metaphor. They weren't (couldn't be) at all any solution of any problem. They were, at best, a means for keeping oneself alerted to what may happen.

I didn't then write them $\dfrac{\text{Tenor}}{\text{Vehicle}} = \dfrac{T}{V}$.

I'm doing so now in the hope they may help in thinking about complementarities. Once again they are no *answer* to any question; they are just a way of generating possibly useful questions.

Pictorially, $\dfrac{T}{V}$ suggests that something (the Tenor) is sort of riding in, being carried by, a car $\dfrac{}{V}$. I am going to assume here that as a rule, a change in V results in some change in T (in some respect and degree). The change in T may be *relevant or not* to what is going on. V is a way of presenting T. How we apprehend T depends in some measure on V, though, of course, it depends on any number of other things too.

So V isn't just a pointer pointing to ? something, though it normally includes pointers. In addition to pointing, it is a way of saying, feeling, doing, etc., something about what is pointed to. V is an instrument, a piece of intellectual apparatus, for dealing with T. Thus its character affects T. But a mere pointer doesn't. The pointer may vary a lot but, provided it points, that doesn't matter.

This contrast between discourse which primarily *points* and discourse which, in one way or another, in some degree *depicts*, is, of course, parallel with many accounts of contrasts between sciences and poetries, which, I take it, are attempts to describe our chief complementarity predicament. It suggests, perhaps, why sciences are translatable but poetries not. And why—with both—it is *unnecessary* and *dangerous* to have and depend on one *Vehicle*. As I say this, you will be recognizing that in countless important matters, this finding and trusting to one Vehicle has been most people's favorite ambition. Nay, more, in what have been considered the most important matters, this has been officially taught as man's first duty (and with all sorts of horrible sanctions—from hellfire on up—behind the teaching). I have, perhaps, suggested enough that whole orders—*and trades*—of philosophic debate would be just out forever, if thinkers would study the complementarity principle more—may I say?—Mooreishly. I mean by that more *devotedly*.

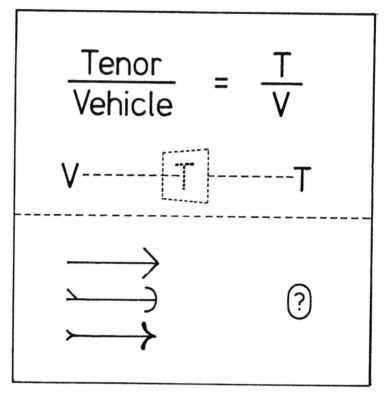

Figure 4

You know, looking back to those long-ago days when Alec and Marjorie Mace and I were trying to learn to philosophize, I have a queer feeling that the fashionable POSE or STANCE we were expected to assume was one of regarding all previous philosophers as comparatively FOOLS. Nobody seemed to care at all really about the HISTORY of the philosophic activity. One of the things Alec Mace did was to FREE his students from that sort of silliness.

A general cultivation of and acquiescence in complementarity positions can be expected to make no little difference to human activities.

I fancy Moore would have considered all this complementarity stuff to be gravely obstructive nonsense. I'm not sure of this, because he could wobble. He could suddenly give up long-held doctrines and then be quite at a loss as to why on earth he had ever for a moment done so. But on the whole, I'm nearly sure he would have thought complementarity notions pernicious. Once, when I was lecturing at Princeton on the interinanimation of words, I saw Moore unexpectedly in my audience.[20] I had been taking Donne's stanza from "The Extasie," one of the most discerning as it is one of the noblest of utterances on the great theme:

When love with one another so
   Interinanimates two soules
The abler soule which thence doth flow
   Defects of loneliness controules.

I had been saying that words too, when suitably commingled, could generate and convey meanings far beyond what any single word in its loneliness could utter. Moore's comment at the end of the lecture opened perfectly with "Of course, I don't agree at all with anything you said." This with his characteristic air of deprecation and his shy and tender smile. He was doing his duty as ever.

Anyway I want to close (this main prose body of my lecture) by recalling again how much Alec and Marjorie Mace and I have owed to our master, who took philosophy of mind so seriously and set us standards of scrupulosity and pertinacity we couldn't do much more than dream of living up to. Needless, I suppose, to add that without *all* that anyone can do by way of living up to such standards, none of the various point-of-view presentations that the complementarity position asks us to take account of can be developed far enough to be compared and combined.

I am finishing up with a further example of complementarity explorings, carried out experimentally *in verse*.

You may perhaps have felt about Moore's pronouncement on the *very simple cause* to which philosophic difficulties and disagreements are, he thought, due, that a supplementary pronouncement might be offered that they often come from the application of *methods unsuited to the aim*. Moore himself repeatedly expressed, in his later life, doubts whether his own procedure was appropriate. "I think it is a just charge against me that I have been able to solve so few of the problems I wished to solve." Perhaps, he thought, he had "not gone about the business . . . in the right way."[21]

I find it helpful and salutary to wonder how Moore would have taken a suggestion that no *philosophic* problem has ever, in all the history of thought, been *solved*—in any relevant sense. Mathematical problems are; and physical questions are shifted. But the great philosophic challenges? No. They may lapse through change in fashion. But are they *solved?* If they were, the contrast surely between advances in philosophy and advances in physics, physiology, and psychology would be ludicrous.

Whether owing to Moore or not, few have been more aware of these doubts than Alec Mace, and for these and doubtless other reasons I am ending up this evening in an odd fashion. I have long felt that the central philosophic problems—those of ethics, psychology, methodology, and ontology—ought to be handled rather in verse than in prose. The suitable verse, I have felt, should be intricate, formal, exacting, lucid, and compact. But it is hardly useful to profess such opinions without experiments in practicing what they would preach. So here is a short presentation and illustration of some major complementarities in what tries to be such verse. The problems these poems examine are knowledges of other people and knowledges of our own selves. And of the extreme mutual dependences (interinanimations, if you like) of these knowledges. This is the side of philosophy of mind that, I believe, Alec Mace—interested though he was in all sides of psychology—was most interested in.

Poem I ends with a question which poem II tries to treat.[22]

Complementary Complementarities

I

The properties of the instruments or apparatus employed enter into . . . belong with and confine the scope of the investigation. (*Speculative Instruments*, p. 114)

This picture I take
Is the camera's view,
Not mine: not you.

Change the instrument,
Change the film or screen,
And you, you're seen

Otherwise. So
—You will find—
With my camera mind:

Film varies there
Minute by minute
And you as fast in it.

Where are you then?
Which infra-thought you
Am I now talking to . . .

Ultra-sentiment you?
Among such how to see
How any you can be?

II

Two seemingly incompatible conceptions can each represent
an aspect of the truth . . . They may serve in turn to represent the facts without ever entering into direct conflict.
(Louis de Broglie, *Dialectica*, II, 326)

Film's a surface thing
My sense-taken *you's*

Bring only a skin
Round a void;
Set me to cling
To a vestige as thin.

What though what I sense
Select its takes,
Install, control,
Wreck and remake;
How was it thence
You acquired a soul?

So I might divine
—Create?—my *you,*
Planted in me
Through what you show:
A you only mine
Isolatedly.

This film-thin shot
At substituting
'What A does' for 'A'
Breaks down on you:
Truly you're not
Just 'what you display.'

But why need I tell
You this   who should know
Well enough   how all
Who   take the shadows
For substance   dwell
In this cinema hall.

You've your own *you* too
Which you never touch,
View, taste, or scent,
Though sometimes hear
Saying for you
What you ought to have meant.

That self-same you
—Summoned whence
To the chromosome dance?—
Before your heart beat
Set up a do
Out-reaching chance:

As the CONCEPT here
Has chosen its word
Sheer through the maze
Of the eddying web
Whose balancings clear
Or block its ways.

Two languages:
As of the soul,
As of the cell,
Take it in turn;
In new pages
Each other spell.

III

Words like 'thoughts' and 'sentiments', equally indispensable
to illustrate the diversity of psychical experience, pertain to
mutually exclusive situations characterized by a different
drawing of the line of separation between subject and object. (Niels Bohr, *Dialectica*, II, 318)

Grave news, my dear!
Our mutual thought
Must of all sediment be clear.
For Proof: they redefine
The elements of our design!

Here's a formula will build a
High efficiency philtre-filter.

Conversely, to enjoy
The customary fellow feeling,
Each last least germ of thought destroy
As too revealing.

Who may this formula employ
And to what end
And through what schooling
There's no precluding
However finely it intend.

IV
One must draw the line somewhere!

My love, my grief, my fear, my hate,
Dear Fate, do either root in you,
Or I,
Idly driven, idly spy.

Where you end
And I begin
Or any else, in fine,
On such dichotomies depend
There's no one left to draw a line.

Poems V and VI are a verse summary of what Werner Jaeger
in *Paideia* describes (I think rightly) as the ideal design for man and
the unique contribution of the Helleno-centric culture.[23] It is the
pattern for the individual and for society first presented in *The Republic*. With pedagogic and mnemonic intent, they are given some
metrical impetus.

The affections and faculties correspond to what we may call
the Sentiments, the affective-volitional system, which Shand[24] and
others have described in such detail. Donne, I believe, took his doctrine here directly from *The Republic*. I add a diagram displaying
the key relationship. The Sentiments (like Plato's guards) mediate
between Reason or Intellect (the Guardians) and the Senses: de-

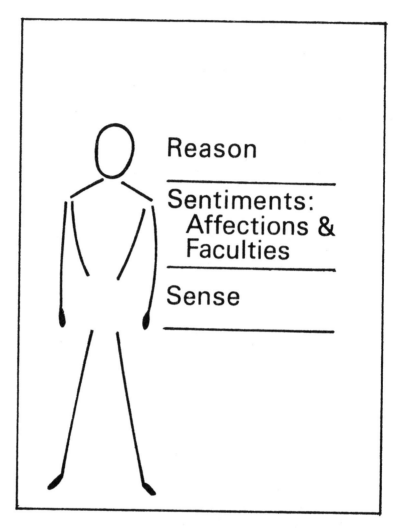

Figure 5

sires, appetites, the energy supply. It will be noted that the grammar here goes both ways: "The A & F can reach down and *control* Sense" or "Sense can reach up and take in what the Sentiments tell it." But Sense cannot itself know that Thought contemplates. One of the great commentaries on this position is in Coleridge's penultimate paragraph of *Biographia Literaria,* Chapter 14, describing

"The poet in ideal perfection" where he writes of the "gentle and irremissive *controul*" needed, using still Donne's spelling.[25]

V
So must pure lovers' soules descend
T'affections and to faculties
Which sense may reach and apprehend
Else a great Prince in prison lies.
      (John Donne, "The Extasie")

So 'a great Prince in prison lies'
   His servants disaffected:
The affections and the faculties
   Disabled and dejected.

How we could feel, how act:
   The SENTIMENTS—whose rank
Held only by their pact—
   Now have themselves to thank

If the Virtues scowl and skulk,
   While their Helpers helpless droop:
Courage complaining in a sulk
   To Faith, the nincompoop.

Yet between THOUGHT and sense
   The SENTIMENTS have stood
Upholding both, their staunch defence
   Let come what would.

VI
Our task can only be to aim at communicating experiences
and views to others by means of language in which the practical use of every word stands in a complementary relation
to attempts at its strict definition. (Niels Bohr, *Dialectica*, II,
318)

Thought can be a driving rage
   And longing be a mirror;
Each must be both; so stage
   No conflict here, no error.

This line that's no dividing line,
   Dug in, throws all agley;
And they that would that Prince confine
   Can lock him up this way.

Though most who'd separate
   Subject from object so
Have it at heart to liberate
   The known from those who know.

And knowers too from what is known;
   Pure knowing on one hand
And on the other, all alone,
   A sacred *gegenstand.*

But that's not how the show is run:
   This independent mind,
Unkingdom'd, might as well be none—
   As countless Lears find.

And that brave circumstance,
   Untinctured by the eye,
As indistinguishable dance
   Flits vainly by.

Through what we've learned we learn
   And rule through what we rule:
Cartesian doubts can swiftly turn
   A sage into a Fool.

So be you not neglectful
   Of incompatibility;
We ARE because we went to school
   To views we could not see.

The very different procedures of verification appropriate to the sciences and the poetries—so different that mutually exclusive uses of the word "true" are in play—were among Alec Mace's deep concerns and I believe he would have found a proposal to treat this as a complementarity situation not uncongenial. He would certainly have encouraged experimentation along such lines.

13 The Enlightening Eye

This piece seems still too recent for me to comment. I will repeat, however, that the overhaul of our fundamental assumptions and underpinnings, the revision or complementarity-wise plural viewing of the old tripartite (knowing-feeling-trying ◄———► *asserting-exhibiting-acting) distinction, here suggested, seems to me badly needed and likely to lead to greatly improved, that is, far more effectual, conceptions of ourselves than are current. And here, finally, I would once more invite deeper exploration of all the meanings of "conception."*

Lecturing in the 1920s in England, T. S. Eliot found that the poem which went down best was T. E. Hulme's "Fantasia of a Fallen Gentleman on the Embankment":

Once, in finesse of fiddles found I ecstasy,
In a flash of gold heels on the hard pavement.
Now see I
That warmth's the very stuff of poesy.
Oh, God, make small
The old star-eaten blanket of the sky,
That I may fold it round me and in comfort lie.[1]

It is a poem which deserves to be better known; in any case, it is a compact type specimen through which to consider poetic imaginings. How securely it relies on indirect meanings needing,

Review of Denis Donoghue, *Thieves of Fire* (New York: Oxford University Press, 1974), and Justus Buchler, *The Main of Light: On the Concept of Poetry* (New York: Oxford University Press, 1974). Reprinted, with additions, by permission of the publisher from "The Assertive, the Active, and the Exhibitive," *Times Literary Supplement*, November 29, 1974, p. 1343.

for that scene and period, no explication: that "fallen gentleman" of
the title, those gold heels and the miracle-working "star-eaten"!
Yet, for a reader for whom such implications do not work, how little any elucidations can do; and, for others, how easily they may
merely smutch its delicacy.

Nonetheless, for almost all its words and phrases questions
arise about how much of their meaning must in some measure be
perceived and explored, and in what ways. Take the musical sense
of "fantasia": "an instrumental composition characterized by freedom of fancy unrestricted by set form." How much of that perfectly fitting description of the poem will, ordinarily, be openly or
covertly active in a good reader? What other nouns that might
follow "fallen" should add their flavor? How much should be recalled of the chill river airs that breathe on the occupants of those
Thames-side benches, before "warmth" gets to work? Does the card
player's usage of "finesse" take a part? Does the unuttered "moth-
eaten" connect with a realization that clear nights are colder than
cloudy ones? And is a thought that heaven might "peep through" at
all in place?

Both the books under review here have inevitably much to
do with such questions and indeed in each of their titles we are
being challenged to divine much that is not discussed or hardly
more than touched on, if that, in their pages. *Thieves of Fire?* Mr.
Donoghue does, it is true, remind us, and forcibly, that if we stress
that Prometheus *stole* the human gifts for man, if we make him a
criminal and ourselves become fences receiving wrongfully acquired goods, we get a drama very sharply opposed to Shelley's.
Quoting Rimbaud, "Donc le poëte est vraiment voleur de feu," he
turns his four chosen Prometheans—Milton, Blake, Melville, Lawrence—into open and unrepentant followers of Eve, profiting from
and emulating her disobedience, rebels and malignants still.[2] As
such they make good foils to Eliot of whose position as well as
theirs Mr. Donoghue has much that is both timely and of permanent import to say, not least when he points out (p. 50) that we are
dealing here with "incorrigible questions of life and death." And it
is against that background that we do well to recall that Prometheus may also be conceived as no thief, but as justly bringing to
men needs wrongfully withheld. All this behind one word in Mr.
Donoghue's title.

Mr. Buchler's title has its infinitely explorable mysteries too. It comes from Shakespeare's sonnet 60.

> Nativity, once in the *main of light*,
> Crawls to maturity, wherewith being crown'd
> Crooked eclipses 'gainst his glory fight.

This is Shakespeare, at even *his* most provocative and baffling, writing on the most provocative and baffling of all our problems. How are we to read these lines and what do they tell us of the book to which they supply a title? What is this "nativity" which "once" had such place? And what may we look for, with its warrant, in a work that has, as subtitle: *On the Concept of Poetry*? It will, I think, be agreed that rarely have two books with such challenging titles appeared together on so supreme a theme. I hope to suggest that they justify their bold invitations to our speculation, deeply opposed though they may seem. Perhaps the hopes some have entertained for criticism are after all to be fulfilled.

"Once in the main of light": of what promise (and frustration or prevention) may this remind us? Is "once" here, more than "as soon as"? Can it be an anticipation of the "Intimations" theme?[3] But against that there is the force of "crawls" evoking the newborn's clumsiness. Or are we not rather to realize anew with what a sunrise the creative drive comes up in us? Should we perhaps compare the "nativity" of a Homer with the "maturity" of sonnet 60, and may the "crooked eclipses" be (among all else) the troubles poetry has had to struggle with since? More specifically, are they those misconceptions of the nature and role of poetry which this most preveniently resourceful essay in metaphysics would correct?

In his first four chapters, Mr. Buchler attacks "an unaccountably persistent . . . group of ideas, rendered sacrosanct by long tradition . . . hardened into a sterile language" which "continues to talk about poetry in terms of 'the imagination', 'reality', 'unity', 'inner experience', 'form and content', and the like." After this considerably destructive engagement, "a just theory of poetry" is constructed. This theory aims "to be 'faithful' "; "Such fidelity ultimately lies in a theory's directive power, its ability . . . to enhance the identifying grasp, the awareness, of each manifestation."[4] This aim is adequately ambitious and it will be found, I think, that it is pursued with high success.

Fundamental to this is Mr. Buchler's division of "utterance or judgment" into three modes, assertive, active, and exhibitive. This last covers the arts, within which the poetries are a subclass. This is, I think, the moment to issue an alert to the reader: this division is inviting us to think anew and to think deeply. An identification of "judgment" and "utterance" goes with it. "Or" here is playing one of its tricks: "utterance" and "judgment" are two names for the same thing, not for alternative, different things. A kick, e.g., is a judgment-utterance. I should perhaps add that *The Main of Light* manages to make itself unusually clear, exacting though its invitations are. On the delineation of these modes Mr. Buchler lavishes delicate and often exquisite care, seeing that their clarification requires the exposure of "a number of stiff philosophical bulwarks that will doubtless endure forever."[5]

Among these erroneous notions are: that judging can be limited to "occasions of intention or voluntary choice"; that judging "is necessarily deliberative," that it is a *mental operation* in a man, rather than the man himself, that judges; and that judging "always takes the form of thinking something or saying something about something else." Through these misconceptions "still another unfortunate transition has taken place: 'utterance' has acquired a eulogistic import." But "utterance is manifested by concentration camps, bombs, and child-beating along with agriculture, medicine, and poetry."[6] Here again, however, a misapprehension has been shown to be possible. Mr. Buchler has been taken as saying that all or most utterances praise. What he says is that utterance as such (i.e., human activity) has *by careless people* been supposed to be, in general, good.

The three modes of judgment-utterance are to be understood in terms of the way "in which human products [i.e., what you do] *function*," for, under varying conditions, a product may function in all three ways: thus a drawing of a dancer may either "state," or "direct," or "contrive-invent," i.e., present a possibility. Each instance of judging is "at bottom an attitude or 'stance.' " It may be an "affirming" (with a truth claim), an "acting" (morally assessible), or a "creating" (right or wrong); and—I think Mr. Buchler would allow—it may be all three of these together.[7] There are many cases where what appears to have one function may actually have another. We should recognize all three functions as equally judicative and equally fundamental. The "assertive" only occupies first place because traditionally it has been given an illegitimate priority; the "active" and the "presenting-shaping-exhibiting" modes are just as much ways of judging. They all, to a radical degree, entail commitment.

Mr. Buchler is concerned in *The Main of Light* with exhibitive judgment as manifest in poetry. Others of his writings present the frame within which this liberating and illuminating conception has its place. What he does here is to provide us with an intelligible philosophic *articulation* of this useful and salutary meaning. "Exhibitive judgment . . . is that process whereby men shape *natural complexes* and communicate them for assimilation as thus shaped." Two expressions I have italicized here call for explanations: "articulation" and "natural complexes." I can best give them in Mr. Buchler's words: "The meaning of a judgement, in any of the three modes, is grasped only through articulation of that judgement, and there is no foreseeable terminus to the process of articulation."[8] We may see in this, I think, a favoring influence from C. S. Peirce (on whose empiricism Mr. Buchler wrote in 1939). Roman Jakobson, in *On Translation* (edited by R. A. Brower, Harvard University Press, 1959), thus alludes to Peirce's stress on what is, I think, very nearly Mr. Buchler's articulation: "For us, both as linguists and as ordinary word-users, the meaning of any linguistic sign is its translation into some further, alternative sign, especially a sign 'in which it is more fully developed,' as Peirce, the deepest inquirer into the essence of signs, insistently stated."[9] "Natural complex" is the name Mr. Buchler gives to "whatever is, and therefore to whatever can be dealt with; to what is produced by men as well as to what is not." "Natural" warns us that "all complexes are aspects of nature"; that "no complex can be dismissed or exorcized." In spite of which, and very refreshingly, the term "complex" "eliminates the idea that there are or that we may be concerned with 'simples' . . . The simple, the seamless . . . is in effect the traitless . . . A simple could not be."[10]

So finespun a complex of philosophic distinctions might give a sampling reader a false impression: that *The Main of Light* is remote from minute and intimate explorations of actual poetry. Such a reader should therefore take note of the selection of poems with which Mr. Buchler exemplifies his positions. His choices are to me enviably apposite and discerning. He is as much at home when commenting on what a specific poem is doing, and how, as in discussing theoretical errors about poetry in general. As he gracefully remarks: "At certain points I have dealt in a somewhat unceremonious way with positions or formulations put forth by writers whom I otherwise admire."[11] Among many others, these include Shelley, Coleridge, Valéry, Santayana, Hegel, Whitehead, Eliot, and Auden. The overall impression is that of highly discriminating fairness as well as of an acute concern with actualities. Thus: "Cognitive gain may or may not be moral gain. There is a great deal of knowledge which has made men unhappy and that makes human woe possible. A major problem of man is the co-ordination and harmonization of judgments that arise in the different modes."[12] How to prevent the assertive, the active, and the exhibitive functions of utterance from corrupting and bedeviling one another as they do, for example, so often and so typically, in advertising? It is very likely this, with its ever encroaching novelty and its protean guises, both political and cultural, which may prove the grimmest threat so far offered to the human effort.

The Main of Light is essentially a philosophic search for "a unique over-arching 'quality of wholeness in man.' "[13] By contrast *Thieves of Fire* is a study of one of the chief divisive struggles between possible human attitudes or stances. My own feeling is that Mr. Buchler, though he rightly remarks, "In no philosopher is the scope of exhibitive judgment so great as it is in Plato," misses, as the key to his chief difficulties with Coleridge's "whole soul of man," the exhibit of human wholeness offered in *The Republic*. So too Mr. Donoghue, though he defends his "duality of imaginative types" with precedents from Wörringer, Nietzsche, and Jung, may be underrating the hazards of such oppositions in criticism, "a country," he says, "noted for liberality and tolerance."[14] He himself here exemplifies these virtues, but the more we note how his Prometheans and their opponents have discussed one another, the better we relish his phrasing.

At the same time Mr. Buchler achieves and secures his flexibilities of treatment through his metaphysical resources. He can speak of a complex "being rotated, so to speak, delineated successively in a number of perspectives."[15] It is possible to miss the implications of "rotated" here. It is a compact metaphoric way of indicating that *everything* whatever (i.e., every "natural complex") can be looked at from many angles—as we may, to learn more about it, turn an object over in our hands. This applies *throughout*, though often, of course, great changes in our presuppositional scaffolding may be required. The resulting liberations may be immense, as we will realize if we recall that the aim of thought (as of persecution) has from age to age been to discredit and destroy, if possible, all but one single position. And in how many classrooms is that not still the case?

Mr. Donoghue gains a similar compass and detachment by means which superficially may seem to oppose and deny Mr. Buchler's distinctions. On the diversity of the "attitudes or stances" taken in *Paradise Lost* to Satan, to Eve and Adam, to the whole plot indeed, he is admirable, rotating, so to speak, Milton's complex for us most revealingly, using Kenneth Burke's acute observations and Milton's own prose positions to bring out its deep ambivalences. Such an "account of the poem," he says, "is inescapable."[16] We may agree while remembering how many Milton experts have somehow escaped it. That he does these things in terms of Milton's *assertions* should not mislead. "Milton is asserting eternal Providence, and the necessity of assertion is the first sign that he, too, has lost a paradise." And again, "The first mark of Milton's style is the necessity under which it labours . . . of asserting what once had only to be sung."[17] But these assertings are not preclusively Mr. Buchler's assertive function; they are ways in which Milton exhibits.

For Mr. Donoghue "in a secular age . . . imagination is the secular equivalent of God as creator, including especially God as self-creator, in Coleridge's phrase, 'the infinite I AM.' "[18] For Mr. Buchler "the connection between the view that poetry is the human simulacrum of divine creativity and this [Coleridgean] view, that poetry activates all human powers, is (painfully) clear."[19] Between them thus they rotate Milton's own prime question. As Mr. Donoghue puts it: "in some respects he is the most modern of moderns, demanding that God will act with our sense of reason and justice; in other respects he yields his will to the arbitrary will of God."[20] If this prime question is "incorrigible" need that be so too of the "knowledges" from whose clashing it proceeds? As products of exhibitive rather than of assertive judgments (as poetry not science) may they not be more cooperative and consentaneous than we would suppose?

As is appropriate in these T. S. Eliot Memorial Lectures at the University of Kent, Eliot himself is, after Milton, the author on whom Mr. Donoghue comments with most sympathy and penetration. At a time when old adages about troughs and waves are being brought to mind, to meet pages that are as fresh, as modest, and as discerning as these on Eliot's later poetry will be occasion for gratitude to many. They may even for some be medicinal: "Milton was always, to Eliot, what Eliot is to contemporary poets, a formidable presence, a Master."[21]

Any general account of modes of judgment, any deep contrast of fundamental positions, would seem to need to ask: what is this account itself—in which of the modes of judgment are we judging here *about* these judgments?.And what is any such contrast itself *doing*? Which side of the quarrel is it itself exemplifying? I have the impression that these questions are seldom asked and even less answered, adequately or not.

And yet, surely, a comprehensive enough account, a calm enough contemplation of them, should not only include their exploration, but also find in this exploratory activity useful controls over all querying and all judgment. The Vedantist ruling of Yadnyawalknya that "you cannot see the seer of seeing . . . or know the knower of knowing" looks from this position, itself partisan.[22] I have above ventured the opinion that Mr. Buchler may allow some judgments to be assertive, active, and exhibitive at once. In doubting Yadnyawalknya's declaration am I not, simultaneously, claiming-for-true, directing a moral effort and shaping a possibility, i.e., exercising the three modes together in coordination? Does not the doubt thus *rotate* our chief mystery?

Objection will, of course, claim that, in the assertive mode, "cannot" and "can" would destroy one another. "You can" and "you cannot" are contradictories. So, we may agree, they would be if the two propositions they deal with were in all other respects entirely the same in meaning. But though the words in them are the same we can ask, are *they*? and in this perhaps come closer again to seeing (i.e., being?) the seer of our seeings. He is truth-seeking (and sometimes truth-claiming), but he is also responsibly directive and the shaper of that which is being shaped.

Yet what of the sense of guilt which may so often attach to such pursuits? Mr. Donoghue rightly observes that when Lawrence speaks of the sun he is not talking physics; the scandal is that he tries to seem to be doing so. The most poignant page of *Thieves of Fire* is about this trouble: "Theft of the divine fire of knowledge made reflection possible and therefore necessary; it made men self-aware, self-conscious, it made the human race a multitude of reflexive animals." And further: "The reflexiveness of mind, which is in one sense its glory, is in another a token of its criminality, its transgression at the source."[23] How challenging is this ellipsis, this way we have of talking as though old stories were somehow History! The source here is a myth, a traditional story, itself reflecting . . . what? Both "re-" and "flect" ("flectere"), "back" and "bend," have their comments on this, fitting into those offered by the etymons of "straight," "true," and of "right" and "wrong." We may also reflect again on the significance of taking *fire*, of all fearsome destroyers, as a symbol of knowledge. Recalling how Coleridge haunts all this with "the infinite I AM" and with "the whole soul of man," in those references to the analogy (so to speak) between poetic and divine creativity, he may again offer us light in Aphorism 9 of his *Aids to Reflection*, and the passage may serve as a further gloss on Mr. Buchler's title.[24]

" 'And man became a living soul.' He did not merely possess it, he became it. It was his proper *being*, his truest self, *the* man *in* the man . . . This *seeing* light, this enlightening eye, is reflection. . . . This, too, is *thought:* and all thought is but unthinking that does not flow out of this, or tend towards it."[25]

II Practice of Criticism

14 Gerard Hopkins

Written before much comment beyond Bridges' had appeared or any of Hopkins' theoretical work had become available, these immediate impressions benefited from no clues as to how the poet would have wished his verse to be read. "Take breath and read it with the ears" was all I had. I had found out already in lectures that uncommon supplies of breath were needed. (Only Shelley, in "The West Wind," had asked for more.) Of Hopkins' recommendations as to intonation I had no inkling. Later, my friend C. K. Ogden became a virtuoso in such reading. He would recite "The Wreck of the Deutschland" in its entirety, following what he hoped was Hopkins' advice meticulously. Listening, I recognized that, had I not known it all nearly by heart myself, I would barely have understood a stanza. What I had tried to do, in lectures, was to bring out the sense and the movement as fully as my voice might. I am inclined now to think that several different styles of rendering of even Hopkins' verse may, in their own ways, be equally rewarding.

Modern verse is perhaps more often too lucid than too obscure. It passes through the mind (or the mind passes over it) with too little friction and too swiftly for the development of the response. Poets who can compel slow reading have thus an initial advantage. The effort, the heightened attention, may brace the reader, and that peculiar intellectual thrill which celebrates the step-by-step conquest of understanding may irradiate and awaken other mental activities more essential to poetry. It is a good thing to make the light-footed reader work for what he gets. It may make him both more wary and more appreciative of his reward if the "critical point" of value is passed.

Reprinted by permission from *The Dial*, 81 (1926), 195-203.

These are arguments for some slight obscurity in its own
right. No one would pretend that the obscurity may not be excessive. It may be distracting, for example. But what is a distraction in
a first reading may be nonexistent in a second. We should be clear
(both as readers and as writers) whether a given poem is to be
judged at its first reading or at its nth. The state of intellectual inquiry, the construing, interpretative frame of mind, so much condemned by some critics (through failure perhaps to construe the
phrase "simple, sensuous, and passionate") passes away once its
task is completed, and the reader is likely to be left with a far se-
curer grasp of the whole poem, including its passional structure,
than if no resistance had been encountered.

Few poets illustrate this thesis better than Gerard Hopkins,
who may be described, without opposition, as the most obscure of
English verse writers. Born in 1844, he became a Jesuit priest in
1868, a more probable fate for him then—he was at Oxford—than
now. Before joining the Order he burnt what verses he had already
written and "resolved to write no more, as not belonging to my
profession, unless it were by the wish of my superiors."[1] For seven
years he wrote nothing. Then by good fortune this wish was expressed and Hopkins set to work. "I had long had haunting my ear
the echo of a new rhythm which now I realized on paper . . . However I had to mark the stresses . . . and a great many more odd-
nesses could not but dismay an editor's eye, so that when I offered
it to our magazine . . . they dared not print it."[2] Thenceforward he
wrote a good deal, sending his poems in manuscript to Robert
Bridges and to Canon Dixon. He died in 1889 leaving a bundle of
papers among which were several of his best sonnets. In 1918 the
Poet Laureate edited a volume of poems with an introduction and
notes of great interest.[3] From this volume comes all our knowledge
of his work.

Possibly their obscurity may explain the fact that these
poems are not yet widely known. But their originality and the
audacity of their experimentation have much to do with the delay.
Even their editor found himself compelled to apologize at length for
what he termed "blemishes in the poet's style." "It is well to be clear
that there is no pretence to reverse the condemnation of these
faults, for which the poet has duly suffered. The extravagances are
and will remain what they were . . . it may be assumed that they

were not a part of his intention."[4] But too many other experiments
have been made recently, especially in the last eight years, for this
lofty tone and confident assumption to be maintained. The more
the poems are studied, the clearer it becomes that their oddities are
always deliberate. They may be aberrations, they are not blemishes. It is easier to see this today since some of his most daring
innovations have been, in part, attempted independently by later
poets.

I propose to examine a few of his best poems from this angle,
choosing those which are both most suggestive technically and
most indicative of his temper and mold as a poet. It is an important
fact that he is so often most himself when he is most experimental. I
will begin with a poem in which the shocks to convention are local
and concern only word order.

Peace

When will you ever, Peace, wild wooddove, shy wings shut,
Your round me roaming end, and under be my boughs?
When, when, Peace, will you, Peace? I'll not play hypocrite
To own my heart: I yield you do come sometimes; but
That piecemeal peace is poor peace. What pure peace allows
Alarms of wars, the daunting wars, the death of it?

O surely, reaving Peace, my Lord should leave in lieu
Some good! And so he does leave Patience exquisite,
That plumes to Peace thereafter. And when Peace here does
    house
He comes with work to do, he does not come to coo,
    He comes to brood and sit.

Hopkins was always ready to disturb the usual word order
of prose to gain an improvement in rhythm or an increased emotional poignancy. "To own my heart" = to my own heart; "reaving" = taking away. He uses words always as tools, an attitude
toward them which the purist and grammarian can never understand. He was clear, too, that his poetry was for the ear, not for the
eye, a point that should be noted before we proceed to "The Windhover," which, unless we begin by listening to it, may *only* bewilder
us. To quote from a letter: "Indeed, when, on somebody's returning me the *Eurydice*, I opened and read some lines, as one commonly reads whether prose or verse, with the eyes, so to say, only,

it struck me aghast with a kind of raw nakedness and unmitigated violence I was unprepared for: but take breath and read it with the ears, as I always wish to be read, and my verse becomes all right."[5] I have to confess that "The Windhover" only became all right for me, in the sense of perfectly clear and explicit, intellectually satisfying as well as emotionally moving, after many readings and several days of reflection.

The Windhover

To Christ our Lord

I caught this morning morning's minion, king-
    dom of daylight's dauphin, dapple-dawn-drawn Falcon, in his riding
    Of the rolling level underneath him steady air, and strid-
    ing
High there, how he rung upon the rein of a wimpling wing
In his ecstasy! then off, off forth on swing,
    As a skate's heel sweeps smooth on a bow-bend: the hurl and gliding
    Rebuffed the big wind. My heart in hiding
Stirred for a bird, —the achieve of, the mastery of the thing!

Brute beauty and valour and act, oh, air, pride, plume, here
    Buckle! AND the fire that breaks from thee then, a billion
Times told lovelier, more dangerous, O my chevalier!

No wonder of it: shéer plód makes plough down sillion
Shine, and blue-bleak embers, ah my dear,
    Fall, gall themselves, and gash gold-vermillion.

The dedication at first sight is puzzling. Hopkins said of this poem that it was the best thing he ever wrote, which is to me in part the explanation. It sounds like an echo of the offering made eleven years ago when his early poems were burnt. For a while I thought that the apostrophe, "O my chevalier!" (it is perhaps superfluous to mention that this word rhymes strictly with "here" and has only three syllables) had reference to Christ. I take it now to refer only to the poet, though the moral ideal, embodied of course for Hopkins in Christ, is before the mind.

Some further suggestions toward elucidation may save the reader trouble. If he does not need them I crave his forgiveness.

"Kingdom of daylight's dauphin"—I see (unnecessarily) the falcon
as a miniature sun, flashing so high up. "Rung upon the rein"—a
term from the *manège*, ringing a horse = causing it to circle round
one on a long rein. "My heart in hiding"—as with other good poets
I have come to expect that when Hopkins leaves something which
looks at first glance as though it were a concession to rhyme or a
mere pleasing jingle of words, some really important point is involved. Why in hiding? Hiding from what? Does this link up with
"a billion times told lovelier, more dangerous, O my chevalier!"?
What is the greater danger and what the less? I should say the poet's
heart is in hiding from Life, has chosen a safer way, and that the
greater danger is the greater exposure to temptation and error that
a more adventurous, less sheltered course (sheltered by Faith?)
brings with it. Another, equally plausible reading would be this:
renouncing the glamour of the outer life of adventure the poet
transfers its qualities of audacity to the inner life. ("Here" is the
bosom, the inner consciousness.) The greater danger is that to
which the moral hero is exposed. Both readings may be combined,
but pages of prose would be required for a paraphrase of the result.
The last three lines carry the thought of the achievement possible
through renunciation further, and explain, with the image of the
ash-covered fire, why the dangers of the inner life are greater. So
much for the sense; but the close has a strange, weary, almost exhausted, rhythm, and the word "gall" has an extraordinary force,
bringing out painfully the shock with which the sight of the soaring
bird has jarred the poet into an unappeased discontent.

If we compare those poems and passages of poems which
were conceived definitely within the circle of Hopkins' theology
with those which transcend it, we shall find difficulty in resisting
the conclusion that the poet in him was often oppressed and stifled
by the priest. In this case the conflict which seems to lie behind and
prompt all Hopkins' better poems is temporarily resolved through a
stoic acceptance of sacrifice. An asceticism which fails to reach
ecstasy and accepts the failure. All Hopkins' poems are in this sense
poems of defeat. This will perhaps become clearer if we turn to

Spelt from Sibyl's Leaves

Earnest, earthless, equal, attuneable, / vaulty, voluminous,
. . . . stupendous

Evening strains to be tíme's vást, / womb-of-all, home-of-
all, hearse-of-all night.
Her fond yellow hornlight wound to the west, / her wild
hollow hoarlight hung to the height
Waste; her earliest stars, earl-stars, / stárs principal, over-
bend us,
Fire-féaturing heaven. For earth / her being has unbound,
her dapple is at an end, as-
tray or aswarm, all throughther, in throngs; / self ín self
steppèd and páshed—quite
Disremembering, dísmémbering / áll now. Heart, you
round me right
With: Óur évening is over us; óur night / whélms, whélms,
ánd will end us.
Only the beak-leaved boughs dragonish / damask the tool-
smooth bleak light; black,
Ever so black on it. Óur tale, O óur oracle! / Lét life, wáned,
ah lét life wind
Off hér once skeíned stained véined varíety / upon, all on
two spools; párt, pen, páck
Now her áll in twó flocks, twó folds—black, white; / right
wrong; reckon but, reck but, mind
But thése two; wáre of a wórld where bút these twó / tell,
each off the óther; of a rack
Where, selfwrung, selfstrung, sheathe- and shelterless, /
thóughts agáinst thoughts ín groans grínd.

Elucidations are perhaps less needed. The heart speaks after
"Heart, you round me right" to the end, applying in the moral
sphere the parable of the passing away of all the delights, accidents,
nuances, the "dapple" of existence, to give place to the awful di-
chotomy of right and wrong. It is characteristic of this poet that
there is no repose for him in the night of traditional morality. As
the terrible last line shows, the renunciation of all the myriad temptations of life brought no gain. It was all loss. The present order of
"black, white; / right, wrong" was an afterthought and an intentional rearrangement; the original order was more orthodox. "Lét
life, wáned"—the imperative mood carries through to the end; let
life part, pen, pack, let life be aware of. "All throughther" = each
through the other.
        I cannot refrain from pointing to the marvelous third and

fourth lines. They seem to me to anticipate the descriptions we hope our younger contemporary poets will soon write. Such synaesthesis has tempted several of them, but this is, I believe, the supreme example. Hopkins' technical innovations reach out, however, into many fields. As a means of rendering self-consciousness, for example, consider this:

> Only what word
> Wisest my heart breeds dark heaven's baffling ban
> Bars or hell's spell thwarts. This to hoard unheard,
> Heard unheeded, leaves me a lonely began.[6]

Or this:

> Soul, self; come poor Jackself, I do advise
> You, jaded, let be; call off thoughts awhile
> Elsewhere; leave comfort root-room; let joy size
> At God knows when to God knows what; whose smile
> 's not wrung, see you; unforeseen times rather—as skies
> Betweenpie mountains—lights a lovely mile.[7]

My last quotations must be the sonnets which most, I think, represent the poet's inner conflict.

> Not, I'll not, carrion comfort, Despair, not feast on thee;
> Not untwist—slack they may be—these last strands of man
> In me ór, most weary, cry I *can no more*. I can;
> Can something, hope, wish day come, not choose not to be.
> But ah, but O thou terrible, why wouldst thou rude on me
> Thy wring-world right foot rock? lay a lionlimb against
>   me? scan
> With darksome devouring eyes my bruisèd bones? and fan,
> O in turns of tempest, me heaped there; me frantic to
>   avoid thee and flee?
>   Why? That my chaff might fly; my grain lie, sheer and
>   clear.
> Nay in all that toil, that coil, since (seems) I kissed the rod,
> Hand rather, my heart lo! lapped strength, stole joy,
>   would laugh, chéer.
> Cheer whom though? the hero whose heaven-handling
>   flung me, fóot tród

Me? or me that fought him? O which one? is it each one?
    That night, that year
Of now done darkness I wretch lay wrestling with (my
    God!) my God.[8]

No worst, there is none. Pitched past pitch of grief,
More pangs will, schooled at forepangs, wilder wring.
Comforter, where, where is your comforting?
Mary, mother of us, where is your relief?
My cries heave, herds-long; huddle in a main, a chief
Woe, world-sorrow; on an age-old anvil wince and sing—
Then lull, then leave off. Fury had shrieked "No ling-
ering! Let me be fell: force I must be brief."

    O the mind, mind has mountains; cliffs of fall
Frightful, sheer, no-man-fathomed. Hold them cheap
May who ne'er hung there. Nor does long our small
Durance deal with that steep or deep. Here! creep,
Wretch, under a comfort serves in a whirlwind: all
Life death does end and each day dies with sleep.[9]

    Few writers have dealt more directly with their experience
or been more candid. Perhaps to do this must invite the charge of
oddity, of playfulness, of whimsical eccentricity and wantonness.
To some of his slighter pieces these charges do apply. Like other
writers he had to practice and perfect his craft. The little that has
been written about him has already said too much about this aspect.
His work as a pioneer has not been equally insisted upon. It is true
that Gerard Hopkins did not fully realize what he was doing to the
technique of poetry. For example, while retaining rhyme, he gave
himself complete rhythmical freedom, but disguised this freedom as
a system of what he called sprung rhythm, employing four sorts of
feet (-, -∪, -∪∪, -∪∪∪). Since what he called "hangers" or "outrides"
(one, two, or three slack syllables added to a foot and not counting
in the nominal scanning) were also permitted, it will be plain that
he had nothing to fear from the absurdities of prosodists. A curious
way, however, of eluding a mischievous tradition and a spurious
question, to give them a mock observance and an equally unreal
answer! When will prosodists seriously ask themselves what it is
that they are investigating? But to raise this question is to lose all
interest in prosody.

Meanwhile the lamentable fact must be admitted that many people just ripe to read Hopkins have been and will be too busy asking "Does he scan?" to notice that he has anything to say to them. And of those that escape this trap that our teachers so assiduously set, many will be still too troubled by beliefs and disbeliefs to understand him. His is a poetry of divided and equal passions— which very nearly makes a new thing out of a new fusion of them both. But Hopkins' intelligence, though its subtlety with details was extraordinary, failed to remold its materials sufficiently in attacking his central problem. He solved it emotionally, at a cost which amounted to martyrdom; intellectually he was too stiff, too "cogged and cumbered"[10] with beliefs, those bundles of invested emotional capital, to escape except through appalling tension. The analysis of his poetry is hardly possible, however, without the use of technical language; the terms "intellectual" and "emotional" are too loose. His stature as a poet will not be recognized until the importance of the belief problem from which his poetry sprang has been noticed. He did not need other beliefs than those he held. Like the rest of us, whatever our beliefs, he needed a change in belief, the mental attitude, itself.

15 The God of Dostoevsky

It is sometimes thought (is it not?) that a critical essay should describe, analyze, display, characterize, even assess and evaluate the literary work it deals with. Perhaps always but certainly when the work is great enough, it is as well to wonder whether the weight be not upon the other limb. Experimental science is crowded with examples in which the instruments of inquiry, not the matters inquired into, are developed or shown up. So far from the criticism illuminating the work, is it not often the other way round with the work throwing new light on the critical apparatus being used?

"Every word," Robert Louis Stevenson remarked, "looks guilty when put into the dock." Most pronouncements (might we not go on to say?) sound a bit blatant if listened to carefully enough. The terms I was using in 1927 were not up to the job I was asking them to do.

Of reading Dostoevsky, I have never, I believe, been so massively invaded and obsessed by any other writer as I was in my first year as an undergraduate, sixteen years before this essay appeared. Such possession has its price. I suspect that when I first lectured at Harvard (in 1931), Stavrogin had become for me even more enigmatic. But then I came there fresh from Peking and was lecturing alternate days on The Possessed *and on "the blue lavatory" as we used to call* Ulysses *from the paper-backed first edition. I have been told these were the first public academic lectures to be offered on that book.*

A new current of religious speculation appears to be sweeping through the world. It may be a sign of superficiality in modern literature that our chief writers avoid it, or, if they are touched by it, become at once banal or jejune. Perhaps they are afraid of it,

Reprinted by permission from *Forum*, 78 (1927), 88-97.

victims themselves of a secret dread. Whatever the reason, we certainly lack prophets. Mr. Lawrence is almost the only contemporary
novelist-prophet, for Mr. George Moore in *The Brook Kerith* wrote
of piety rather than of religion.[1] But a more charitable explanation
of this dearth of prophets is also possible. The problem that faces
the modern writer may be for the moment too difficult. Either he
must leave his work confused or he must content himself with a
type of solution—some official or unofficial creed—which no
longer satisfies.

That this is the right solution is suggested by the fate of Dostoevsky. A great number of books have been written, especially in
the last few years, about Dostoevsky's religion. As so often with
prophets a bewildering variety of interpretations can be forced
upon him. The bewilderment arises, I believe, from forgetting that
he was, before everything else, a novelist or forgetting what a novel
can become in a great writer's hands. "Dostoevsky's novels are not
novels at all," wrote Mr. Middleton Murry. "It is foolish to attempt
to retain Dostoevsky as a novelist for it can only be done by failing
to recognize him for what he is. The old expressions he charged
with a content that was fantastical; his Christianity is not Christianity, his realism not realism, his novels not novels, his truth not
truth, his art not art."[2] This amounts to saying that inadequate
ideas about realism, novels, truth, and art do not apply to Dostoevsky, but no more do they apply to any great author. The very
same ideas which we need if we are to discuss Shakespeare, Goethe,
Aeschylus, Dante, or Tolstoy are needed if we are to understand
The Idiot, The Possessed, or *The Brothers Karamazov.* These ideas
in fact are the clue to his work.

Mr. Murry is right in saying that Dostoevsky was not a
Christian. In the creative period of his life he was not a believer.
Belief in God as a person, the faith of the Christian religion, was
impossible to him for two main reasons. Here is a passage from one
of his letters: "I want to say to you about myself, that I am a child
of this age, a child of unbelief and scepticism, and probably,—
indeed I know it,—shall remain so until the end of my life. How
terribly it has tortured me (and tortures me even now) this longing
for faith which is all the stronger for the proofs I have against it!
And yet God gives me sometimes moments of perfect peace; in such
moments I love and believe that I am loved."[3]

One ground for this unbelief is that to which he alludes by

saying that he was a "child of this age," the general argument for
scepticism which derives from the fact that modern man knows too
much about the universe and about his own place in it. The second
ground was his peculiar aliveness to and preoccupation with Pain,
and is more important. In *The Idiot* Myshkin and Rogozhin halt
together before a picture of Christ at the moment when he is taken
from the Cross. Rogozhin suddenly says "I like looking at that picture." "At that picture!" cries Myshkin, struck by a sudden thought.
"At that picture! Why that picture might make some people lose
their faith." "That's what it is doing," Rogozhin assents unexpectedly. All readers of Dostoevsky will call to mind other passages
which show how terribly this central fact of Pain haunted Dostoevsky. It was, I think, the main source of his disbelief. Yet he was at
the same time consumed with a desire to believe. The very fact of
Pain, the fatal obstacle, itself made the need for a belief more over-
mastering. This emotional dilemma is one with which most people
have struggled in their own experiences. But we tend to escape it
either by growing callous or by handing over the responsibility.
Dostoevsky did neither. He followed what is the essential procedure of the great artist and grappled with it himself in a lifelong and
appalling struggle. The stages of this struggle are his novels.

So far all is clear and comprehensible. The difficulty begins
when we seek for particulars about this process of grappling with
the emotional dilemma, for there are two ways of grappling with
internal conflicts; the way of the intellect and the way of feeling
and attitude. The way of the philosopher and the way of the artist.
We can either try to hit on a thought which reconciles the conflicting aspects or we can try to hit on a mode of feeling and action—a
way of life which allows the rival impulses to combine, which re-
solves the clash into a cooperation. Usually, of course, the two
processes of thinking a problem out and working it out emotionally
are inextricably entangled. This was so with Dostoevsky.

I say "entangled" to suggest that the two processes of thinking out an intellectual solution and of reorganizing our feelings can
get in one another's way. There are obviously some problems
which *can* be thought out and can be solved in no other way.
Mathematical problems, for example. This no one will dispute. But
there are others which cannot be solved by thought, *because they
are not, essentially, problems of thinking.* And all the problems

with which Dostoevsky struggled are, I believe, of this kind, together with nearly all the problems with which theologians and philosophers have been struggling as far back as our records reach and indeed far further. And, I suggest, not only can these problems *not* be solved by thought, but there is ground for believing that the endeavor to think them out has made them more difficult to solve in other ways. Yet today we have the habit of trying to think them out so firmly incorporated into the functioning of our nervous system that any other mode of solution seems to us fraudulent.

I suggest that long, long ago, very soon after the development of language, a disastrous attempt to *understand* the universe began. To understand it—not in the sense of finding out how it works, that is a task in which science is being admirably successful —but to comprehend it, to grasp what it is and what we are who are parts of it. We all know moments when we seem to grasp this, but such moments pass, and what it is that we have grasped we fail to say. If we look more closely we find that these are moments of feeling and that the "knowledge" they seemed to yield was not like our "knowledge" that fire burns and water quenches but rather an immediate sense of clarity, serenity, and energy. We build up a set of beliefs to justify these feelings, all-important as they are, and persuade ourselves that it was the truth of these beliefs that we grasped in the moment of vision through which we seemed to understand the world.

This is, of course, an incomplete analysis but sufficient for the moment. I call this attempt disastrous for two reasons. First, because these beliefs tend to be overthrown whenever we find out more about how things work or about the history of the world. And since we have pinned many of our most valuable feelings and ways of behavior to these beliefs, the feelings tend to be damaged when the belief is overthrown. This has been happening lately on a large scale but we ought to realize that what has happened already is nothing to what is likely to happen if the youngest of the sciences, psychology, should at last begin to make headway. It is probable that the whole fabric of our accredited ideas about ourselves will go down in the near future—it is cracking already—and if this should happen a moral chaos such as man has never experienced may be expected. Raskolnikov and Smerdyakov can be considered advance samples of this chaos.

But there is another reason for thinking this attempt to understand the universe disastrous. It is that the attempt itself has complicated our feelings in ways which are unfortunate. Originally, I conceive, beliefs of the kind I am discussing now arose as *rationalizations* of feelings and practices which had a deep root in human circumstances and necessities. The feelings came first, and the belief is just something which, if it were true, would make such feelings seem reasonable. But the belief once established has a back-wash influence upon the feelings which were originally its ground. It combines with other beliefs of different origin and becomes distorted. It gets worked up into a system, and then it may happen—I believe it has constantly happened—that the feelings it fosters become *unnatural*, they no longer spring from man's needs. The feelings fostered by a belief in hellfire are a glaring instance, but there is a case for thinking that nearly all religious feelings are in this sense nowadays unnatural. They do not appear to arise in the child until he has been subjected to the influence of beliefs.

There is another side to all this, of course. Probably this characteristically human aberration has been from time to time invaluable to man. Many of his best traits would never have developed without religion. But perhaps it is only those of his religious feelings which are least *unnatural*, least disturbed by beliefs, that are really to be praised. A great deal has certainly come into his mind by the same means which he would be better without.

I am thinking of certain forms of callousness, of discontent, of homesickness for heaven, of nostalgia, of yearning after the impossible; of much pride, vainglory, and hypocrisy; and at the same time of much cultivated and unjustified humility. These are vices of the mind which we owe in large measure to religious beliefs.

The names of three of these feelings which may be regarded as among the unfortunate products of religion are: (1) spiritual pride or megalomania; (2) nostalgia for the ultimate or yearning after the other world; (3) self-abasement or self-humiliation.

They bring us sharply back to Dostoevsky. No other writer has put so much of these three into his books. All his most distinctive figures (with the exception of Myshkin and Dmitri Karamazov), are made monsters through exaggerations of one or the other of these three feelings, spiritual pride, nostalgia for the ultimate, and the enjoyment of self-humiliation—the three are not independent. Moreover it is these exaggerations which make them unlike the characters of any other writer.

There are, I admit, forms of spiritual pride, nostalgia for the ultimate, and gusto of self-humiliation which are not religious in origin. For example, the forms normal to adolescence. But I suggest that the special forms which have so prominent a place in Dostoevsky are specifically due to religion. They are the cosmic forms of these feelings and spring from the fact that he was so preeminently a "God-tormented man," one who had the feelings of religion without the beliefs and one for whom the impossibility of the beliefs was devastating, since, *for him*, it left the feelings without their justification.

With a suitable set of beliefs these feelings are *comparatively* harmless. Spiritual pride can become the sense of an immortal destiny (of a life to come which will justify these exorbitant feelings of importance). Nostalgia for the ultimate becomes the love of God. Gusto of humiliation can become either penitence or the fear of God.

But without such beliefs the feelings may turn into disintegrating forces and play havoc with the personality. Their proper counterbalances do not come into play. This happens again and again with Dostoevsky's characters and would have happened probably to Dostoevsky himself but for his power as a creative artist, a way of salvation denied to his heroes. Ivan Karamazov, it is true, tried the same way out, but Ivan was only an amateur.

Let us consider rather closely the character in which Dostoevsky carried this disintegration farthest, Stavrogin the hero, Lucifer-like in his beauty and his pride, of the book called *The Possessed* whose real title is *The Devils*. What is Stavrogin essentially? Several theories have been put forth. According to Mr. Murry he is essentially the Conscious Will which has cut itself completely loose from the life of instinct; he is the limiting point of consciousness and his suicide is the logical outcome of the purely conscious life, the end to which pure consciousness must always come. Stavrogin, by this theory, is purely a Will seeking always more and more extreme tasks to perform. A Will testing its strength to the uttermost. Therefore when this spoilt darling of Saint Petersburg society has exhausted the possibilities of ordinary experience he turns to debauchery, not because it attracts him—nothing attracts him on this theory—but because it doesn't. His debauchery is part of his policy of trying everything. And afterward he turns to exploit the possibilities of the ridiculous. He secretly marries a lame idiot girl, he pulls a pompous clubman's nose, he bites the governor's ear, because these feats are still more arduous tests of his strength. So finally he publicly denies his marriage (knowing that soon he will publicly confess it) and, crowning triumph, he refrains from killing his disciple Shatov when Shatov, because of the lie which Stavrogin has just told, strikes him in the face. This last act of self-conquest is for Mr. Murry the end of Stavrogin. His Will has triumphed over his pride and in so doing it has slain itself. Henceforeward he is only an empty shadow, a dead man already, to whom all things are the same.

This is a very plausible theory. Unfortunately, since Mr. Murry wrote, an additional chapter of *The Possessed* has been published. I refer to "Stavrogin's Confession," an addition which throws a flood of light on Stavrogin's psychology and incidentally on Dostoevsky's own. So far from Stavrogin's experiments in the ridiculous being supreme tests of his will power they are seen to have another source. Stavrogin himself is speaking: "Every unusually disgraceful, utterly degrading, dastardly, and, above all, ridiculous situation in which I ever happened to be in my life, always roused in me, side by side with extreme anger, an incredible delight . . . It was not the vileness that I loved (here my mind was perfectly sound) but I enjoyed rapture from the tormenting consciousness of the baseness." With Dostoevsky's other books in mind there is nothing in this that need surprise as Stavrogin's lust for a consciousness of vileness links up with his pride and the two together are the key to his religious dilemma.

According to Shatov (who through his resemblance to Myshkin and Alyosha Karamazov is certainly the character in *The Possessed* who has the most authority and the best claim to speak the final word) Stavrogin is "an atheist because he is a snob, a snob of the snobs. He has lost the distinction between good and evil because he has lost touch with the common people."[4] The true Russian is untouched by the difficulties and dilemmas of the intelligentsia because he has his work to do.

"Listen," Shatov says, "Attain to God by work, it all lies in that. Peasants' work, ah, you laugh, you're afraid of some trick."

But Stavrogin was not laughing.

"You suppose that we can attain to God by work," he repeated, "reflecting as though he had really come across something
new and serious which was worth considering." Shatov with his
belief in Russia, in the new advent, in the Russian Christ (views
which Myshkin before and Alyosha afterward also expound and
which were Dostoevsky's views also as a publicist) represents a past
phase of Stavrogin. A faith which Stavrogin had himself tried in
vain to hold. But even Shatov, and here he is speaking for Dostoevsky himself, cannot believe.

When Stavrogin challenges him Shatov can only stammer,
"I, —I will believe in God."[5]

Not one muscle moved in Stavrogin's face. Stavrogin too
did not believe in God, and as the "Confession" makes clear he had
given up trying. What he is trying to do instead is to find a way of
forgiving himself. He is tormented by remorse for the crime he con-
fesses to Bishop Tikhov, a crime which Dostoevsky could invent
for him to have committed. For Stavrogin at this stage God would
have been primarily a means by which he could have been pun-
ished and forgiven. But he knows this and such a belief seems to
him too easy a way to forgiveness. His self-contempt is so great
that, even if Christ could forgive him, he, Stavrogin, cannot. This
self-contempt again remarkably resembles pride.

Two years before the crisis of the story Stavrogin had two
disciples, Shatov and Kirilov, both men of fine simplicity and inno-
cence. To both Stavrogin had seemed little less than a Messiah.
Simultaneously, but without either knowing about the other, he
had indoctrinated them with utterly dissimilar creeds, Shatov with
a faith in the Russian God and Kirilov with views which in the
interval have been worked up into the conviction that it is his duty
to kill himself because God does not exist. Since God does not exist
he, Kirilov, must be the supreme Will in the universe, and as such
he is bound to show self-will and the highest self-will is the destruc-
tion of that Will by itself. But Kirilov like Shatov has not lost touch
with the common people. His social impulse is still strong. He kills
himself in order to prove that man is God, and to make it unnecessary for other men to kill themselves. Once he has proved this, the
Man-God will arise, the earthly paradise will come about.

For Stavrogin this strange argument takes a parallel form,

but with a difference. Since God does not exist he, Stavrogin, must take on God's functions. He must punish himself in order to forgive himself. In the end he too kills himself. But not to show the way or to inaugurate the reign of the Man-God. He is evil and knows that he is evil, in just the sense in which he himself says that Kirilov is good. Stavrogin has lost his social instincts. They have gone, together with everything else which makes life possible, in the total devastation of his personality. So he "brushes himself off the earth like a nasty insect." But originally Dostoevsky meant to save Stavrogin, to convert him and to restore him to grace. He found in the end that he could not. The decay in Stavrogin had gone too far. The artist in Dostoevsky—something stronger than the prophet, the philosopher, the teacher—intervened. Stavrogin's end was the only one which could be accepted by the whole of Dostoevsky's mind (as opposed to the desperate efforts of a part of his mind, the part which struggled to believe in God).

This is what I meant at the beginning by saying that the clue to Dostoevsky is that he was an artist. All sorts of partial impulses toward edification, toward optimism, toward the preaching of a premature beatitude, toward a simple salvation through faith in the Russian God, were always tugging at him but his sense of life as a great artist, the sense of life as it came to the whole of his mind, not a part only, forced him to take another way. This, incidentally, is why he makes Myshkin, his perfect man, an idiot, a thing that has bewildered many readers. He makes Stavrogin (whom he admired perhaps even more than Myshkin) "brush himself off the earth like a nasty insect" because he felt that there was no possible way of life open to him. His pride, his nostalgia for the ultimate (taking the form of introspection), his lust for self-contempt, had eaten away everything and there was nothing left to be saved.

But to put it this way suggests that Stavrogin is no more than an awful warning of the dangers of disbelief. You can of course make him such a warning if you like, but to do so is to miss the point. Stavrogin is a work of art; we shouldn't look at him as an exhibit in a chamber of horrors or as a specimen in a psychological laboratory. Dostoevsky is not using Stavrogin in order to point a moral. He is doing something much more difficult and much more important than that. Stavrogin is there, not as an object lesson nor as an instance, he is there in order that we may imagine him and, while imagining him, become more completely ourselves.

In so doing we do not necessarily become more like Stavrogin or less like him (though this will depend obviously upon what we were like before). The whole conception that art works by making us copy or shun the examples held up before us can today be rejected as mistaken. What happens is something more difficult to describe. In contemplating Stavrogin, the more fully we realize him and imagine him as Dostoevsky saw him, a change takes place in ourselves. We can express this change by saying that we feel in the presence of beauty. Not that Stavrogin or his suicide or his entanglements in the lives of the other characters are beautiful, far from it; but the whole thing has a combined effect upon the reader, and it is this effect which matters. It was for this that Dostoevsky created him, his history and his fate.

I know that to call this effect the sense of the presence of beauty is misleading. It is only a way of signaling that the effect is valuable in a certain way and if you ask what this way is, I can only say that it makes a fuller and completer life more easy. Impulses in ourselves which make life difficult or narrow it down into an affair of pretenses and evasions become, through such works of art as Stavrogin's story, more manageable. Feelings and impulses for which we have no better names than horror, despair, shame, desolation, pettiness, futility, doubt, and fear get, not pushed out of sight, but somehow reconstituted so as to become parts of a possible way of accepting existence. In other words we find a way of life. This is what God was for Dostoevsky. As Mr. Murry very finely says, "God was for him the possibility of acceptance, the hope of a way of life. He knew that belief in God as a person, the faith of religion as we understand religion, was denied to him forever. He asked no more than a way of life."[6] My own view is that he found it through his work as a creative artist. At the end of his life he wrote in a letter: "There is only one cure, one refuge,—art, creative activity";[7] and I believe that for those who are less creative the answer is the same.

Yet in this very letter this quest for a way of life is confused once again with the problem of the existence of a Deity. Dostoevsky, never as a thinker in the narrower sense but only as a creative artist, got the two problems separated. He never understood that the way of life which he sought could be its own sanction and that it needs no sanction from a belief in God. The great dilemma which recurs so often in his work—"If God does not exist then all things are lawful"—the dilemma which drove Ivan Karamazov mad, never gave up its secret to him, yet it is really not a dilemma but a riddle, a verbal ambiguity. If there is no God in the sense of no way of life, no scheme of values, then indeed everything is lawful. But a scheme of values, a way of life, is not dependent upon the existence of a Deity, though historically the two questions have been fused together. Our accepted values, which repose finally upon our needs as social human beings, can, of course, gain a powerful support from a belief in a Diety. But this support is inessential and it is one which Dostoevsky himself when he was most fully alive found himself compelled to do without.

16 A Passage to Forster

It looks as though that critic, trying nearly fifty years ago to live by his pen in New York, was not far off from becoming one of the "very large proportion of deserters" from Forster he notices. He seems, indeed, to be remarkably aware of discomforts in his reading of his novelist. It will be worth stressing, therefore, that he had been for over a decade very deeply a devotee, ready to let Longest Journey *and* Howards End *shape as they could his outlook and even his life. Nothing in this essay should be read as reneging that great debt. But the critic had not long before been in India and had seen something of what those who were then trying to rule India were managing somehow to do. This explains perhaps the paucity of his references to* A Passage to India *though this would be the book that most of his readers would most want to hear about. He may even have been feeling, as later and increasingly, that India should be among things listed by Blake in his Proverb of Hell as "portions of eternity too great for the eye of man."*

Turning over the leaves of a public library copy of *Where Angels Fear to Tread* I find, neatly scribbled on the margin of the seventeenth page, "What is it all about?" This seems an early page for such a query. Later on it might appear less surprising; but in any case Mr. E. M. Forster is not a writer whom we should naturally suspect of obscurity. In his ultimate intention, his philosophical goal, yes, perhaps, but not in his preliminaries, his superficial layout, the ordinary page by page texture of his writing. His prose seems, on the contrary, the clearest and simplest possible. And yet, like a mote in the eye, this scribbler's query has made me uneasily conscious of things that we ordinarily take for granted. There *is*

Reprinted by permission from *Forum*, 78 (1927), 914–920.

something odd about Mr. Forster's methods as a novelist, and this oddness, if we can track it down, may help us to seize those other peculiarities which make him on the whole the most puzzling figure in contemporary English letters.

The oddness has to do with the special system of assumptions he tacitly adopts from the very first page in each of his books. Every writer, perhaps, starts with assumptions which he leaves the reader to discover. They make up his intellectual individuality and differentiate his angle of vision from that of the next man. The moment in our perusal when we first pick up these assumptions and feel our minds fit in, or fail to fit in, with his is the moment when we begin to judge him as an author, to decide whether we like his book or not. But in Mr. Forster's case the assumptions are less obviously aside from the conventional center than in most cases, and for this reason they are the harder to pin down in words. Yet they influence his handling of every scene. Where another writer possessed of an unusual outlook on life would be careful to introduce it, gradually preparing the way by views from more ordinary standpoints, Mr. Forster does nothing of the kind. From the start he tacitly assumes that the personal point of view is already occupied by the reader, who is left to orient himself as he can.

This may lead to lamentable misunderstandings. For example, once we have picked up the author's position we see that the characters in his early books, Mrs. Herriton, Harriet, Gino, Mr. Eager, Old Mr. Emerson, are less to be regarded as social studies than as embodiments of moral forces. Hence the ease with which Miss Abbott, for example, turns momentarily into a goddess. *Where Angels Fear to Tread* is indeed far nearer in spirit to a mystery play than to a comedy of manners. This in spite of the astonishingly penetrating flashes of observation by which these figures are sometimes depicted. But to understand why, with all his equipment as an observer, Mr. Forster sometimes so wantonly disregards verisimilitude we have to find his viewpoint and take up toward his characters the attitude of their creator.

For some readers the task is easy. A mute conspiracy becomes at once established. This is why, although there is no Forster Society, and although no little handbooks have yet been written expounding a Forster philosophy, something very like a cult early grew up around his books. When with *A Passage to India* he burst into public notice, many of his admirers undoubtedly felt an obscure grievance. Unconsciously they had allowed their admiration to take on a snobbish tinge. But they may have felt, also, and rightly, that a great number of his new admirers were scarcely aware of their author's presuppositions as these show themselves in his earlier books, and that if they had understood them better they might have felt less in sympathy.

For the underlying bias in Mr. Forster's work is not one which a reader as sincere as Mr. Forster would wish his readers to be will find easy to accept or to adopt. Mr. Forster never formulates his criticism of life in one of those principles which we can adhere to or discuss. He leaves it in the painful, concrete realm of practice, presenting it always and only in terms of actuality and never in the abstract. In other words, he has no doctrine but only an attitude, differing in this from such exponents of current tendencies as Mr. Shaw or Mr. Wells. He resembles an Ibsen rather than a Ruskin—to name two authors with whose viewpoints Mr. Forster's has some analogies.

It is a commonplace that English readers like pinpricks, but they like them in the form of direct accusations or in the tickling form of satire. They take to Mr. Shaw or to Samuel Butler as to an agreeable stimulant. They are much less ready to listen to criticism when it comes from the more wounding hands of an artist. For this reason Mr. Forster's novels are unlikely ever to become a vogue. And even the small cult which I have mentioned may be noticed perhaps to have a very large proportion of deserters, and to contain not a few adherents whose motives are open to suspicion. For Mr. Forster is a peculiarly uncomfortable author for those who are not content merely to enjoy the surface graces of his writing and the delicacies of his wit, but make themselves sufficiently familiar with his temper to see life to some degree with his eyes. His real audience is youth, caught at that stage when rebellion against the comfortable conventions is easy because the cost of abandoning them has not been fully counted. So as time passes Mr. Forster's admirers tend to forget him or to see him in quite another guise from that in which he first appeared to them. We become less enthusiastic for the light of truth as we realize how high a maintenance rate even a modest installation entails. The divine beam comes to seem merely hurtful to the eyes.

These may seem strange terms in which to discuss so suave
and polished a writer. It is Mr. Forster's peculiarity that he offers
his discomforting vision with so urbane a manner. He is no "holy
howl-storm upon the mountains." He has no thunders, no hoots,
no grimaces, nor any of the airs of the denunciating prophet, yet at
the heart of his work there is less satisfaction with human existence
as he sees it than in the work of any other living writer I can call to
mind. The earliest of his books, *The Longest Journey*, is perhaps an
exception to what has just been remarked about his manner. It has
the rawness and crudeness and violence we should expect in the
work of a very young writer. Those who have not realized the
intensity of the dissatisfaction behind Mr. Forster's work would do
well to read it. There is much there, of course, which time has mel-
lowed. But the essential standards, the primary demands from life,
which still make unacceptable to him so much that ordinary people
find sufficient, have not altered.

Mr. Forster's peculiar quality as a novelist is his fiercely
critical sense of values. What was, in the days of *Longest Journey*, a
revolt has changed to a saddened and almost weary pessimism. He
has, in his later writings, in *Pharos and Pharillon* and in *A Passage
to India*, consoled himself to some degree by a cultivation of the
less militant and more humorous forms of irony. He has stepped
back to the position of the observer from which in his *Where
Angels Fear to Tread* he was at such pains to eject his Philip. But his
sense of values remains the same. He has the same terribly acute discernment of and the old insuperable distaste for what he once called
"the canned variety of the milk of human kindness" and for all the
other substitute products that in civilized communities so interfere
between us and our fellows. Most people after a while develop a
tolerance, if not even a liking, for these social conveniences. Offi-
cialdom, overt or disguised, ceases to offend them. The imperson-
ality of the doctor, for example, his lack of any but a professional
interest in their case, comes to strike them as natural and even
desirable. The artificial, inculcated brand of bonhomie and com-
radeship, to take another example, upon which in certain American
universities social life is deliberately built, is for them a satisfactory
modus vivendi. And the patriotism which springs from the suggestive power of a slogan is counted as better than nothing. These
things appear to them the inevitable consequences of large com-

munities, and life not to be vitiated because such substitutes enter into it. But to Mr. Forster life does seem constantly vitiated by automatism, by official action, by insincerity, by organization when it touches charity, or any of the modes of human intercourse which once were governed, in small communities, by natural human feeling alone. That nothing itself would, after all, be better than the only life which now seems possible for millions, appears to be his final position. I am curious to know what Mr. Forster's Ansell, if he had outgrown his Hegelianism, would have thought of it.

We can trace to this horror of automatisms in human affairs, to this detestation of the non-spontaneous, very much that might seem unconnected and accidental in his books. The passion for the Italian character which animates *Where Angels Fear to Tread* and *A Room with a View*, the unfairness to the medical profession which crops up so markedly from time to time, as in *Howards End*, the exaggeration which mars his depiction of schoolmasters (apart from Fielding), clergymen, and others in authority, his sentimentalization of Old England, and his peculiarly lively flair for social coercion in all its forms—all these spring from the same source. And I believe that the theme which more than any other haunts his work and most puzzles his attentive readers has the same origin.

A special preoccupation, almost an obsession, with the continuance of life, from parent to child, with the quality of life in the sense of blood or race, with the preservation of certain strains and the disappearance of others, such is the nearest description of this theme which I can contrive. In itself it eludes abstract presentation. Mr. Forster himself refrains from formulating it. He handles it in the concrete only, or through a symbol such as the house, Howards End. (Mrs. Wilcox, the most mysterious of his creations, was a Howard, it will be recalled.) This preoccupation is extremely far removed from that of the Eugenic Society—which would be, precisely, the canned variety; the speculations and calculations of the geneticist do not bear upon it, for it is to Mr. Forster plainly a more than half mystical affair, a vision of the ultimate drift or struggle of the universe and the refuge into which an original strong tendency to mysticism has retreated. The supreme importance to him of this idea appears again and again in his books and it is when automatisms such as social pressures and insincerities threaten to intervene here that he grows most concerned—witness *A Room with a View*. In *Longest Journey*, Rickie's mother appears to him in one of the most dreadful dreams in fiction. "Let them die out! Let them die out!" she says. His child has just been born a hopeless cripple. Gino in *Where Angels Fear to Tread* stands "with one foot resting on the little body, suddenly musing, filled with the desire that his son should be like him and should have sons like him to people the earth. It is the strongest desire that comes to a man,—if it comes to him at all,—stronger even than love or desire for personal immortality . . . It is the exception who comprehends that physical and spiritual life may stream out of him for ever." Compare also the strange importance in *A Passage to India* of the fact that Mrs. Moore's children are Mrs. Moore's.[1]

But the most fascinating example of the handling of this theme is in *Howards End*, the book that still best represents the several sides of Mr. Forster's worth, and in which its virtues and its occasional defects can best be studied. Two different aims are combined in *Howards End*; they have their interconnections, and the means by which they are severally pursued are very skillfully woven together; but it is true, I think, that the episodes which serve a double purpose are those which are usually regarded as the weakest in the book. One of these aims is the development of the half mystical, and inevitably vague, survival theme which we have been considering. The other is the presentation of a sociological thesis, a quite definite piece of observation of great interest and importance concerning the relations of certain prominent classes in modern England. For that matter, they can be found without trouble in every present-day community. To this second aim more than half the main figures of the book belong. A certain conflict between these aims is, I suggest, the source of that elusive weakness which, however high and distinguished a place we may find for *Howards End*, disqualifies it as one of the world's greatest novels.

It will be convenient to begin with an instance of this weakness, a passage where the two aims come together and where there is a curious forcing of the emotional pitch of a kind which, were there no other explanation, we should be inclined to describe as sentimentality. Margaret Schlegel has just told her sister Helen of her engagement to Mr. Wilcox. The scene is a slope of the Purbeck Hills.

Helen broke right away and wandered distractedly up-
wards, stretching her hands towards the view and crying. . .
England was alive, throbbing through all her estuar-
ies, crying for joy through the mouths of all her gulls, and
the north wind, with contrary motion, blew stronger against
her rising seas. What did it mean? For what end are her fair
complexities, her changes of soil, her sinuous coast? Does
she belong to those who have moulded her and made her
feared by other lands, or to those who had added nothing to
her power, but have somehow seen her, seen the whole
island at once, lying as a jewel in a silver sea, sailing as a
ship of souls, with all the brave world's fleet accompanying
her towards eternity?[2]

This is a passage which, I am afraid, has gone home to many
hearts and bosoms, yet if we consider it carefully, weighing especially the exact effort of that "somehow seen her" and the results of
the sudden appearance of the adjective "brave," can we help but
regard it as affected? It is a mild but a clear case of that literary
imposture known colloquially as "putting it over." Mr. Forster has
always had a peculiar gift for charging his sentences with a mysterious nervous shiver. The scene of the idiot messenger in *Where
Angels Fear to Tread* is a notable example. So, too, is the Wych
Elm scene towards the close of *Howards End*. In these instances
and, indeed, in all but a few places, nothing could be more admirable. But his admirers have not been without a fear that this gift
might tempt Mr. Forster to overwork it, a fear which some of the
Mrs. Moore scenes in *A Passage to India* have not lessened.

But, to return to *Howards End*, the few passages which
awaken this discomfort in the reader are, I believe, all consequences of the mixing of the two aims of the book, the half mystical preoccupation with survival overforcing the emotion in scenes which
have apparently only to do with the sociological thesis. It is time to
expound this thesis more fully. It concerns the two kinds of people
mentioned in the passage I have quoted—the able, competent,
practical, effectual Wilcoxes, and the speculative, contemplative,
critical, and imaginative Schlegels. It concerns the relations of these
two sorts to one another in the community, the separation and
antagonism of people of vision and people of action. The situation
is illustrated by their reactions toward a third sort of person, one
which is the result, ultimately, of their separation and antagonism

—Leonard Bast, who is both crude as compared with the Schlegels and feeble as compared with the Wilcoxes, but a victim and horribly alive. The presentation of Leonard Bast, in its economy and completeness and its adequacy to the context, would be enough by itself to give any novelist a claim to enduring memory. Consider only chapter 6, the description of Leonard and his "wife" Jacky in their semi-basement flat. It is only ten pages long, but what other novelist, though taking a whole volume, has said as much on this theme or said it so clearly?

While Leonard remains what he is here, the tragically revealing instance of Mr. Forster's thesis, no admiration is too much. But something happens, he becomes needed for another purpose. The other aim of the book, Mr. Forster's peculiar personal preoccupation with the continuance of life, claims him. A string of incidents is developed in which he becomes no more than a dummy. His collision—it is little more—with Helen, his last brief appearance when he is killed by Charles Wilcox, these do not match with the rest. There is a disaccord, and in a minor degree the same thing happens with the other figures in the book, with Helen and Margaret and Mr. Wilcox. They are used for a double purpose, and the two aims do not quite agree. Only Mrs. Wilcox and Charles Wilcox are free from the subtle inner disharmony, because each is claimed only by one purpose—Charles only by the thesis and Mrs. Wilcox only by Mr. Forster's incommunicable idea, his glimpse of the mystical significance of life. With this incommunicable idea, *Howards End* closes. It is purely, I think, to let Leonard live on, that he is so willfully given a child. There is something in Leonard which Mr. Forster will not let die. Leonard himself being worthless is killed violently, and flung aside, but he lives on in Helen's child. This event is Mr. Forster's confession of faith.

17 Nineteen Hundred and Now

*Reading Malory as a child I was, I recall, much troubled
about the connections between "a full hardy knight"—
clearly praise—and "foolhardy." My puzzling was further
perplexed by the dialect of a groom who restrained me, from
a jump I thought my pony could take, with "Don't be
fulardy! Don't be fulardi!"*

*Rereading this piece—a period piece it knew itself from
the start to be—that old uncertainty comes up again. My
feelings about what was worth risking oscillate widely from
declaration to declaration. Sometimes I have to remind
myself that what I said about Yeats, for example, was
written before* Words for Music Perhaps *had come out. And
then again I find myself having to recognize that I ought to
have been far more foreseeing. I suppose that anyone who
writes of contemporary trends can do so only by forgetting
for the moment how likely to be mistaken our notions of
what is coming must be.*

A well-known Max Beerbohm cartoon serves me in place of
an exordium. In it the Eighteenth Century, wigged, silk-stockinged,
and rapiered, stands gazing with pained eyes at its imagined successor—a shadowy, etiolated replica of its own self, the decadent
ghost of an achieved perfection. Below, the actual Nineteenth Century, burly, bland, and extremely solid, is beaming through cheer-
ful but calculating spectacles at a larger, even solider, even cheer-
fuller self—a Twentieth Century facing the whole stretch of time
with unshakable confidence, proud in the simple certainty of righteous might. In a third picture, beneath these two lucid summaries
of modern English history, appears the actual Twentieth Century, a
slender, hesitant, nerve-racked young man with features bearing

Reprinted from *The Atlantic*, 140 (1927), 311-317.

some resemblance to those of Mr. T. S. Eliot. About him and before him is spread darkness, broken only, at the point where the vision should appear, by a faintly luminous query.

A reproduction of this picture wriggled in the drafts above my fireplace for a long while before I finally twitched it from its pin and dropped it into the flames. It had been annoying me for some time. A singularly numbing full stop rounds off the best of Max Beerbohm's jeux d'esprit. Turn them over in the mind and your smile suddenly seems to become a smirk. With the twentieth century a quarter way through, and its tendencies declaring themselves more clearly every week, that stooping, puzzled figure lost his point; he became the representative, not of this century, but of the tail end of the last.

The literary critic is usually anxious to disclaim the possession of any fortune-telling ability. But, if the wandering Cagliostro, or Professor Buncombe, who plies so brisk a trade in his booth at the village fair, really does no more than read his clients' tendencies, the critic ought to recognize himself as a fellow member of the craft.[1] For every author who is worth considering gives us in his work a sample of current tendencies. If he does this unwittingly, as the poet and novelist may, so much the better. But we cannot in any case appraise his merits without, consciously or unconsciously, estimating these tendencies. Every critic worth the name is a minor prophet by vocation.

Before trying to sum up the chief happenings to the spirit of man in this first quarter of our century let me first point for a moment to some of the snares which beset the rash venture. We must beware of mistaking a surface tendency for one which works more deeply. Tolstoy—rejecting Shakespeare in favor of *Uncle Tom's Cabin* because Mrs. Stowe claimed to be preaching the brotherhood of man but Shakespeare did not—made himself an awful warning for all time through just this error.[2] It is not the tendencies which an author professes, but those which actuate him, that we must use as our guide; and to discover these is no light undertaking.

Equally dangerous is the fallacy of the procession. Starting from the reflection that we are not all living in the same era, either intellectually or morally, we pass readily to the image of mankind as an army, guides, vanguard, main body, and laggards, advancing like a procession or writhing by like a snake. But this image is very inexact. The mind grows in many directions at once. An octopus would be a better image than a snake, and a tree is perhaps the best of all. Poets and original writers are the growing points of this tree. If we assume that, in spite of its prehistoric roots and sturdy strength, the mind of man is still a sapling, we shall feel free to watch for those stirrings of growth in the upper branches which indicate where the main boughs will spread in the future. A subtle and incessant rivalry between different trends is necessary for this growth. Forking and ramification are not a calamity, but a condition of health. Our question here is simply: Where is the sap most vigorously flowing?

A third danger, harder still to guard against, is the following. Sometimes influences which loom very large and appear very important pass by rapidly and leave no deep or permanent effect. Others, less salient but as it were more massive, pervade the community for long periods and modify our outlook without being much noticed. The Russian Ballet, for example, made an immense disturbance when it first came to London. It rapidly won over the "advanced guard" while merely antagonizing the main body of taste and opinion. But a few years later it had become a fashion spreading with characteristic rapidity to all classes and types. Today its only opponents are the new "advanced guard." It has set its stamp upon the wholesale furnishing houses and replaced a dingy type of commercial decoration by less restful schemes, but its success is probably symptomatic of nothing with which we need be concerned here. An instance of the other kind of influence, powerful, permanent, but unobtrusive, is the growing interest in psychology. With these 'warnings' duly noted—we shall have occasion to look back to them—let us proceed.

The chief, the dominant trend is toward a reversal of the roles of intellect and feeling. Bergson led the way in this, but, great though his influence was when backed up by William James, the causes of this revolution probably lay deeper than he alleged.[3] It was neither the failure of intellectual philosophy, bankrupt though it was, nor the psychology of instinct, as this was understood when Bergson wrote, that prompted the revolt against logic. I should trace it myself to the currents that for more than a century have

been sweeping against religion, flowing down from the uninhabit-
able polar zones of science. Indeed, just as the meteorologist founds
his study of cyclones upon the assumption of an inflow of cold air
toward the equator, so the contemporary critic must, I believe,
always remember that religion, hitherto man's chief means of
envisaging the universe, is being challenged and affected even for
believers. Complications of course ensue, and the currents are often
found flowing in the opposite direction. But, directly or indirectly,
science has disturbed us all. Man's trust in the universe is probably
less today than it has ever been, as it is certainly harder to rational-
ize. At times he feels himself to be alone in a queer place. Nonetheless there are hours when he feels secure, but these hours are not so
much climaxes of thought as states of feeling. Thus feeling, but not
necessarily religious feeling, comes to be regarded as our chief
guide and support.

    This trend toward feeling rather than thought is not con-
tradicted by the fact that the young so often seem more intellectual-
ized than ever. The discussion of principles tirelessly continues, but
it follows a new set of laws. Formerly a few principles stood fairly
solid and the feelings were more or less in revolt against them. The
contest *circled* about them. Nowadays more principles are in the
field and they shift and change at the prompting, less and less disguised, of rival feelings which are the main disputants. We can see
the difference very clearly if we set the discussions with which
Kingsley used to exercise the Victorians against those with which
Mr. Aldous Huxley indulges us. Mr. Huxley is peculiarly the philosopher of the Oxford freshman. In the mounds of last season's
talk which are piled so high beneath *Those Barren Leaves* the enthusiastic young reader scents the comfort of a confirmation in his
own half-rationalized confusion of impulses. Eased from the smart
of his own provincialism, but unable to perceive the something
more—it is not as much as it should be—that Mr. Huxley attempts,
he contents himself with trying to be as witty and as complex as his
original. Mr. Huxley, indeed, excellently represents the most frequent predicament of the Anglo-American (or Anglo-New York?)
intelligentsia: the feelings neither simple enough, strong enough, nor
sufficiently rooted to win a stable poise, and the intelligence merely
a clever subordinate, abetting—like the servant in an old comedy—
all the rival machinations of the principal figures in rotation.

I have turned the discouraging side of the picture to the front, making very free with Mr. Huxley for the purpose. But there is a very different side to be examined. Twenty years ago, and this is a symptom of great importance, Mr. Huxley's most cordial admirers would have been disciples of Mr. Wells. *The New Machiavelli* (1911; the date seems worth inserting, so fast does the mental landscape change today) was regarded on its appearance as a very daring and shocking book. Daring it was, in view of the then current mentality, a mentality which Mr. Wells has played his part in changing; but that it should have shocked proves very clearly how immense a load of unhealthy inhibitions has been lifted in recent years. But this often remarked and much discussed tendency away from prudery is not the one upon which I wish to insist. Mr. Wells, with his passion for explicit statements, for programs, policies,and concrete prophecies, is a perfect example of the habit of mind away from which we have been trending. In spite of the scepticism of logic which he sometimes shows (we have to remember our first 'warning' above), and in spite of such safety-valve outbursts as produced his *God, the Invisible King*, Mr. Wells retains the outlook of Thomas Huxley, the confidence that hard thinking is by itself a sufficient guide in life. That is why the younger generation no longer reads him with the same enthusiasm. Mr. Wells is in fact a rationalist; and the sons and daughters, the nephews and nieces, of the generation that eagerly adopted his world outlook have exhausted its emotional possibilities. Add the disillusionment coming from the war, and it ceases to be surprising that Mr. Wells, by addressing himself to human reasonableness, should seem to them to be missing the point.

But there is a further explanation for this failing influence. Mr. Wells, as *The History of Mr. Polly* and the early romances show, might have been a great creative novelist if he had not chosen instead to be the first educator of his age. We are all immensely indebted to him for saner and better-informed views upon innumerable social problems, but his carelessness as an artist has made his later books look 'thin' to the eyes of a more self-conscious and self-critical generation. General disorientation, preoccupation with feeling, and the increasing mixture of cultures have made us more introspective. The contemporary young man has more information about himself than he can handle. His bewilderment is quite different from the social and political problems with which Mr. Wells is concerned. It is in fact the bewilderment with which only the artist can grapple. We feel a need for order in our own minds before we can set about ordering the affairs of men in general, and only the artist can give us this order that we can no longer win from religion. Thus the decline in Mr. Wells's influence is partly due to his perhaps deliberate renunciation of the task of the artist.

A similar "thinness" is also the accusation brought against Mr. Shaw, who seems equally, in spite of great popular successes, to be vanishing over the horizon. It is a commonplace of criticism that Mr. Shaw's plays show no natural command of emotion. He is a master of those feelings that are struck out by the clash of ideas, but hardly ever comprehends the feelings which lie behind the ideas. And his set emotional pieces, the death of Dubedat, for example, in *The Doctor's Dilemma*, are so plainly factitious that they cast a fatal doubt upon his authority as a guide to life. Our age has learned a great deal from him, but its deeper concerns do not come within his province.

The passing of these two rationalist gods of the dawning century is significant. It is doubtful, though, whether we can be so optimistic as Emerson. When half-gods go it is less likely that the gods arrive than that other half-gods take their place.[4] Or, what is more probable in this case, merchants with new gods for sale may appear. The decline of Mr. Wells and Mr. Shaw is deplorable if it means only more room for crude mysticisms. But to describe Mr. D. H. Lawrence, in spite of *The Plumed Serpent*, as a merchant with gods to sell would be very unfair. For Mr. Lawrence's sincerity, in the deepest sense of this abused word, is awe-inspiring. Its quality makes him a very significant contrast to Mr. Shaw. (Again we have to remember our first warning against mistaking a surface tendency or doctrine for a deeper trend.) Mr. Shaw talks in *Back to Methuselah* of the Life Force; Mr. Lawrence feels it, whatever it is. And when Mr. Lawrence writes about it, as he is too apt to do, we still feel that he has known what he is talking about; but Mr. Shaw's Life Force is never anything more than an excogitated hypothesis.

No one better than Mr. Lawrence represents the still largely inarticulate yearning of the moderns for a closer contact with life, or, to speak more clearly, for a fuller, less inhibited, and more natural response in feeling. The conventions of a morality which has largely lost its social and religious sanctions press upon us more and more. Whether we applaud or regret it, the fact now stares us in the face that our needs are altering. By changing the conditions of our lives the industrial revolution has changed us too. Our morality begins more and more to be a misfit—too tight in some places, and not nearly tight enough in others.

How far we have changed already from the morality of our forefathers may be seen by comparing even so conservative a book as *The Old Wives' Tale* with *David Copperfield, The Scarlet Letter,* or *Tom Jones.* Over every act of each of Dickens' characters (I except Mr. Micawber as being not a character but a fantasy—about as real as Rumpelstiltskin) there hangs a clear moral judgment. They did right or wrong, were well or ill advised according to a moral plan in Dickens' mind as definite as a chessboard. So also with Hawthorne and with Fielding. These men possessed moral principles fully qualifying them for a seat on the Bench at the Day of Judgment. In comparison Arnold Bennett is utterly unprincipled, but we may still consider that the morality—not an affair of principles, but purely a morality of sympathetic feeling—that rules in his great novel is more adequate to life as we know it.

The moral misfit has its comic possibilities. Mr. Shaw, nicely dressed after an eighteenth-century fashion, can be content to exploit them, with now and then a whiff of scorn or commiseration for ugliness and discomforts which he does not share and only imperfectly divines. But Mr. Lawrence, who is alive to all the real horrors which a misfitting morality entails, and who feels to the uttermost both the unnatural tension and the lack of support, is inevitably agonized. It is his power to present this agony, rather than any positive contribution toward a new morality, that makes Mr. Lawrence so significant. He is gifted with a sensitiveness which few have equaled and with a vigor which makes his most emotional contemporaries seem dilettanti beside him, but the characteristic failing of his generation has nonetheless betrayed him. He has not been content to let his feelings work out a salvation, as a poet of equal endowment in a happier age might have done. In spite of his revolt against those traditional doctrines or principles or ideals that try either to stifle feeling or to force it in ways no longer sanctioned by our circumstances and our needs, he has not been able to refrain from manufacturing new doctrines, equally if not more disturbing in their interference. The purity and freshness of the best parts of his early work, of *The White Peacock,* for example, have given place to the murky mysticism of *Phantasias of the Unconscious.* Harking back to the primitive mentality described in *The Golden Bough,* he has constructed an artificial framework of doctrine which acts like a forcing house to his feelings. Hence the dreary exaggerations of so much of his later work. The doctrinaire has tyrannized over the poet, and Mr. Lawrence's return to reality has ended too often in a worse falsification than that against which he originally revolted.

Before proceeding let us glance back over the ground so far covered in this triangulation of contemporary consciousness. One result of the subordination of reason to feeling may be the state of affairs which I took Mr. Huxley to illustrate—feelings too slight and too shifting to dictate any steady or consistent view of life. At the other extreme is the state of affairs exemplified in Mr. Lawrence—feelings so deep and strong that the reason becomes a mere slave in their service. Confusion, shallow or profound, seems to be the outcome in either case, but against this we may set the increased fidelity to our fullest experience that the reascendance of feeling has brought about. In an age of confusion it is not surprising that our most representative authors should be bewildered.

But confusion need not be the outcome. To prove this we can turn to the work of the best of our younger poets. We have, of course, great poets such as Mr. Bridges or Mr. Housman, who have kept, more or less deliberately, out of the stream of current tendencies and influences. But their poems might have been written as well, or better, eighty years ago; to recall our image of the human tree, their work is a blossoming upon side branches rather than a stirring upon the main lines of growth. And we have poets whose work, however admirable, is significant chiefly as a confession of defeat—Mr. de la Mare harking back always, when he writes well, to a child's world untroubled by contemporary problems, or Mr. Yeats in his later poetry retreating from actuality behind a smoke screen of occultism.[5] There are innumerable ways of dodging the issue, of sheltering from the storm, but our interest here turns to those who make their poetry not a refuge from the present hour but a means of gathering together their faculties to win a new order from the turmoil. Picking out, as before, a chief figure to indicate a general tendency, let us attempt to plot a curve with the aid of Mr. T. S. Eliot.

The first impression made by Mr. Eliot's poetry is perhaps one of an unexampled confusion. No rational scheme seems to unite the items. Allusions, quotations, materials of every imaginable kind, seem to jostle one another at random, and the reader usually completes his first perusal without attaining even a dim idea of what the poem is "about." Nonetheless, if he is a reader used to great poetry, and if he has read the lines slowly and carefully enough to give them time to take shape to him *as sounds*, he will probably have received another impression very rarely made by anything but great poetry. The words have a final and authoritative ring. They sound both passionate and sincere, as though the choice were strictly governed by feeling and as though that feeling were deep, intricate, and coherent. Between this first impression and the conquest of the poem, which may require many readings and even a lapse of years, a double process takes place. It is partly an imaginative realization of the feeling governing the choice of words, partly a work of detective intelligence exactly parallel to the more creditable feats of Sherlock Holmes. This happy guesswork supplies those links in the poet's thought which would, if supplied by him, have impaired the concentration of the poetry and deadened the astonishing emotional resonance of his phrasing. They might, however, have been given in a gloss to be read apart from the poem at the reader's discretion.

It may be objected that this is a strange amount of trouble to take over a poem and an exorbitant demand for a poet to make. "Beauty is simplicity," someone will remark, forgetting that some very simple effects can only be produced by very complicated means. It is much easier to produce a noise, for example, than a pure musical tone. But indeed there is nothing in this account of Mr. Eliot's poetry that does not apply to many other poets—to Donne, to Milton, or to Shelley at his best (the Shelley of *The Triumph of Life*), to name three who differ as widely as possible from him and from one another. That it may take even a very serious and gifted reader years to master a good poet need surprise no one. Even with the help of all the commentators not a little of Shakespeare at his best still requires seven readings. It must be so, if the poet is not merely exploiting our ready-made feelings, but is weaving them into new patterns that have never existed before. In brief, the creative poet has to create something in us and we must not blame *him* if this costs *us* trouble. The only question is whether it is worthwhile.

Ours is an age of mixed feelings; so is Mr. Eliot's poetry a poetry of mixed feelings. But the mixture may be ordered or random. And the method by which we attempt to right the disorder must be judicious, or worse ensues. If the signs of the times as revealed in literature point to anything it is this: that no doctrine today has any power to free us. Disordered feelings cannot be purified by preaching. Nor can we escape by quashing those of our feelings that are troublesome. A wider acceptance of life is, in fact, the only way out. Thus when Mr. Eliot sets some august example of ancient passion beside some tawdry fragment of contemporary existence it is not to point scorn at the present or to glorify the past. In his hands, when he makes such a collocation, the past does not seem so glorious, nor the present so debased, for the same currents of life are felt to flow through them both. Without a whiff of doctrine and merely by a more balanced inclusiveness, the counterpoising feelings have been added to our experience. The miracle is simple enough; two conflicting feelings meet and coalesce.

But the poise, the serenity, the capacity to see life steadily and see it whole, will not ensue in the reader unless he starts where Mr. Eliot started. To some readers Mr. Eliot's best and longest poem, *The Waste Land*, so significant in its title, does not bring any release, but only an increased sense of disillusionment and despair. Still more does this reflection apply to Mr. James Joyce's *Ulysses*, the other supremely representative work of this third decade. Only those who are unprepared for nothing, however painful, repellent, or abhorrent, that life can offer will escape shock, perhaps severe shock, from its titanlike convulsions. This is the justification of the censorship which has been exercised against it. But upon those who are ripe its robust acceptance of everything has an enheartening, calming effect that comes like a culmination of all the tendencies of the century. The quiver that welcomes release from illusion is so close to the horror of disillusionment as to be sometimes indistinguishable from it. If our increasing knowledge of ourselves shows much to distress us, the antidote or counterpoise is also uncovered. If acceptance is sometimes terrible, so that Mr. Eliot once said that *Ulysses* was written to put the fear of God into us, it is really an end and not a beginning of terrors.

This third decade, if I have chosen its spokesmen aright, sees us with much better mental foundations if with less towering edifices. The whole quarter century has been a period of deflation. Hopes are not so lofty, ideals less in evidence, and faith, if we distinguish this from knowledge, much declined. All this, however, applied to those only who stand out preeminently in our literature. Among lesser writers, those of less sincerity and clear-sightedness, the opposite characteristics are often manifest. But if, as we may reasonably assume, the clearest spirits set forth what is obscurely present in the souls of others, this phenomenon may be understood. Strong convictions often mask a secret hesitation. I should add finally that, although one of my instances is an American, only the spiritual history of England comes within this survey. It would be more difficult to write the equivalent chapter for America. The cultural background, the economic present, the probable future issues of the two countries, are so diverse that separate treatment is unavoidable.

18 *Herbert Read's* English Prose Style

My chief recollection about this review for the Criterion *is
of T. S. E. telling me, in characteristically cryptic tones, that
he was very glad to have it "because they think we all agree
all the time." Just who "they" or "we" might be was undis-
closed. Since I had been at some pains to sweeten what I said
about the book as much as, in conscience, I could, I
wondered whether he might have been even gladder if I had
shown more entirely what I thought. This I did a few years
later and at length in chapters 5-8 and in the appendix of*
Interpretation in Teaching *(by far, I think still, my most
originative book, with the best chances of being in due time
useful to causes that matter). And later—elsewhere, but I
have failed to locate it—I made an attempt, in a complementarity spirit, to conceive points of view from which
Herbert Read's odder utterances might have seemed to him
not merely permissible but even obvious. I regret that I
cannot now recapture what came of this bold and exciting
venture.*

The merit of any systematic treatise on such a matter as
prose style must, at present, lie more in the quality of the provocations it affords than in the results established. The methods available in discussing the various mental activities that govern the character, order, and movement of words are as yet too conjectural for
this to be otherwise. It will not then appear as a reflection upon Mr.
Read's inquiry if this review concerns itself chiefly with the psychological assumptions and constructions he uses.[1] The recognition
"that a philosophical and psychological basis does exist for, and
does explain" the phenomena of prose style is a very satisfactory

Review of Herbert Read, *English Prose Style* (London: G. Bell and Sons,
1928). Reprinted from *Criterion*, 8 (1928), 315-324.

feature of the book. But other satisfactory features have left Mr. Read too little space, in his chosen limits, to expound this basis as clearly as we should wish. In a short book he has included quite a hundred pages of extracts—admirably chosen, and commented upon with excellent good sense and discernment. Some of the detailed critical discussions which follow these extracts are very good indeed. The comments upon Mr. Churchill's eloquence, for example, or upon the secret of Jane Austen's attraction, though it may be doubted whether in the passage quoted from *Persuasion* the flaw is so "entirely a question of style." Something very wrong in its conception may also be suspected. All these good things prevent Mr. Read from giving us his fundamental conceptions in any very precise form. Yet the whole argument of the book depends upon them and its value and interest lie in this dependence. It is to be hoped that Mr. Read will convert the book in some future edition into a voluminous affair, a really generous exposition of his psychological conceptions and their application to prose literature. As it stands it neither does Mr. Read justice nor serves as an elementary introduction to the subject for teachers and others, an aim he may have in view. For it contains too many passages which, although they *may* be justifiable if given a recondite meaning, are misleading and confusing in their more obvious senses, the senses which will certainly be given to them by readers who are not specialists. This is not Mr. Read's fault, it is a consequence of his confined space and the general level of reflection on these matters. He will have the sympathy of everyone who has attempted to discuss any large subject briefly.

A too condensed statement is sometimes as dangerous to the writer as to the reader. It invites confusions which an expansion reveals. Mr. Read seems not altogether to have escaped this danger. His division of Prose and Poetry in his introduction is an example. There seems no good reason why he should not define these words as he does though the consequences would be rather more surprising than he seems to allow. It suits his purpose and provides a healthy linguistic exercise for his readers, an exercise that the various controversies which have already ensued shows to be needed. But when he goes on (p. xi) to say that Poetry may be "an affair of one word, like Shakespeare's 'incarnadine,' " and that therefore it may be without rhythm whereas living prose must have rhythm, he draws a quite unwarranted conclusion. "Incarnadine" by itself is *not* poetry, though the American lipstick merchant hopes that it is. Only *Shakespeare's* "incarnadine" is poetry; and Shakespeare's "incarnadine" is merely this word in its context of "multitudinous seas." It becomes poetry only in this context, the poetry comes about only through the co-presence in the mind of all the words of the line, with their rhythm. We need not experiment with "the extensive ocean incarnadine" and so forth, to be convinced of this. The mistake is due to the too condensed form of Mr. Read's definition: "Poetry is creative expression . . . In poetry the words are born or re-born in the act of thinking." If he were to expand "creative," "expression," "born," and "thinking," to display fully what he understands by these terms, he would, I believe, find nothing to justify his mistaken conclusion. What would appear would be the peculiarly close interdependence between the poet's whole state of mind and the core of words round which it grows. In poetry, as we shall all admit, the words can hardly ever be changed without the poetry's being vitally changed also. In prose we can often change words without important consequences—and the measure in which this is not true is the measure (or should be, I suggest, on Mr. Read's definition) of the intrusion of Poetry into the prose. But Mr. Read seems to me to describe this close interdependence very unfortunately. In poetry, he says, "there is no time interval between the words and the thought." A very rash assertion indeed. For if Shakespeare one morning, while busy with his accounts, happened upon the word and recognizing it as just what he had been wanting, cooly slipped it into his unfinished passage without "thinking" it through over again, we should have to conclude that the line is a bad one. Mr. Read will have to deny that this could possibly have happened; he would do well to reflect long and carefully before he does so. Plainly it is not the physical or even the psychological conditions of composition that decide whether a passage is poetry but the relation of the words to a state of mind and the qualities of that state of mind itself.

In this part of the introduction (and no reader should allow himself to be prevented from reading further through dissatisfaction with a section which is unequal to the rest) the influence of Italian speculations is also unfortunate. When Mr. Read says "The thought is the word and the word is the thought, and both the thought and the word are poetry" he is talking in the idiom of Croce, an idiom fatal to profitable reflection on these matters.[2] For either he is loosely affirming a close interdependence, or he is giving away a trick to the behaviorists just where those naive theorists least deserve to win one. The whole prospect of a clearer understanding of Poetry depends upon distinguishing the words from the "thought" and investigating their relations; and phraseology such as this (it recurs occasionally later in the book, e.g., p. 164) produces either a dead stop in the mind or a fuddled (or ecstatic) feeling of ultimate truth, according to our philosophical antecedents. In neither case is the result fruitful, for if this *were* all that could be said in the matter it might as well not have been said.

The main body of the book is divided into two parts under the headings Composition and Rhetoric. The chief interest lies in the second part. For an *objective* examination of the use of language—without, that is to say, paying attention to the purposes for which the language is being used—cannot yield very much. Mr. Read, however, makes a good job of this discussion of words, epithets, figures of speech, sentence and paragraph structure, and so forth. He escapes the dry incurious dogmatism of the textbooks very successfully, not of course without giving occasion for dissent here and there over points of detail. It is in the hope that an expanded edition may follow that I shall continue to quarrel with him over these details rather than select the many excellent observations which might with equal ease be instanced.

Mr. Read makes a sound division of metaphors into *illuminative* and *decorative*, a division which might be carried further, for there seem to be several kinds of decorative metaphor, some unimportant, but some very powerful both in poetry and prose. "Decorative" metaphors he would exclude from pure prose. "These are generally introduced either to display the poetic tendency of the author's mind, and are therefore out of place; or to give an alternative expression to a thought which has already been expressed in direct language. In this case they are redundant" (p. 28). But surely this is to overlook at least two very important services that metaphors render in prose. The expression of our feelings about the subject we are discussing; and the control of tone, our attitude toward those we are addressing. I suspect, from this and some other passages in the book, that Mr. Read *thinks about* utterance[3] with too much abstraction. To take *tone* first, what we say in metaphor may be either less or more offensive than if said in plain words (examples might range from "How much salt do we need with this?" to "Who pulled your chain?"). This whole aspect of speech Mr. Read, I think, too little considers. It is hidden from him by his choice of the word "persuasion" to cover all the countless different purposes for which men may write.

But the use of metaphor to convey our feeling about what we are speaking of is still more important. On page 29, Mr. Read rewrites a flowery passage on the Oxford Movement and in doing so gives us one of the few examples of imperfect sensibility to language that this book—no slight test—contains. In his translation of this passage into direct language a very important part of its meaning is certainly lost—the whole expression of the author's feeling towards the Oxford Movement, the Anglican Church, and the Church of Rome. "The Anglican sands" is certainly not equivalent to "the looser elements of the Anglican Church." The first expresses the feelings of a Romanist, the second those of an Anglican. Similarly "failed to uncover any rock-bottom underlying them" (the Anglican sands) is not equivalent to "failed to reach any fundamental body of opinion." No more is "the Rock of Peter" equivalent to "the Church of Rome." Mr. Read was nodding when he made this paraphrase; the original presents one set of sympathies, the paraphrase another. I suspect in part a prejudice against elaborate metaphors in prose as the explanation, but also the influence of ideas about "meaning" which are altogether too simple. This over-simplicity, a very serious handicap in discussing any of the problems of style, is largely due to his use of the word "Thought." To this word however we must return.

While upon the subject of synonyms a slighter example may be mentioned. Mr. Read (p. 7) takes "flood" and "deluge" to be synonyms, and makes the use of the one or the other by Jeremy Taylor to be a matter of sound and rhythm. His observations on these are just, but surely the words have also a marked difference in sense—"deluge" having come to stand for the catastrophic downfall of the water and "flood" for its relatively static overwhelming presence? And with this difference in one kind of meaning go others; the feelings the two words evoke are different.

That Mr. Read's conception of meaning needs improvement

is indicated also by his use of the word "visual" in many passages. A word in *prose* he says "must *mean* the thing it stands for, not only in the logical sense of accurately corresponding to the intention of the writer, but also in the visual sense of conjuring up a reflection of the thing in its completest reality" (p. 3). Here the first definition of "meaning" is as much too loose as the second is too narrow. Again (p. 104), "The object of narrative is to transmit to the reader an exact visual account of the object or action represented." Perhaps Mr. Read is himself a visualizer or dependent upon his visual images in his realization of meanings. But there are many people who use visual images very little and lose nothing by their abstention. No doubt the eye is our most important sense organ, but to prescribe generally this or any other mode of concrete presentation is to mistake what is *sometimes* an invaluable means for an end. Examples can be found, among the extracts Mr. Read gives us in this very chapter on Narrative, where this form of evocation is not used at all. In the story of the Prodigal Son and the paragraphs from Fielding there is no attempt "to transmit to the reader an exact visual account." We can picture the action if we please, but the authors do not picture it for us. They merely say what happened. One can understand why Mr. George Moore once rather foolishly described *Tom Jones* as "an empty book . . . giving us no glimpse of the world without." Mr. Read is too sensible to press his demand for "visual clarity" to this point. Nonetheless it leads him to object for the wrong reasons, to some phrases of Mr. Kipling's on page 105. The passage he quotes is "overdone," it is true, but that something is there described that probably no one really saw is an unjustified complaint and incidentally it ignores the intention of the passage. This is always the danger of these arbitrary prescriptions. "Visualize," except in very special instances, is in fact a metaphor; by synecdoche one form of concrete presentation stands for any form: and not even concreteness (much less any special form of concreteness) can be insisted upon as necessary in prose, or as always a merit. The extraordinary abstractness* of the

---

*Mr. Read seems to be a little confused as to the relations of abstractness to precision. "To add an epithet of *quality* is to progress from the abstract and therefore vague entity of *substance* to the definite entity of *sense perception*" (p. 15). But an idea may be as abstract as you please without therefore being indefinite or vague, as any logician or mathematician would explain to him.

language of Henry James at his best, as in the passage Mr. Read quotes ("a sort of wrought effect or bold ambiguity for a vista," "the influence rather of some complicated sound, diffused and reverberant, than of such visibilities as one could directly deal with"), might be instanced, if proof were needed. But probably Mr. Read did not mean what he wrote nearly so seriously as I have taken it. I have lingered with it because it is just the kind of rememberable and applicable principle which teachers find useful, and with which they too often persecute their pupils.

The last chapter of the part devoted to Composition discusses Arrangement. Mr. Read rightly insists that arrangement "is mainly a question of rhetoric," yet makes a reservation. "In rhetoric we consider arrangement as a means to secure a particular effect; from the point of view of composition we have to consider arrangement as an end in itself, as a pattern of aesthetic worth, independent of the ideas expressed." I find nothing, however, in the chapter to convince me that Mr. Read is really doing this. His very judicious comments all seem clearly to discuss the matter with reference to some effect more or less particular. And it is very doubtful indeed whether there is such a thing as "the point of view of composition," whether aesthetic worth, "pure form" independent of the ideas expressed or some other purpose, is not merely a remnant of one of the idler speculations of the last century. Mr. Read makes little or no use of the idea; it is one of the virtues of his book that he eschews it. I wish he could be persuaded in a second edition to omit this concession to the aestheticians.

Passing now to part II we encounter at the threshold a formidable table of the types of rhetoric:

	Thought	—	Sensibility
	I		I
Logic	Exposition	—	Narrative
	I		I
Speculation	Fantasy	—	Imagery
	I		I
Emotion	Intelligence	—	Personality
	I		I
Character	Eloquence	—	Tradition (taste)

$\sqrt{2}$ stands for a highly abstract but a perfectly definite and precise idea. The passage this citation is from is an unusually weak spot, for its psychology is as

In material and in method this table is scholastic in origin. My difficulty with it is that I cannot persuade myself that these divisions correspond with any facts in nature. Mr. Read seems by their aid to say a number of interesting things about particular pieces of prose, and a number of things that are almost certainly true. But that may be because he has an interesting mind, not because these distinctions are really sound or helpful; and I am a little doubtful whether he really uses them, whether he could not have got on quite as well without them. The difficulty arises most over the Thought-Sensibility division, the one which Mr. Read most fully expounds—he gives it in all about four pages. It is true that he says "These terms are not used with any particular philosophical or psychological bias," but this remark must be merely in the nature of a defensive smoke screen, for if they are not so used they become so vague as to be nearly useless. In any case, as Mr. Read will agree, they are not used in any of the several senses current in modern non-scholastic psychology, a fact which in view of Mr. Read's economies in explanation makes the whole matter obscure. If it is suggested that we all know sufficiently what they mean without going into any theories behind them, I can only urge that they are in fact vague and ambiguous, that Mr. Read makes a display of using them with precision, and that if we wish to follow what he does with them we must discover, if we can, what, for him, they are.

The distinction between Thought and Sensibility corresponds, we are told, to the scholastic distinction between internal and external acts of the will. Internal acts are directed towards an end, external acts towards an object. The distinction is further equated, hesitatingly, with the distinction between introversion and extraversion. Seeing how extremely rough this last division is Mr. Read does well to hesitate. These definitions—we are given scarcely any further explanations—do not, I think, greatly illumine the table. We must look then at the use Mr. Read makes of Thought and Sensibility if we are to arrive at a precise understanding of his meaning. But we find that he makes surprisingly little use of his dis-

---

confused as its logic. I venture such remarks because these are not large debatable philosophic matters, but elementary distinctions agreed upon by all trained students. The mistakes I deprecate here are like blunders in simple arithmetic.

tinction. In his discussion of Exposition I cannot discover that he makes any reference to internal acts of the will, directed towards an end. He seems to use "Thought" here in the ordinary sense of "thinking"—that is, the activities of comparing, discriminating, generalizing, constructing, and inferring, which are the subject of chapters in all the textbooks of psychology. An end doubtless is implied but in no sense in which the construction of a narrative does not imply an end. But is there really any reason to suppose that a treatise on ancient law or upon gastronomy does not imply reference to an object, to the world of external objects (sensibility) even more than, for example, the introspective expatiations of Ivan Karamazov or almost any paragraph of Mrs. Virginia Woolf's later novels?

My point is that Mr. Read's distinction between Thought and Sensibility does not really help him to separate Exposition from Narrative, or to describe either of them. Narrative may perfectly properly concern itself with a material which has little or no trace of "sensibility" (if sensibility is an affair of the influence of the external world). It may concern itself with wishes, for example. I am inclined to think that Mr. Read is not altogether consistent in his use of the word. In one place (p. 177) he seems to make it an affair of our bodily response; in another (p. 203) he speaks of "a particular kind of sensibility, a sensibility not only to historical continuity, but also to historical wholeness, or integrity." Why not a sensibility to logical fallacy or to mathematical elegance? Here "sensibility" and "thought" seem almost to have changed places.

I feel a similar difficulty with Mr. Read's other divisions. The division between Fantasy (fancy) and Imagery seems to me in Mr. Read's pages to stand on its own feet and be very little assisted by his references to Thought and Sensibility (p. 137). Fantasy can certainly be as sensuous in every way as Imagery, a point which Mr. Read's allusion to the *Thousand and One Nights* as "the greatest work of fantasy that has ever been evolved by tradition," well brings out. And I would submit that it is also in parts as "instinctive" (p.137) as any writing could be. Mr. Read, however, has a special sense of his own for "instinct" (pp. 71, 94) which seems a pity when so much labor has been devoted to making it a more useful word.

This chapter on Fantasy is the least interesting in the book, partly because Mr. Read has here departed from his subject, prose style, in order to recommend a literary form which he believes has been unduly denigrated. The examples he gives, if they are compared with those given in the other chapters, will not, I think, bear out his contention. And his accusation that "This aspersion of Fancy is entirely sentimental in origin" (p. 151) tempts one to retort in kind. Mr. Read, however, shuffles about his remarks on Imagery, Imagination, and Fantasy very confusedly. Imagery is a type of his own creation, named and set up but not defined, for Mr. Read's effort at a definition (on p. 152) is too much of the blunderbuss order.

The last chapters contain much excellent criticism, but again the theoretical scaffolding seems rather to be ornamental than useful. The impression lingers that the book has been written with too much haste, and that its statements have not received from the author as much deliberation as their solemn manner invites the reader to bestow. Slips are frequent. "A personal style may be clear and concrete, but it is not *ordered*. The images, though hard and distinct, are haphazard. They form a picturesque ruin, not a symmetrical structure. The details of this *order* we may call the idiom of the writer" (p. 178). "In fact, all that is necessary for clear reasoning and good style is personal sincerity. A sincere mind can and does reject facts which do not fit into its hypotheses" (p. 96). Surely Mr. Read meant to write "A sincere mind can and does reject hypotheses which do not accord with its facts." And can this be a Freudian *lapsus calami?* In any case this sincerity doctrine— though it wins ready applause from those who are less clear about what they mean than sure that they mean it—will not bear examination. Its formulation here is a disproof of its truth. No one would suggest that Mr. Read was not sincere in every sense when he wrote it, yet the ambiguities of the word "necessary" have tripped him up and confused his reasoning. "All that is necessary" may mean "The only thing that is required" or "The only thing that is indispensable." In the first sense the statement is plainly untrue. In the second it seems possible that in some recondite sense it may be true. Mr. Read must, I think, have had this second sense in his mind first, and then proceeded in his argument from the other. A very cautious attitude to words and lively constant awareness of their ambiguities seems certainly as much required for clear reasoning as any kind of sincerity. "Lucidity, simplicity, and system" may be, as Sir Henry Maine suggested, the characteristics of a good expository style.[4] But we must especially beware lest system should too much domineer. The provocations—which I have unduly stressed—seem to me largely the result of too intense an effort toward system. Many of the remarks with which I have quarreled would pass well enough in conversation, or if set out with a less impressive manner, but so much talk about precision does invite precise reading. Behind this theoretical apparatus, however, is a body of observation, discernment, and criticism from which all who study is *closely* will profit. But the book, as it stands, can only have a bad effect upon hasty or average readers. It is much to be hoped that Mr. Read will recast his book, and make, in later editions, more use of the methods and slowly won results of academic psychology which can restate many of his distinctions less arbitrarily and with more illumination. It would be sad should his fine gifts for *detailed* criticism be permanently impaired through a strategic error in his choice of intellectual equipment.

19 Notes on the Practice of Interpretation

I am of opinion now that this sort of verbal activity is a waste of everybody's time. It is too tempting a game, with no one to keep any score any more than with shuttlecock and battledore. The culprit is not converted, though he may be irritated. The fuming victim is not, in reality, relieved. Worse still, he is often badly infected himself by the diseases he is professing to cure. The detached (let us suppose) reader is not assisted. I do not see that any but the editor, the publisher, and the printer profit from the free copy so provided. Having mentioned the editor I should add that I never could imagine how the Criterion *allowed this contributor entry into its pages. Anyone curious about this should look into the first seven pages of chapter IX, "The Bridle of Pegasus," of my* Coleridge on Imagination. *The "representative present-day critic" there exhibited is Montgomery Belgion. How the paragraphs there quoted got into the* Criterion *is truly a literary problem.*

As to this piece here reprinted my present feeling is that I felt I had to defend passages in Principles *I have had no interest in since. All the terms used were too unreliable for any useful purposes. It was a pillow fight in a fog of escaped feathers.*

As to why my pages in Coleridge on Imagination *are more effective, my suggestion is that I had in the interval been reading S. T. C., working at* Interpretation in Teaching, *and learning a little more about reading and writing.*

Few writers fail to be accused of absurdities which they did not commit, but when this occurs of pages as responsible and authoritative as those of the *Criterion* even the most stoical will be tempted to reply.[1] The temptation is strengthened when the views for which the writer is reproved are views he has written against for

Reprinted from *Criterion*, 10 (1931), 412-420.

years. And since many more readers derive their information as to an author's opinions from periodicals than from his books, almost a duty of self-defense arises. This must be my excuse for entering upon a form of controversy which is, as a rule, neither dignified nor useful in advancing a subject. Mr. Montgomery Belgion's interpretations of my opinions, however, are so mistaken and so calculated to misinform readers of his article as to what I do say, that some notes upon them are, I think, justified. They may also have a less personal interest as a contribution toward the study of interpretation, a subject which Mr. Belgion seems to think is not in need of further examination by critics.

My critic finds for example (p. 124) that in *Science and Poetry* I "endorsed Matthew Arnold's familiar dictum that what is valuable in religion as in science, is art." Readers of that little book will remember, however, that I endorsed no such dictum. My endeavor there was to set what is valuable in religion (and poetry) and what is valuable in science as far apart as such unlike kinds of activity with their unlike kinds of value should be set. The whole essay was, in fact, an argument against confusing them.

Mr. Belgion goes on: "That dictum is, when you examine it, the statement of an extraordinary doctrine. For what can the dictum mean? It can only mean that the emotions we obtain through seeing, hearing, or reading, the results of the artistic treatment of religious and scientific matters, are what make religion and science valuable. But Mr. Richards now appears to be arguing on the basis of a theory even more preposterous." I do not think many people who are likely to be reading this will have difficulty in thinking of other things which the dictum might mean. It might, for example, be saying that what was valuable in religious and scientific thinking was some kind of intuitive insight also found in the artist; or it might be saying that if we are to derive valuable experience from scientific and religious utterances we should regard them in the ways that we regard poetry. It might reasonably mean other things. Some of these interpretations are interesting. I should *endorse*, I think, none of them, though I could discuss them. But Mr. Belgion's interpretation to me is undiscussable. He asserts that the *only* meaning for the word "art" which he can use in such a context makes it equivalent to "emotions resulting from artistic treatment." Such a confession of linguistic limitations is remarkable. It explains, I suppose, why he has to give my poor attempts at clarifying these matters a series of interpretations "even more preposterous." What he gives me to say is that only "good" art (i.e., in his sense of "emotions resulting from artistic treatment") is valuable, and nothing else is, in our whole emotional life. I can only say that if I met anyone saying anything like this I should drop the conversation abruptly—unless in a mood for the study of psychopathology.

How Mr. Belgion puts this rubbish upon me is worth noting: quoting my remark that "there is no gap between our everyday emotional life and the material of poetry," he comments "Now what is being asserted in this passage is by no means clear. One can only diffidently suspect that, underlying Mr. Richards's claims for what poetry can do for us, is a notion that poetry and life are somehow equivalent." Why all this diffidence? All the books of mine which Mr. Belgion cites contain tiresomely elaborate descriptions of the connections between poetry and life which seem to me to hold, and of the facts and arguments by which this view can be recommended. It is impossible, however, to understand these descriptions unless the definitions of "poetry," "life," and "experience" used in them are understood. Mr. Belgion has clearly had no success at all in his efforts to understand them.

Having thus burdened me with a ridiculous opinion, Mr. Belgion, page 125, (unwittingly I believe) confuses it with another—an old and by no means absurd one—and so links it with the rather big claims I have tried to revive for poetry. "But poetry cannot be employed by us for the ordering of our minds; nor, likewise, are any of the rest of his claims on behalf of poetry justified. Not one of them is justified because the supposition underlying them is false. The emotion which a poem can produce in us is not identical with what we should feel if we experienced in actual life what the subject of that poem seems to be."

Now the supposition in the last sentence is again not one that I have ever held. I have indeed in the larger books argued repeatedly and expressly against it. Nor does it in any way underlie the claims I have put forward for poetry. No such assumption is required for these claims. For them it is enough if the emotions a poem produces can influence in certain indirect fashions emotions produced in other ways.

Mr. Belgion makes only one attempt to convict me of this supposition by citation. I must quote his whole paragraph:

> A theory bearing on this point has recently been advanced by the distinguished French novelist, Mr. Jean Giraudoux, the theory, viz. 'Il n'est pas un sentiment en Racine qui ne soit un sentiment littéraire.' His argument is this. In the youthful period during which are stored those indelible impressions that later become the artist's inspiration, Racine was afforded no experience of actual life; consequently, the exclusive data for his work were the classics upon which his Jansenist teachers had nourished him. To show, moreover, that this is so, Mr. Giraudoux examines the behaviour of a number of the most famous characters in the great tragedies. Of course, the theory may not be true; enough that it is made plausible. For let Mr. Richards ponder what that plausibility means. He, in his book, says (p. 263) that there are writers who 'lose sight of the real sanctions of the feelings in experience', although he neglects to mention why experience should yield 'real sanctions' for imaginative literature. Are we then to consider if Racine, the master of the French stage, the author of a tragedy which Voltaire called 'the masterpiece of the human mind', never put into his work a single feeling taken direct from life, that he did not know what was, and what not, legitimate material for literature? Is it not more likely, on the contrary, that Mr. Richards misunderstands the nature of aesthetic emotion, and that that emotion, not only is different from the emotion we should have if we experienced the poem's subject in actual life, but can be produced without having originated from life at all? As again Mr. Eliot says: 'And the emotions which he (the poet) has never experienced will serve his turn as well as those familiar to him.'

Three points may be noticed here. First, that Mr. Belgion takes experience in an odd and special sense, a literary man's sense, which contrasts it (but without defined boundaries) with literature. Witness what he reports Mr. Giraudoux as saying about Racine's early days. Can anyone seriously suppose that anyone's "exclusive data" could be the classics? Not the worst psychologist ever could be so silly. In any case such a sense of "experience" with its derived senses for "life" and "poetry" is too vague and unconsidered by far to be used in this kind of argument. This sense of "experience" must, I think, be a main source of Mr. Belgion's queer interpretations of my pages.

Secondly, he quotes me from a passage where I am trying to suggest how "sentimental" poetry gets written by people who, in ordinary life, are not markedly sentimental. He evidently takes me to mean by "the real sanctions of the feelings in experience" that those actual feelings must at some time have formed part of non-literary experience, have been "taken direct from life," and he makes this misinterpretation fundamental to what he calls my view. I suggest he look up "sanctions" in some good dictionary. However, on the point whether he is right in attributing to me the supposition that everything in a poem must be taken, in his sense, from "life," he might read the following: "Many of the finest and most widely significant experiences, and those therefore most suitable for poetry, come nowadays, for example, through reading pieces of advanced research"—*Principles of Literary Criticism*.[2] Or he might read the following from a passage where I am discussing the relation of the feelings in the poem to the poet's own feelings. "The feelings need not be stated or even openly expressed; it is enough if they are hinted to us. And they need not be actual personal 'real live feelings'; they may be imagined feelings. All that is required for this kind of insincerity is a discrepancy between the poem's claim upon our response and its *shaping* impulses in the poet's mind. But only the shaping impulses are relevant. A good poem can perfectly well be written for money or from pique or ambition, provided these initial external motives do not interfere with its growth."[3] I may well have had Mr. Eliot's remarks in *The Sacred Wood* in mind when I wrote these phrases. (Incidentally I should doubt very much if Mr. Belgion—after quoting from Mr. Eliot that "the business of a poet is not to find new emotions, but to use ordinary ones, and, in working them up into poetry, to express feelings which are not in actual emotions at all"—is correct in adding "That is to say, the emotion obtainable from a poem is to be found in the poem and nowhere else." For this is either a tautology or very disputable, whereas Mr. Eliot's analysis of *one* method of poetic composition is both interesting and acceptable.)

In addition to overlooking these statements as well as scores of others which directly imply a difference between the experience as it is worked into the poem and "ordinary experiences of the street or of the hillside," Mr. Belgion unhappily pays no attention to the chapters in *Principles* or the pages in *Science and Poetry* where this heresy of his of "specific aesthetic emotions" is discussed and when some of the evidence that it is a heresy—contradicting the views of the chief "experts" of critical tradition—is set out.

Thirdly, with Mr. Belgion's suggestion that I mistake the emotion we get from the poem with the emotion we might have if we experienced the poem's subject I have dealt already, but since he harps upon the matter I must do so too. "Thus Mr. Richards must be regarded, in this matter of the nature of the aesthetic emotion, as doubly mistaken. The experience which the poet offers to his auditor, or reader, is not the original experience which has provided him with a subject for his poem" (p. 128). This, however, is a remark which I have myself, in several places, ventured to make; for example, on the very page from which he quotes my "sanctions in experience" phrase (*Practical Criticism,* p. 263): "If we separate out the subject or theme of the poem, *A girl bewailing her lost or absent lover,* and take this, abstractly, as the situation, we may think that it sounds sufficient to justify any extremity of sympathetic emotion. But this abstracted theme is nothing in itself, and might be the basis of any one of as many different developments as there are kinds of girls." (Also see pp. 191 and 297). My critic might have taken the precaution to consult either the index or contents of the book before dealing me out such A.B.C. blunders. (And while I am making references let Mr. Belgion ponder a passage on "thinking," pp. 249-251.)

He says, however, I am doubly mistaken. I not only think the poem just hands over some happy or unhappy half hour of the poet's emotional life—but I somehow also think that the reader gets just what went on in the poet's mind while he was writing the poem! He gives me the second of these incompatible mistakes by a similar piece of interpretation. He quotes a footnote of mine defining the "aim" of a poem (p. 204). "I hope to be understood to mean by this whole state of mind, the mental condition, which in another sense *is* the poem. Roughly the collection of impulses which shaped the poem originally, to which it gave expression, and to which, in an ideally susceptible reader, it would again give rise." (He omits what follows in the footnote: "Qualifications to this definition would, of course, be needed, if strict precision were needed, but here this may suffice." Evidently it didn't.) He then goes on: "Here the error consists of assuming that that to which the poem can give rise, even in 'an ideally susceptible reader', is the collection

of impulses which led the poet to shape it originally." That the collection of impulses which shape a poem and the collection which
lead a poet to shape it are different collections is perhaps a subtle
point for Mr. Belgion. But the difference is crucial to my definition
for reasons which the reader will notice if he compares the remarks
on the growth of a poem quoted above.

What I call the "shaping impulses" and also "the poem" in
this footnote is what I take Mr. Belgion to call "what a work of art
exists to produce." It is something we have to define, more or less
exactly, if we want to talk about particular poems at all. Why it
should be all right for Mr. Belgion to inform us later (p. 129) that
the artist does have an intention and a single intention, and the
poem a one and only aim, and so very stupid of me to say the same,
is a mystery I cannot penetrate. If he had really wanted to know
what I thought about an admittedly difficult point, he could easily
have glanced at the chapter entitled "The Definition of a Poem" in
Principles. There (pp. 225 and 227) he would have found an analysis distinguishing four starting points. "We may be talking about
the artist's experience, such of it as is relevant, or about the experience of a qualified reader who made no mistakes, or about an ideal
and perfect reader's possible experience, or about our own actual
experience. All four in most cases will be qualitatively different.
Communication is perhaps never perfect, so the first and the last
will differ. The second and the third differ also, from the others and
from one another, the third being what we ought unrestrictedly to
experience, or the best experience we could possibly undergo,
whereas the second is merely what we ought to experience as things
are, or the best experience that we can expect." He would have
found also a general formula for a definition of a poem: "namely,
as a class of experiences which do not differ in any character more
than a certain amount, varying for each character, from a standard
experience." For reasons which go deep into the theory of interpretation it would be a mistake to fix the standard experience for all
occasions. For some purposes it is useful to make some reader's
experience the standard: for other purposes the poet's experience,
such of it as is relevant, is better; for actually we do read (interpret)
in these two ways, now to what the poem means, now to what the
poet meant. Badly written poetry brings out the problem plainly.

But this may be treating the subject too elaborately for Mr.

Belgion. What he does (p. 137) is to cry "forget the poet." (I won't accept any responsibility for encouraging him in this.) And talks in the very next sentence about "the full emotional effect which this sonnet *exists to produce*," and in the next but one of "its intended effect." But neither its intended effect nor, I think, the effect it *exists to produce* can be *defined* without reference to the poet. Of course they can be *experienced* without thinking of the poet.

These, I regret to find, are by no means all Mr. Belgion's difficulties with my pages. He complains (p. 129) that I leave him in the dark as to what I refer to by "personality," while quoting on page 129 and page 130 sentences standing amid contexts which make this for most people, I still think, sufficiently clear. I prefer to leave it to the unguided judgment of the reader, stressing only that for Mr. Belgion (p. 129) *"we are left altogether without a clue* as to what he means." He couples this assertion in the same sentence with another: "He does not even mention to which school of psychology he belongs." As it happens, I did include a whole section explaining just this (part 4, pp. 321-322.)[4]

One further point only—not to weary the reader—for there are others. Mr. Belgion quotes (p. 130) a series of passages in which he says I deny that what a work of art "exists to produce" is an identical effect in all its spectators. This, we have seen, is something I should never deny once it had been properly stated and "exists to produce" analyzed. And these passages do not, except for Mr. Belgion, bring it up. But he proceeds to expound the middle passage and answer certain questions about it on my behalf. "What are the excellent reasons for which it is possible to like the 'wrong' poems and dislike the 'right' ones? His answer (Mr. Richards's) is, of course, that we are liking or disliking a poem for reasons which are excellent, when we thoroughly understand what is said in it, and to that we respond 'directly', with 'the choice of our whole personality.' "

This answer for me is just nonsense as applied to my remark. Mr. Belgion seems to be confusing what the poem "exists to produce" and what we do with this when it has been produced. I am talking about the latter, and my remark is to be interpreted with another which stands exactly opposite it in my pages (348-349): "What is good for one mind may not be good for another in a different condition—with different needs and in a different situation."

This may stand perhaps as a summing up of these notes, since it applies to more things than poems. Whether Mr. Belgion's reasons—in view of his condition—for disliking my remarks are excellent or not I am unable to judge. The important thing is to make clear that the opinions he attributes to me are all of his own concoction—not of my expression.

20 Lawrence as a Poet

When the court action against The Rainbow *was
reported, I wanted, very badly, though I could not, to go to
call on him and at least shake his hand. His books, from* The
White Peacock *on, had mattered so much. Incidentally, I
have not known, as a lecturer, passages that could still and
move an audience more than the "til the heralds come" paragraphs of the funeral scene there. (Maybe some of* The
Brook Kerith *could do likewise. Could there be authors
more unlike?) Little by little, however, it became grievously
evident—though by no means to some—that things in this
potentially great writer were going agley. Readers are typo-
logically almost as various as writers. This little comment
may, however, record what many who once looked to Lawrence as to few others came to think about him.*

A fundamental fact about Lawrence's poetry is that its reader
cannot escape the problem of belief. By all but a small special part
of it he is forcibly invited—and the energy of the poetry is the force
of this invitation—to do something in his response for which "believe" seems to be the appropriate word. The "do you-don't you?"
"will you-won't you?" challenge is more insistent with his than with
any other poetry I can think of—and this is so whether the doctrine
is being argued in take-it-or-leave-it, literal language or being uttered through symbols of experience which are themselves made
symbolic. In either case one is invited to "believe"—and yet a great
part of this doctrine is of a kind that no one, without doing violent
damage to himself, can "believe." Are there two "believes" here,
different in sense though the same in feeling? This is the capital
problem with most of Lawrence's poetry.

Review of D. H. Lawrence, *Last Poems* (Florence: Orioli, 1932). Reprinted
by permission from *New Verse*, 1 (1933), 15-17.

If there are two kinds of believing here (let us call them "adopting the attitude as good" and "accepting the doctrine as true"), readers of Lawrence will sort themselves out by the degree to which these activities are separable in their minds. There are those who can follow him in his attitudes to life without agreeing that his doctrines are true. And there are those who cannot separate them—who must take them or reject them, attitude and doctrine, together. It will be idle for men of these different sorts to dispute about his poetry: they should be disputing about the uses of language and the senses of "belief" instead.

For those who can separate kinds of beliefs, Lawrence's poems fall into a number of classes, according to whether his own queer dealings with himself in restricting his own outlook on the world did or did not vitiate the poem. His was a singularly all-round mind at the beginning of his course, with an intellectual equipment and logical aptitudes not inadequate to the prodigious sensibility, plasticity, sincerity, and courage that made him Lawrence. But quite early he took to shutting up these intellectual faculties whenever they threatened his system of intuitions. He deliberately turned his intellect into a giant slave of his intuitions instead of making it a partner, and the result was a loss of sanction that ruins a large part of his work. Whenever his own experience was alone relevant—being universally normal experience—there was no loss of sanction, as in "The White Horse" in the Death poems here.

> The youth walks up to the white horse, to put its halter on,
> and the horse looks at him in silence.
> They are so silent they are in another world.

And it is so in scores of slighter though longer poems where, also, Lawrence is not reaching out beyond the field of his own marvelously deepened and clarified experience. But when he does reach out of it, and passes from "feeling something" to "feeling *that* so and so"—where the so and so involves other men's other experience as well as his own—his prophet's trick of despising evidence too often betrays him. It does so here in some poems of political doctrine ("The Cross" is a good example) as it did in his earlier poems that are *arguments from* his experience of sex. "Birds, Beasts and Flowers" escapes this danger, since the arguments there are not made to follow from the perceptions but to display them.

The danger is two-fold. The poem becomes, *as doctrine,* false (which might be a slight matter except insofar as acceptance of it as true is required); secondly, and much more serious, the attitude to life in the poem becomes peculiar to Lawrence, *merely his,* or at best sectarian. Instead of a poem proceeding from "the all in each of all men" we are left with a document—often a very moving one, but essentially a piece of a case history. Lawrence's loyalty to his gift, to his intuition, was sometimes a disloyalty to his completer humanity—a fault as bad as being, for example, *only* a Frenchman. It forced him to write out of much less than his whole self.

These are the (fairly well known) problems which Lawrence's "Last Poems" bring up as violently as any of his earlier. Here 30 serious poems may stand with his best, and there are about 250 utterances of the Pansy kind—all in the colloquial, unrhymed, sometimes meditative, sometimes argumentative manner of his later work. Even in the best the reader must be prepared for those patches of prose which Lawrence took no particular care to clear out of his verse. Few of these poems are memorable in the narrow sense in which what you remember are the words—first, last, and always. What remains is the sense of passionate awareness that opened as you read. If poetry requires "an identity of content and form," Lawrence was not a great poet. But this is a question *either* of definition *or* of the technical ways appropriate for certain purposes. "Do not let us introduce an Act of Uniformity against poets."[1] Lawrence's ways were right for his purposes whenever his purposes had behind them as much of himself as they required.

21 Literature, Oral-Aural and Optical

This was an optimistic (essentially politically minded)
utterance on one of the most frightening of the technological
threats to the human future, the supplanting of man's chief
humanizing instrument, writing. This is no place in which to
develop the opposing view or to attempt the due reconcilia-
tion. Those concerned with how this threat may be guarded
against may be referred—regarding current inadequacies of
conceptions of what writing-readng does for us and regard-
ing current attacks on literacy—to The Written Word, *Sher-*
idan Baker, Jacques Barzun, I. A. Richards, Newbury House
Publishers, Rowley, Massachusetts, 1971. And as to how we
might make still wiser use of writing—that man-creating
and man-maintaining invention—to Techniques in Language Control, *Christine Gibson and I. A. Richards, from*
the same publisher, 1974. Both of these say much that on the
occasion of this talk would have been out of place. We may
remind ourselves that broadcasts are for occasions, but
written utterances are for any time.

My title is itself a miniature example of the problem I would
discuss: "Literature, Oral-Aural and Optical."

I think man must love confusion. Otherwise he wouldn't
pronounce "oral" and "aural" alike, as if there were no difference
between speaking and hearing and no point in separating the
doings of the mouth and the ear. Writing, of course, distinguishes
them. Any reader can see the difference between "oral" and "aural".
But as most people, I believe, most often say them, they sound the
same. Speech takes them and their meaning together, in a large
loose sort of unity. Writing, in this instance, tries to use their etymons to clear things up.

A talk delivered on BBC Radio on October 5, 1947, and printed in the *Listener*, October 16, 1947, pp. 669-670.

I want to speculate a little in this talk on some of the differences between speech and writing when used for their most ambitious purposes: for poetry and philosophy. I am talking still in a writing-conscious era when in spite of radio, tape, and the soundtrack, the WORD is still, first and foremost, the written word, and more specifically the printed word, not the utterance of a voice. And the sentence is still something that offers itself to the eye in static precision—there before us to be examined—frozen stiff, as it were, to be sliced up and dissected by the leisurely, piecemeal, analytic mind served by the corresponsive eye, whenever we chose to linger and explore. The written sentence and its meaning stand over against the eye—to be looked into. But to the ear a spoken sentence is more like a fluctuant, resonant pulse of our inner history, gone by almost before it is completed. That is the great contrast I want to play with. It may be rather important now that speech and the ear are getting their chance to stage a comeback.

This contrast has had more than a little to do with the history of literature. Isn't it remarkable—as the great Chadwick[1] complained when writing of the Heroic Age—that we haven't any word for "literature before writing"? Isn't it monstrous that one should have to talk about aural literature or preliterate literature, meaning by that something that isn't necessarily ever written or read, needn't be any concern of the man of letters, isn't made up out of letters but out of sounds, isn't literature at all, but direct vocal utterance? This shows, doesn't it, how thoroughly *writing* has stolen the show? The very mother-art from which literature sprang hasn't even a name among us.

Literature is born and reborn on the summit of Everest. It is a very odd thing, but in literature the best in each kind comes first, comes suddenly, and never comes again. This is a disturbing, uncomfortable, unacceptable idea to people who take their doctrines of evolution and of progress over-simply. But I think it must be admitted to be true. Of the very greatest things in each sort of literature, the masterpiece is unprecedented, unique, never thenceforth challenged or approached. The rule seems to be that stated in the refrain of "Green grow the rashes, O": "One is one and all alone and evermore shall be so."

Think of the *Iliad*, of the Book of Job, or in prose of the earliest "J" narratives in Genesis or of the "Court History of David" in

2 Samuel 9-20. That court history is the first historical narrative there is, written about 1000 B.C.—500 years before Herodotus, the "Father of History." The scholar's judgment on it seems to be that as narrative prose it is utterly unmatched in its kind by anything later in the Old Testament. The same thing seems to hold of later masterpieces, each in its own kind. There is no rival to Plato or to Vergil or to Dante, or to Cervantes, and no second Shakespeare or Milton. I don't know any satisfying explanation of this strange general rule. It feels as if it were somehow deeply significant and seems to herd with myths of the Fall of Man and the Golden Age. But it is not a myth, I believe, but a historical generalization.

We pen-conscious and print-minded people have to make no slight effort if we are to imagine what happened in the minds of speakers and listeners before writing came in. Our habits and attitudes are shaped by our experience as readers and by our optical training in analysis. We are ready to compare and connect and distinguish and abstract in a thousand ways which were hardly, if at all, possible to the pre-literacy listener.

All this has its advantages and disadvantages for us, both as speakers and listeners. It helps us, sometimes, to avoid some sorts of nonsense, though it may well expose us to other sorts. It lets us interfere consciously with our minds in their work of grasping the meaning. It makes the whole job of understanding—or misunderstanding—more complicated than it need be. These habits of comparing and abstracting, which come from the way in which words (and their meanings too, as we think) stand before us separately in print, enable us to ask pertinent questions, but they invite us also to raise points which have nothing to do with what is going forward.

In contrast, for the pre-literate's *ear*, words in discourse are not separate items, open to time-free contemplation, they are crests or troughs in a stream, parts of a wave pattern. It is arguable that the pre-literate could swim, as it were, in the sea of meaning while we only paddle and splash along its edges. However this may be, my point is that the reading mind and the speech-centered pre-literacy mind tackle apprehension in different fashions.

Homer illustrates the difference well. Readers coming to Homer under their own steam are often puzzled by a lot of things which this difference may help to explain. Homer's similes, for example, adorn the events they are attached to; they do not as a rule present or elucidate the action. They don't make us see *that* more clearly; they ask us to imagine some other event which may be remarkably unlike and unconnected with what is being described. There is usually no scope for the cunning discoveries of deeper correspondencies in which metaphor-curious *readers* of poetry so much delight. Homer's audiences were not looking for such things. They were attending to something else.

Some of the troubles which Plato had with Homer's morality may have had the same explanation. There we have the first and greatest *writing* philosopher turning with what seems a malicious but anguished unfairness against the universal provider, the educator of Greece. Eric Havelock has suggested that we may see in Plato's rejections of Homer the revolt of the writing mind's mode of apprehension against the *pre-literate* mind's other, less abstract and intellectual, ways of ordering itself.[2] The contrast is not simply between poetry and philosophy. Poetry is often, in technique, philosophical; and the aims of philosophy may be poetic. Moreover, the origin of philosophy, like that of poetry, is in aural not in optical composition.

Socrates—as against what Plato wrote—didn't write anything. He conversed instead. What he said is something we have more or less to guess at. Whatever it was, and whether Plato reported of it accurately or not (first-class opinions have been poles apart on that) Socrates' conversation does really seem to have done more for philosophy than all the writings of all the philosophers ever since. For it settled what sort of thing philosophy, or the discourse of reason—as it has been practiced in the West—was to be.

Socrates, in a word, invented philosophy. If John Burnet was right, he also invented something else—which goes with philosophy and has been even more influential. He invented the soul.[3] Before Socrates, so Burnet thought, nobody ever anywhere had had any conception of what, ever since Socrates, has been in mind when the word "soul," in his meaning for it, is considered. When, at his trial, Socrates says that the only thing that matters is to care for one's soul, the best that his judges could have made of that, Burnet suggests, is something like "Be good to your ghost!"—without any of the implications that one's soul really is oneself and is what knows and chooses.

Now whether we like reason and the soul—and believe in

them—or not, there is no doubt that they are among the most decisive inventions ever made. They are not obvious or natural discoveries by any means. They are not chairs or shoes; they are more like
the electron. And they seem to belong to the Western tradition and
are unparalleled in other traditions. Without them, *we*, of the tradition, would not, any of us, be what we are. The questions we ask
and the sorts of ways in which we try to answer them . . . the very
we's we take ourselves to be and the sort of thing we take *thinking*
to be . . . all these are outcomes of these inventions. So it is interesting that the man who made them didn't write anything.

Socrates may have had a prejudice against writing. Plato
gives him—in the *Phaedrus* (274c-277a)—a very curious little story
about the invention of the letters:

"I heard, then," says Socrates, "that at Naucratis, in Egypt,
was one of the ancient gods of that country, the one whose sacred
bird is called the ibis, and the name of the god himself was Theuth.
He it was who invented numbers and arithmetic and astronomy,
also draughts and dice, and, most important of all, letters. Now the
king of all Egypt at that time was the god Thamus . . . To him came
Theuth to show his inventions, saying that they ought to be im-
parted to the other Egyptians. But Thamus asked what use there
was in each . . . when they came to the letters, 'This invention, O
King,' said Theuth, 'will make the Egyptians wiser and will im-
prove their memories; for it is an elixir of memory and wisdom that
I have discovered.' But Thamus replied, Most ingenious Theuth,
one man has the ability to beget arts, but the ability to judge of
their usefulness or harmfulness to their users belongs to another;
and now you, who are the father of letters, have been led by your
affection to ascribe to them a power the opposite of that which they
really possess . . . you offer your pupils the appearance of wisdom,
not true wisdom . . . for they will read many things without instruction and will therefore seem to know many things, when they
are for the most part ignorant and hard to get along with . . .' "

"Socrates," says Phaedrus, "you easily make up stories about
Egypt or any country you please." But Socrates goes on:

"He who thinks, then, that he has left behind him any art in
writing, and he who receives it in the belief that anything in writing
will be clear and certain, would be an utterly simple person . . .
every word, when once it is written, is bandied about, alike among

those who understand and those who have no interest in it . . . for it has no power to protect or help itself."

Instead of such words, the true teacher will use "the legitimate brother of this bastard [sort of speech] . . . [and sow,] in a fitting soul intelligent words which are able to help themselves and him who planted them, which are not fruitless, but yield seed from which there spring up in other minds other words capable of continuing the process for ever, and which make their possessor happy, to the farthest possible limit of human happiness."[4] Socrates is notably serious here.

There are more modern inventions—aren't there?—of which we can echo Thamus' remark. "One man has the ability to beget arts, but the ability to judge of their usefulness or harmfulness to their users belongs to another."

Radio (and videotape) are technology's long-delayed reply to writing. It might (if the god Thamus were its guide) give us back some of the things we lost by the invention of letters. Not that we can or should give up reading and writing or the useful habits of reflection and analysis and private judgment they have developed and encouraged. These are part of the human equipment now—to be denied to no man. But—if the speakers can resist its temptations and control its vagaries, and if the other conditions which worry the critic of radio are righted—listening might (it is permissible to dream)—listening might give both philosophy and poetry a new communality and with it a new roundness and wholeness, freeing them from the pharisaical regard for the recondite.

Reading, silent reading, is manifestly antisocial activity. When Augustine first saw a man reading to himself silently (it was Saint Ambrose) he was deeply shocked. He knew Ambrose was a good man, what he did couldn't be wicked . . . but still!

Listening, in contrast, tends to communality. What is listened to, by choice, in common, speaks to "the all in each of all men." This may be low and trivial. But it may, as the *Iliad* and Job can remind us, deal with man's highest and most momentous concerns.

The *Iliad* and the pre-writing narratives of the Old Testament were products of public competition. They were the winners, the things which best pleased and continued to please, their audiences through a series of elimination trials. I do not think it is being sentimental or romantic or nostalgic to stand in some awe of the judgment of those early audiences—who listened and judged Homer and the "J" narratives of Genesis. They had this advantage over us. They were expert audiences, experienced in what they judged. They knew the stories. The form and style they were to be told in had been settled. The audiences knew in general what to look for, as farmers do at a sheepdog trial. So they could concentrate on how well it was done. They didn't have to wonder what sort of a game this was, or what the rules, if any, were, or what the player was trying to do. They knew all that, and could devote themselves to judging his play.

The result was a sort of economical functional efficiency, if you like that way of putting the point. Furthermore, the *Iliad* is a collective product—in shaping which the discernible preferences of the audience, shown then and there, had an immediate effect on the poets. Kipling puts it beautifully: "Unless they please they are not heard at all."[5] The poets could not rely on posterity to recognize their unappreciated merits. To address posterity you need a pen. The result was that posterity has been kinder to these aural composers, whose work was breath on the wind, than it has been to any *writers*.

Then, into this mode of composition came the new influence of writing. As to how it came in—that is all speculation. Early inventions often spread slowly and unevenly. Perhaps writing was used in commerce for centuries before poets took it up. When they did the effect was to freeze the traditional stream, making it viscous first, then solid and fixed. We may guess, perhaps, that there was a final stimulative effect before the scribes and the editors took over and speech, the living voice, gave place to the text and the *book* came to the throne.

The early books inherited the powers and organization of the oral tradition. That is a large part of the explanation of their immense influence ever since and of their miraculous massive preeminence. I am thinking not only of Homer and the Bible but of the founding books of most of the great cultures. The Vedas, Analects, and Mencius are good examples. They are the spoken word attributed suitably to Confucius or Mencius, written down later. I am not sure that the preeminence of Plato's earlier dialogues doesn't have the same explanation. Perhaps Socrates knew what he was doing in not writing. But the point is that the new techniques of composition through writing, when superimposed on the old techniques of speech, produced extraordinary results.

Well now. The book, at last, so it is said, is being deposed. Its successor is this microphone before me which looks so inattentive and unresponsive. The question is: whether the new or restored opportunities now offered to speech, when superimposed on the established techniques of reading and writing, can work the miracle again. My own feeling is that they can and may.

Perhaps this attempt to describe what a great book does may help a little to show that writing, when good enough, can do the things that the stage and the cinema—time-bound, as they must be—have to leave to their master art. A book offers to the free, reflective, deliberative mind opportunities for exploration (including self-exploration) denied, technologically, to more coercive means of communication. The more important the theme of the communication the more needed are these opportunities.

Current exploitations of the Gospels via the cinema are familiar. To those who have undergone them and also read The Brook Kerith *and the Gospels at some reasonably leisurely tempo, the moral as to media will be plain.*

The last paragraph of this review may well sum up the concerns so many of these pieces have touched on.

When a writer takes, as it would seem, every imaginable risk in subject, handling, plot . . . opening himself most widely to charges of triviality, sensationalism, imperceptiveness, impiety, and blasphemy, and yet incredibly triumphs over them all, another danger is incurred. The reader may become too curiously interested in *how* the feat has been accomplished to attend duly to what has actually been achieved. Wonderment at the ingenuity of his design, the adroitness of his transitions, the indirections of his presentation, his daring and discretion of invention at all levels, and what else has saved him from so many disasters can becloud our view of what in the end he has done. Not the least of his problems has been to keep all this technical management unobtrusive. *Ars est celare*

Review of George Moore, *The Brook Kerith: A Syrian Story* (1916; New York: Liveright, 1969). Reprinted by permission from *The New York Review of Books*, December 3, 1970, pp. 47-49. Copyright © 1970 Nyrev, Inc.

artem. Yes, but this, as epigrams often are, is itself too showy to be just. The inquisitive and critical eye can usually search out more than a little of the means employed in even what may seem the least contrived performances. The need is, as Coleridge reminds us, to subordinate "our admiration of the poet to our sympathy with the poetry."[1]

The reissue of George Moore's *The Brook Kerith* fifty-four years after its first publication (1916) offers an exceptionally good opportunity to appraise these traditional reflections. An attempt to reassess the book after such an interval brings them into sharp focus. Lecturing and benefiting from an altered and concerned audience's written comments, I had both its dangers and the measures by which it fended them off brought home. But was the outcome, the attainment as much made clear? This new attempt must try to weigh both means and end.

When *The Brook Kerith* was being written Moore was one of the most talked-about literary personalities alive. This was a position he hardly shrank from. Indeed in *Hail and Farewell*, three volumes of it, in *Conversations in Ebury Street*, in *A Story-Teller's Holiday*, he happily and at times magnificently supported and adorned it. From his first Zola-inspired, packthread-stitched parcels, his *Esther Waters* and *A Mummer's Wife*, which he grew fond of contrasting with his dewdrop gossamer style, he had repeatedly been a handler of controversial themes: censorship, the unmarried mother, drunkenness, and gambling. Schoolgirls had to lock themselves up to read about them. But he treated them with a sober and sympathetic discernment unexpected amid the frivolings of his public pose. In *The Brook Kerith* he seemed surely out to shock again: an easy misapprehension which could not be further from the truth. As may be learned from Professor Walter James Miller's excellently discursive and informing foreword, the imaginative creator in Moore sheltered behind the figure of Jesus he took pains to present.

The prime technical problem was to present Jesus *through* an eye which the reader could accept as adequately prepared, *through* a personality with which we could sympathize deeply enough to permit him to be our representative *through* whom we might provisionally perceive and respond, be captured, be bewildered, be despair-struck, agonized, overcome . . . ourselves. And yet the observer had to be a mind rich, wayward, and independent enough to protect our detachment fully.

This medium is Joseph of Arimathea, the member of the Sanhedrin who, according to the Gospels, gave the body of Jesus burial. We first meet him falling asleep on his grandmother's knee while she is telling him of the prophet Samuel. Joseph's grandmother, his father Dan, his teacher Azariah, Galilee, Jerusalem, the gorges through to Jericho, the Essene community, Joseph's stay there, its Head, Hazael, its philosopher, Matthias, the prophets in the deserts about Jordan, Joseph's tradings, journeyings, self-searchings, all his growth through the years before his first true encounter with Jesus—all this in a thousand ways prepares us to feel with Joseph when, as a dutiful son, he cannot become a disciple. At the same time, the incongruities of the disputing apostles exasperate his heartbroken estrangement from the Jesus he watches distantly through the entry into Jerusalem and meets again only in the night when, having begged Jesus' body for Pilate and brought it from the cross to his own new tomb, he detects that the victim is still alive.

When Jesus has sufficiently recovered physically, Joseph accompanies him back to the Essene cenoby where, until his baptism by John, he had served as their shepherd. He leaves him there promising to return, but is killed by zealots in Jerusalem. And with that the second great technical problem arises: the transition as seekers from Joseph to Jesus. It is handled by the hill journey Jesus makes in search of the ram needed to restore the brethren's degenerate flock: an absorbing narrative this, leading into the long years of shepherding, Jesus' memories of old Joshbekasher "who had taught him all he knew of sheep," and in the end the handing over of the flock to young Jacob—who, too, has had a long atonement to make for a fault.

All these years the brethren in the cenoby have known little or nothing of what happened between the baptism by John and Jesus' return. And it is the evening of his handing over that Jesus is moved to tell Hazael, their aged Head, of the unparalleled sin he committed in the near two years of his life unknown to them. But before he can do so a wanderer is seen far off on the opposite side of the gorge making his hazardous way by the cliff path toward them. The brethren fear that he may be a robber and are loathe to open the gate. It is Paul fleeing from his pursuers and it is Jesus who admits him, feeds him with ewe's milk, and bathes his feet.

Next day, while Jesus is away arranging a search for Timothy, who has somehow parted from Paul on their journey toward Caesarea, Paul tells the Essenes the story of his life, of his vision on the road to Damascus, and of his ordeals and triumphs in preaching Christ crucified and the resurrection. (An astonishing replaying, this, of the Acts.) The Essenes tell him in return what little they know of Jesus of Nazareth—by which Paul is more deeply disturbed than he knows. When Jesus comes in with the news of Timothy, Saddoc, one of the brethren, relays some of Paul's story to him while Paul gazes in bewilderment. "A great persecutor of Christians. Of Christians? Jesus repeated. And who are they? . . . Christ is a Greek word, Manahem said, for it seemed to him Saddoc was speaking too much."

When Paul mentions that his Lord Jesus Christ was betrayed in a garden, "at the words, who was betrayed in a garden, a light seemed to break on Jesus' face" and he asks permission to tell the brethren what had happened in those two unknown years. It so interests them that when Paul suddenly cries "A madman! A madman! Or possessed of an evil spirit!" and rushes out "nobody rose to detain him; some of the Essenes raised their heads and, a moment after, the interruption was forgotten." Jesus continues his account. When it is ended, Manahem relates Paul's story in full. Jesus is "overtaken by a great pity for Paul."

Jesus leaves to tell the truth in Jerusalem but on the way he finds Paul lying under a rock with foam on his lips and just coming out of a great swoon. Jesus revives him and guides him through one of the strangest journeys ever told all the long way to Caesarea. When Paul arrives there and meets Timothy again he is about to tell him of the "madman with a strange light in his eyes . . . but was stopped by some power within himself."

So much for samplings and sketchings of the technics, the handling. Can one generalize at all? Perhaps to the extent of noting how continually the chief interest—what it is all about—is forwarded through other, often almost competing interests: refractors and reflectors of that. As a physicist studies his particles and their interrelationships not immediately but through what may seem devious indications, or as we catch at our own thoughts and feelings through words they play with and hide behind, so what this book is primarily concerned for is advanced through differing minds whose idiosyncrasies are in the utmost degree realized, displayed, allowed for. Joseph, Dan, Peter and his fellow fishers, Nicodemus, Esora, Matthias, Hazael, Jesus, and Paul are as different as people can be. Yet they are all, to a compelling degree, living *and* comprehensible. And this is certainly a condition of our being able through them to grasp a little of the mystery within which they, with other living minds, play their parts.

As to the little which we may grasp, a thousand readers would be likely, if required, to find a thousand different ways of trying to indicate it. Unless cruelly pressed few would try to utter it; the book in its own unimaginably complex way manages to do that. Apart from examinations, those relatively recent monstrosities, there is little reason why the attempt should be made. What a book does, if it is good enough, can hardly be done otherwise and talking about it is seldom helpful. In contrast, how it manages itself is an eminently discussable and interesting matter. Questions of *how* are, as it were, anatomy, physiology, and, warily speaking, psychology. But what is done is a moral issue, or better, one of those recognitions out of which moralities arise.

Now that the dust cloud has settled it is easier to think about what Moore was here doing. He was writing a novel about the religious quest. (He had written on a related theme earlier in his *Evelyn Innes* and *Sister Teresa*.) He was not taking part in any doctrinal or historical discussions, not saying his or anyone else's say about the "historicity" of Jesus or about the role of a belief in the Resurrection in a Christian life. The demands of his novel required him to keep it clear from all such concerns; entanglement with them was indeed the most to be feared of all the dangers my first sentence alludes to.

Questions of biblical exegesis had above all to be avoided. In taking the greatest and most familiar religious figure as his hero he was exposing his work to endless interferences from the preconceptions and imaginative routines of his readers. How insulate it? How not affront? How in fact prevent confrontations? We can study his problem concretely by noting how he deals with the little actually said in the Gospels about Joseph of Arimathea. Matthew (27:57) says simply that he was a rich man and a disciple; Mark (15:43) makes him "a councillor of honourable estate who also him-

self was looking for the Kingdom of God"—as member of the Sanhedrin he could not, perhaps, be very openly a disciple? Luke
(23:50) adds that he was "a good man and righteous (he had not
consented to their counsel and deed)"; John (19:38) says that he was
a disciple, "but secretly for fear of the Jews."

Moore uses all this but so leads the reader into Joseph's mind
(or Joseph into the reader's) and so builds up the strain that by the
time Mary and Martha are telling him how they "found the stone
rolled away and a young man in white garments in the sepulchre"
we are listening to them with him and alive with his apprehensions.
Jesus is unconscious, precariously hidden in the gardener's empty
cottage and at any moment a house-to-house search may begin. It
is characteristic that Joseph should fall to "wondering at the answers he would make to Pilate, and at the duplicity of these, for he
had never suspected himself of cunning. But circumstances make
the man, he said, and before Jesus passes out of my keeping I shall
have learnt to speak even as he did in double meanings, as Pilate
did—as indeed all men do."

Few come nearer to their own thoughts than Moore's chief
characters. It may be the roominess and richness of their aware-
nesses of their own thinking that allows the book to retell such a
story with impunity. In the end it is the book's resourcefulness and
honesty with itself that protects it as a critique of religious passion
and reflection.

23 Beauty and Truth

In revising this presentation for print, I find that a number of reflections compete for precedence. Any very familiar poem—especially one much pushed to young readers at school—accumulates a thick deposit of misconceptions, the more so if its meanings are both intricate and deep. For the "Ode on a Grecian Urn" all these conditions are fulfilled. Has it perhaps been buried for too many under too huge a tumulus of nonsensical commentary? Or, to reverse the image, has what should have been a spell to invoke quietude in meditation been turned into a football battleground? A television presentation has to reckon with both these threats. It has to remember that it is not young readers but their mentors, among which it must itself be counted, that can promote the most absurd misreadings. That a poem has been misunderstood is never of course necessarily its fault. In general, may we not think that the greater the poetry the greater the risks it must take?

As this poem, most pointedly in its close, is so eminent an instance of art treating of art, of poetry on poetry, a longer introduction may here be in place.

This text is very much as I gave it on television. To have loaded it with further aberrations of critics would have confused its audience. But the printed page can do much that a vocal performance cannot. So here I add, without comment, another representative oddity of opinion.

I would make two main points with it.

1. Though there is a danger that to some the whole activity of interpreting poems may come to seem just a guessing game in which no secure views are attainable, careful reflection can decisively show that a good poem defends itself from a foolish reader effectively. It does so through words and phrases, in the poem and outside it, of which the misreader has not taken due account.

This misapprehension was in its day much praised. Lest

"Talk Six" of the Sense of Poetry series, broadcast on WGBH-TV, Boston, in the winter of 1957-1958. Rewritten in 1975.

*my reader now dismiss it with a gurgle or a guffaw, I must
report that not a few most esteemed critics heartily accepted
the reading proposed. I am not mentioning their names.
They may have repented and several of them have been and
are among my friends. The misreading became for a brief
span fashionable: a way of being in the swim, one upholder,
editor of the widely used* Critic's Notebook, *calling it "The
only possible critical reading," thereby exhibiting a confidence which happily tells us where we are.*[1]

*Here is the most eloquent of its proponents, the grand
condescension of his regard for the poem and its author
being especially instructive. So is the flip approach, the
misuse of Shelley's great line, "pinnacled dim . . ." But "approach" is here the wrong word. He is receding from the
poem.*

*For generations critics were to be observed "pinnacled dim
in the intense inane," interpreting the close of Keats's "Ode
on a Grecian Urn." I quote the last stanza from "Poems"
1820:*
O Attic shape! Fair attitude! with brede
   Of marble men and maidens overwrought,
With forest branches and the trodden weed;
   Thou, silent form, dost tease us out of thought
As doth eternity: Cold Pastoral!
   When old age shall this generation waste,
      Thou shalt remain, in midst of other woe
Than ours, a friend to man, to whom thou say'st,
   "Beauty is truth, truth beauty,"—that is all
      Ye know on earth, and all ye need to know.

*The critics have spun beautiful cobwebs "without substance
or profit" out of those last two lines. In 1938. however,
Mr G. St Quintin robbed them of much of their imaginary
weft. He interpreted the obscurity as follows: "Keats . . .
says that the Urn will always remain 'a friend to man'
because it will always give the message, 'Beauty is Truth,
Beauty'; and the following words . . . are interpreted
as being addressed to all who are capable of hearing and
understanding it . . . Even allowing for the fact that Keats
was not writing a philosophical treatise and may be vague in
his use of terms, it is difficult to believe that he really meant
this . . . as a significant message to humanity at large.*
   *An alternative suggestion is to assume that the 'ye' of the
last line is addressed to the figures on the Urn. For them
Beauty is Truth because their experience is limited to the*

beautiful as depicted on the Urn . . . This interpretation, of course, requires that only the words 'Beauty is Truth, Truth Beauty' be printed in inverted commas, as in Professor de Sélincourt's edition."[2]

Now how does the poem defend itself from this assault? What in it precisely and finally, for readers who retain a balanced command of its language, precludes this proposed reading?

"Thou": With all three second-person singulars the poem is addressing the Urn, and it is the Urn (not the poem or the poet) which then utters the two final lines. And it utters them as "a friend to man, to whom thou say'st" what follows.

"On earth": One might almost suppose that those who have applauded the St. Quintin-Tillotson "discovery" had never heard or read the words "on earth as it is in heaven." With "on earth" the Urn is fulfilling its duty as custodian of ashes, reminding us of the traditional opposition of before death and after life. But Good Heavens! what on earth could these words mean if addressed to the figures instead of to mankind? What sort of dementia finds this "an admirable sense"? I conclude that the poem—through its sufficiently self-evident grammar—is perfectly able to take care of itself.

2. My other main point is that with a poem of this order, carrying so vast a charge of meaning, inviting its readers to reflect on the deepest of traditional themes, there will be no such thing as any single, one and only, right "solution" as though it were a simple equation or puzzle. As with any living organic whole, there will be many states of relative stability, different positions as its components vary in precedence to one another. Many readers, I fear, find this doctrine hard to take. To them it seems tantamount to letting anything go. But in practice, I believe, admission that there may frequently be more than one valid view of what a good poem is doing makes a reader more rather than less scrupulous and more rather than less on guard against nonsense. In this it accords with other applications of Complementarity principles.

Let us have the Ode itself before us and reread it as reflectively as we can.

Consider again its title: it is on an Urn which has been used to preserve ashes and has been long in the tomb and is thus a strong reminder of death. The poem addressed to it speaks for and to each and every one who "Awaits alike th' inevitable Hour" ("With all that Beauty, all that Wealth e'er gave"). To quote from another line in Gray's "Elegy," this is a "storied Urn" even more than those we may read of there. And when at the end, after the return of the questioning, a reply is given, we should not forget—should we?—that an Urn has no mouth and does not speak; it is not a preacher or a lecturer; it is "still," it is a "silent form." What it may say is what we say for it, say to ourselves, after contemplating what the poem has presented to us: *life* seen from the angle of *death*.

While the last stanza is still in our minds let me recall for you four lines from the Hymn to Pan in *Endymion*, book 1, lines 293-296:

> Be still the unimaginable lodge
> For solitary thinkings; such as dodge
> Conception to the very bourne of heaven,
> Then leave the naked brain.

Compare with that

> Thou, silent form, dost tease us out of thought
> As doth eternity.

That this Ode uses the second-person singular (and "ye") is not unconnected with its use in the prayer book. In these lines it is telling us what it is doing; great poetry has often to do with the boundaries, the limits of "solitary thinkings."

Let us look now at the opening lines:

> Thou still unravish'd bride of quietness,
>   Thou foster-child of silence and slow time.

(To be read, I suggest, very slowly—to allow slow time itself to take part in the presentation as well as to let the immense charge of meaning develop and come through.)

"Still": As in "still waters run deep"? As in "a still small voice," "a voice of gentle stillness" (see 1 Kings 19:12)? As in "Peace, be still!" (see Mark 4:39)? But this sea that is being stilled here is "the sea of Life and Time" ("the bitter waves of this blood-

drenched . . . sickening whirl," to quote Porphyry's report of the
Delphic Oracle on Plotinus) that becomes, in Yeats's "Byzantium,"
"that dolphin-torn, that gong-tormented sea."

Of course, there is the other sense of "still," "not yet," contrasting with and heightening the adjectival senses: unmoving,
soundless, unperturbed. And it is highly active here too, reawaken-
ing awe at the many centuries through which those ashes have been
buried and have "in a yard under ground, and thin walls of clay,
out-worn all the strong and specious buildings above it; and quietly
rested under the drums and tramplings of three conquests" (Sir
Thomas Browne, *Urne-Buriall*, chap. 5). That belongs, that awe
does.

But there is something else which hovers around in many
readers' fancies though it does not belong since it would be but dis-
tractive.

"Unravish'd bride": A willing bride is not ravished, and this
Urn is truly the devoted bride of quietness, devoted in the sense in
which a Hindu Sati devotes herself.

Is there not a further charge of mystery behind this "unravish'd"—some great contrasting background? Is there behind the
line something of the Rape of Proserpine? Here is Milton (*Paradise
Lost*, 4.268) describing that Garden of Eden no other garden can
rival:

> Not that fair field
> Of Enna, where Proserpine, gathering flowers,
> Herself a fairer flower, by gloomy Dis
> Was gathered—which cost Ceres all that pain
> To seek her through the world.

Unwillingly Proserpine is dragged away by the ruler of Hades to be
queen of that underworld in which this Urn has so long been.

"Foster-child of silence and slow time": stillness and silence,
the lines affirm them and reaffirm—in part to bring out the intense
liveliness of the doings depicted on the Urn, echoing thus, as it
were, Marvell's lines from "The Garden":

> Apollo hunted Daphne so,
> Only that She might Laurel grow.
> And Pan did after Syrinx speed,
> Not for a *Nymph* but for a *Reed.*

"The Garden," too, in its very different ways, is about the opposition with eternity of what we "know on earth," "until prepared for
longer flight."

As to the lively doings, it is noteworthy that Swinburne in
the Spring Chorus of *Atalanta in Calydon* parallels very closely
what these first two stanzas and line three of the fifth present, down
to "the trodden weed" ("And the hoofèd heel of a satyr crushes/
The chestnut-husk at the chestnut-root"). His is a "leaf-fring'd leg-
end" too, "With lisp of leaves" and "wild vine slipping down." Here
are his "men or gods" and "maidens loth":

> And Pan by noon and Bacchus by night,
>   Fleeter of foot than the fleet-foot kid,
> Follows with dancing and fills with delight
>   The Maenad and the Bassarid;
> And soft as lips that laugh and hide
> The laughing leaves of the trees divide,
> And screen from seeing and leave in sight
>   The god pursuing, the maiden hid.

It is noteworthy too that this Chorus ends with "The wolf that follows, the fawn that flies," a note which accords with that of the
close of stanza 3 of the Ode. And the chorus is broken in upon by
Queen Althaea herself—in her own way a custodian of death—
with "What do ye singing? what is this ye sing" and with ever bit-
terer words to balance all the Chorus can say of sweetness "with all
its honey in our lips." The Urn too, having presented, almost indeed overstressed, sweetness, has its balancing bitterness to add.
And yet, do not lines 3 and 4 hint already of what the rest of the
poem will do? Are they not well charged with latent irony?

Let us listen again to stanza 2:

> Heard melodies are sweet, but those unheard
>   Are sweeter; therefore, ye soft pipes, play on.

Here is an extreme transvaluation. Poetry, like music, is an art of
sounds. But now, along with the pipes and the song, it is to be silent, and the coming reiterations of "happy" are to insist on and
extend the renunciation. Renounced, they play on,

> Not to the sensual ear, but, more endear'd,
>   Pipe to the spirit ditties of no tone.

If ever a line by its own tone and movement tells us how to take it, this does. "Ditties," a word originally of grave import, is used so by Spenser, nothing light or trifling or merely diverting being suggested; on the contrary, in Wycliffe's Exodus 15:1: "Thanne Moyses soong this ditee to the Lord." There is an implication of musical setting here explicitly removed. Those pipes are "soft" because unheard. The superiority of "the spirit" to "the sensual ear" is firmly asserted, the very renunciation announced by "more endear'd" heightening its value. *Non inutile est desiderio in oblatione.* These Urn-borne silent ditties, which follow through the rest of this stanza and the next, are of acquiescence. They acquiesce in frustration, deprivation, loss. Their movement is not in the least that of self-indulgent daydream (as some critics have condescendingly supposed) but of an alerted cost-counting consent. And yet what is figured on the Urn is to be envied. Why? Because neither for the singer, nor for the leaves, nor for the Lover is there any Fall. For the living there is. The anguish of mutability and mortality is pressed home until, as Keats had written earlier of his Cave of Quietude (*Endymion*, 4.528), although "Woe-hurricanes beat ever at the gate / Yet all is still within and desolate."

All is given up, offered up to become "All breathing human passion far above." It is by this sacrifice that the other side of the Urn as we turn to it becomes so poignantly fulfilling. We need though to remind ourselves of how central to men's hopes and fears his ritual sacrifice of his best has been. In this fourth stanza the silence the poem has been celebrating throughout spreads:

> And, little town, thy streets for evermore
>   Will silent be.

Everything human passes so (to quote from Yeats's "Sailing to Byzantium") "into the artifice of eternity." "Eternity," Blake's Proverb of Hell has it, "is in love with the productions of time." It is through this renunciation and detachment that this "silent form," the Urn, can

>   tease us out of thought
>   As doth eternity.

"Tease": comb the surface of cloth; separate the fibers with a teasel; draw all the hairs or fibers in one direction. No complexity,

no to and fro, no pro and con of thought, no turbulence, no sickening whirl, no tossing waves of Time and Life that

In sequent toil all forwards do contend.[3]

After this, the poem having done what it has done, the last
five and a half lines, I suggest, are more a gloss reflecting this than a
way of saying something further. For what is further, though endless, is not to be said:

He who speaks does not know;
He who knows does not speak.

Now for some critics, busily speaking. I will omit to mention names. Who wrote which of the following comments does not
matter. What matters is that they could write them. I do assure you
that they were highly qualified scholars, leading authorities indeed.
They are talking about the two final lines:

' "Beauty is Truth, Truth Beauty"—that is all
Ye know on earth and all ye need to know.'

I have capitalized and punctuated as best may suit the view I am
hoping to recommend.[4]
Of these lines an authority writes: "But, of course, to put it
solidly, that is a vague observation—to anyone whom life has
taught to face facts and define his terms, actually an uneducated
conclusion, albeit pardonable in one so young." The Urn isn't exactly "so young"—is it? But, of course, this critic carelessly sup-
poses that these concluding lines are uttered by Keats, not by the
Urn.
"To face facts and define his terms," John Middleton Murry,
to whom I owe very much on this and in other ways, points out
that when he wrote the Ode Keats was facing "more than a fair
share of the miseries of the world . . . a brother dead, a brother
exiled, the fear that his new-born love would be denied fulfilment,
his money gone, his health and perhaps his life in question."[5] You
will find the detail (and incidentally the quotations I am using) well
set out in Murry.

However, I think I can guess how this charge that "Beauty is Truth, Truth Beauty" is "actually an uneducated conclusion" happened. I am nearly sure that some at-his-wits'-end schoolmaster had set the lines for comment in a scholarship examination and that our unhappy critic wrote what he did fresh from reading through some scores, perhaps, of hasty scribblings upon them. If so it was the examinees, not Keats, that he was judging, not the Ode but their comments on it which drew "actually an *uneducated conclusion*." As support for this guess may I offer a representative example of the comments I have myself received on these last two lines: "He hears the soundless message and, placing upon it his own interpretation, passes it along to us. I find this somewhat presumptuous of the poet and I resent it. To each his own interpretation—if any."

I will follow him with a more respectful, but still a frankly baffled comment: "This statement of equivalence ("Beauty is truth, truth beauty") means nothing to me. But on re-reading the whole Ode this line strikes me as a serious blemish on a beautiful poem . . . I suppose that Keats meant something by it, however remote his truth and his beauty may have been from these words in ordinary use." What about this "ordinary use"? Could we agree perhaps that there will be many very different sorts of "ordinary use" with such big words as these? Take "Beauty." There is the use, for example, in T. S. Eliot's pub scene near the end of the second part of *The Waste Land* where, on the Sunday on which Albert was home, it is a "hot gammon" the lady was asked in for "to get the beauty of it hot." And there is the kind of use we get in Byron's:

> There be none of Beauty's daughters
> With a magic like thee.[6]

And there is the use of "Beauty" in the titles of Spenser's "An Hymne of Heavenly Beautie" or Shelley's "Hymn to Intellectual Beauty," both poems probably well known to Keats.* Spenser was a chief awakening influence on Keats and in view of all that Keats's letters tell us of his peculiar preoccupation with Beauty and Truth,

---

*What matters here, surely, is *not* surmises as to whether Keats had been rereading Spenser, but that in two minds of their order the same identification of Truth and Beauty was obvious.

it is hard to believe that he had not read Spenser's "Hymne" with uncommonly close attention. Here are its first two stanzas:

> Rapt with the rage of mine own ravisht thought,
> Through contemplation of those goodly sights,
> And glorious images in heaven wrought,
> Whose wondrous beauty breathing sweet delights,
> Do kindle love in high conceipted sprights:
> I faine to tell the things that I behold,
> But feele my wits to faile, and tongue to fold.
>
> Vouchsafe, then, O thou most almightie Spright,
> From whom all guifts of wit and knowledge flow,
> To shed into my breast some sparkling light
> Of thine eternall Truth, that I may show
> Some litle beames to mortall eyes below,
> Of that immortall beautie, there with thee,
> Which in my weake distraughted mynd I see.

For this "Hymne," as you see, Beauty and Truth are together: "thine eternall," "there with thee." Both words come equally in the middle of the middle line of the stanza.

Shall we look in conclusion at the tradition behind these great abstract words? We will see that the Ode is simply using them with their full traditional force: nothing remote or unfamiliar. Both stem from Plato. For the account of Beauty we go to the *Symposium*:

> He who has been instructed rightly in the things of love . . .
> when he comes towards the end will suddenly perceive a
> wondrous beauty (and this . . . is the final cause of all our
> former toils) . . . and the true order . . . is to begin from the
> beauties of earth and mount upwards . . . from fair forms to
> fair practices . . . to fair notions until . . . he arrives—and at
> last knows what the essence of Beauty is. (211)[7]

This ascent, this ladder in "the things of Love," is, in momentous ways, parallel to the ascent—the ladder in modes of Knowledge—up which book 6 of Plato's *Republic* leads us.

> This, then, which gives true being to whatever deep knowl-
> edge is of, and the power to get this knowledge to whatever
> gets it, is to be named the idea of the good. (508e)[8]

Compare:

> This, then, every soul looks for, and for this every soul does all that it does. (*Republic*, 505e)

> this . . . is the final cause of all our former toils. (*Symposium*, 211)

With these in their conjunction we may compare another apex: "We see we saw not whàt did move" (Donne, "The Extasie"). We may be reminded too, as Keats may have been, of another poem in which "Truth and Beautie buried be" (Shakespeare, "The Phoenix and the Turtle"), in which repaire to an Urne is enjoined and in which

> Property was thus appalled,
> That the selfe was not the same:
> Single Natures double name
> Neither two nor one was named.

The wondrous beauty which the lover "suddenly" perceives "when he arrives," and the source of Truth and Knowledge are one and the same.

In brief, the way of Love and the way of Knowledge meet. Here is how John Middleton Murry puts it, and "solidly": "The Soul, for Keats, is that condition of man in which his Mind and his Heart are reconciled . . . in the idiom of Christian spirituality, the condition of the Knowledge and Love of God."[9] There is nothing uneducated or unmeaning here or any occasion for sneers about "initiates" or for the other disparaging remarks that have been fashionable among the hoity-toities. What is puzzling is that learned and well-intentioned men have made such to-do about a position so central, traditional, and familiar. It may however be salutary to recognize that the highest qualification and reputation can on occasion combine with patent and resounding inability to read. How loath we are to be reminded!

Few English poets raise more clearly than Herbert, or in more challenging and explorable ways, deeper questions as to the techniques, conditions, kinds, and aims of poetry and its variant relations to experience. At the same time he is among the most audacious, responsible, and self-searching of writers. It is her full recognition of these characteristics which makes Helen Vendler's study, *The Poetry of George Herbert*, so admirable a continuation of the efforts in recent decades to return Herbert nearer to his due place. Her fine and generous understanding of these efforts combines with her venturesome yet wary percipience to make her a most enheartening as well as a steadying companion in the rereadings of Herbert (and the rethinkings) her work will promote.

Such rereadings, I hope, will be punctuated by recognitions of Herbert's peculiar value as a model from which those who will can learn most about the conduct of verse. He is an innovator of a variety hard to match who shows equal resource and skill (at his best) in detecting, meeting, and eluding the dangers of such radical experimentation. "Wisdom lies," said another bold innovator, Robert Bridges, "in masterful administration of the unforeseen," thus summing up the chief lesson that even *The Testament of Beauty* (taken either as the work of that name, or as its theme itself) can impart.[1] Vendler, it seems to me, is especially discerning as to Herbert's dealings with the unexpected, the reinvented character of so many of his poems, the reconceptions from which their dramatic actions spring.

These reconceptions are most evident within single poems— "The Pulley," for example—but as germinative tensions between

---

Review of Helen Vendler, *The Poetry of George Herbert* (Cambridge, Mass.: Harvard University Press, 1975). Reprinted by permission from *Times Literary Supplement*, November 28, 1975, p. 1417.

poems they are equally remarkable. In these he can take an idea
which seems utterly and uniquely appropriate to one use and turn it
to another, which may, at first sight, seem contrary and incompatible. As an instance, consider what the middle lines of "Vertue" do.
To the "Sweet rose" he is addressing they say:

> Thy root is ever in its grave
> And thou must die.

In "The Flower" we have:

> Who would have thought my shrivel'd heart
> Could have recover'd greennesse? It was gone
> Quite under ground; as flowers depart
> To see their mother-root, when they have blown;
> Where they together
> All the hard weather,
> Dead to the world, keep house unknown.

Only as both poems in their entireties develop does their interplay
make us see how each enhances and confirms the other.

But indeed this mutual support between the poems becomes
with rereadings the most distinctive mark of his most successful
poetry, a feature of his art cultivated by him, in part, no doubt,
because he found it in the Scriptures (as he saw them) and described
it as shown there so admiringly:

> Oh that I knew how all thy lights combine,
> And the configurations of their glorie!
> Seeing not onely how each verse doth shine,
> But all the constellations of the storie.
> This verse marks that, and both do make a motion
> Unto a third, that ten leaves off doth lie:
> Then as dispersed herbs do watch a potion,
> These three make up some Christians destinie.[2]

"Watch" has puzzled many readers. Probably it is a misprint; if
not, we may conjecture that its prime sense here is "attentively wait
for." There will come a time when these as yet dispèrsed (a favorite
word with Herbert) herbs will be enabled to blend their powers to
become the curing potion promised in the final line of this sonnet:
"This book of starres lights to eternall blisse."

I could have found scores of better, if more elaborate, examples of these motions of lines to one another illuminatingly analysed by Vendler, but I wished to find a simple, though typical, instance for myself. The overall effect of these reciprocal controls is to give indeed a new promise of unity to Herbert's best work. And, more than once, as in her analysis of "The Call," which "can serve as a touchstone for one's attachment to Herbert" (pp. 203-209), what almost surfaces in it (a favorite word with her) is a version of Christianity compelling for even the least devotional of readers. It is not surprising that Herbert has had an influence stronger, more salutary, more instructive than that of poets much more famous and more widely read. And not chiefly, perhaps, upon poets disposed to share his piety. Vendler, after quoting Eliot and Coleridge to the effect that the best readers of Herbert should be Christians, quotes Housman: "Good religious poetry . . . is likely to be most justly appreciated and most discriminatingly relished by the undevout."[3]

I find something engagingly comic in this situation. Being myself an infidel, I wish, of course, to deny that my condition is disabling. Both Coleridge and Eliot seem to have been unhappy in their phrasing, Coleridge declaring that to appreciate "The Temple" "the reader . . . must be both a devout and a *devotional* Christian." But S. T. C. himself was no churchgoer; he was the utter opposite of Herbert in that. And Eliot's pronouncement is as risky: "You will not get much satisfaction from George Herbert unless you can take seriously the things which he took seriously, and which made him what he was."[4] What to "take seriously" may be is a large question, but that unbelievers have got immense satisfaction from Herbert is not in doubt. On the other hand---though whether Vendler would agree with me here I am uncertain---we may have to reconceive both poetry and the human mind before we understand how this can happen.

However, the ways in which poets contrary in temperament and persuasion from Herbert can gain from studying him are an easier matter. Here Swinburne can serve as a pertinent witness. That he, like Herbert, had an extreme though opposite concern with death makes the comparison more interesting. Two sample contrasts will be enough. Take the idea in the central lines of "Vertue" quoted above. In his "A Forsaken Garden" Swinburne has:

> Where the weeds that grew green from the graves of its roses
>   Now lie dead.

And here, as well, Swinburne's use of the final three-syllable line can make one think of Herbert. But to feel the opposition and the indebtedness fully we may do well to remind ourselves of other lines from "A Forsaken Garden":

> Shall the dead take thought for the dead to love them?
>   What love was ever as deep as the grave?
> They are loveless now as the grass above them
>   Or the wave.

Inevitably, in thinking of what poets have learned from Herbert, his prosodic explorations must be given their prime place. Is it extravagant to suggest that Swinburne's mastery of monosyllabic lines, as in "The Pilgrims,"

> And we men bring death lives by night to sow
> That men may reap and eat and live by day,

may have owed something to the example of Herbert?

My other example also concerns death. In Herbert's poem of that title, in contrast to "an uncouth hideous thing," Death is re-portrayed:

> But since our Saviours death did put some bloud
>   Into thy face;
>   Thou art grown fair and full of grace,
> Much in request, much sought for as a good.
>
> For we do now behold thee gay and glad

Here is Swinburne:

>   one thing which is ours yet cannot die—
> Death. Hast thou seen him ever anywhere,
> Time's twin-born brother, imperishable as he
> Is perishable and plaintive, clothed with care
>   And mutable as sand,
> But death is strong and full of blood and fair
> And perdurable and like a lord of land?[5]

The lines come in the chorus opening with "Who hath given man speech?" an utterance that, again and again, reads as though it were at root a retort to Herbert. No questions of undue borrowing arise. My comparisons are but to show how Herbert enriched the general resources and how his inventions may be employed for purposes alien and adverse to his. Another example, from a poet as unlike either Swinburne or Herbert as they are unlike each other, will be in place. Here is Walter de la Mare writing about death and using, undeniably, one of Herbert's most impelling themes and one of his major dramatic tensions, but with a deeply opposed outcome.[6] That in his title he refers so pointedly to Keats, writing also of death—these sweet sounds "Pipe to the spirit ditties of no tone"—makes this poem's revolt and acquiescence the more palpable. It is a commentary both on Herbert and on "Ode on a Grecian Urn." How often poems contain observations on other poems and work in part through these whether the poet or his readers knew it or not. Taking up Keats's rhyme "play *on*," de la Mare gives us

Music Unheard

Sweet sounds, begone—
    Whose music on my ear
Stirs foolish discontent
    Of lingering here;
When, if I crossed
    The crystal verge of death,
Him I should see
    Who these sounds murmereth.

Sweet sounds, begone—
    Ask not my heart to break
Its bond of bravery for
    Sweet quiet's sake;
Lure not my feet
    To leave the path they must
Tread on, unfaltering,
    Till I sleep in dust.

Sweet sounds, begone!
    Though silence brings apace
Deadly disquiet
    Of this homeless place;

And all I love
In beauty cries to me,
'We but vain shadows
And reflections be.'

To ask what Herbert would have thought (and what we should think) of the word "vain" in the penultimate line is, I think, a good way of reminding ourselves of the main component of Herbert's best poetry. Our debt to him is for more than for his additions to the stockpile of devices, prosodic, rhetorical, thematic, and dramatic. It is due, as this book so well demonstrates, to his surpassing powers of design and his singular fidelity to what his poem at every stage of its growth needed. More deeply than with most, his conception of his labor as a poet required this of him.

Vendler rightly remarks, "I do not think that there is significant help to be had in understanding Herbert by invoking theories of poetry that detach artifact, as a system of formal signs, from lived experience, recreated in a mimetic form of speech."[7] The reference to speech here is highly appropriate. Herbert's best poems seem so often to be *said* rather than written, and most of all when—as with "Grace" and "Heaven"— only an inconceivable amount of most delicate contriving could have brought them about. Vendler is almost throughout as happy as she is thorough in tracing these complexities, often underlying an appearance of extreme simplicity. And when you feel that she has said, excellently, all that can usefully be said, her next paragraph displays to your unalert eye ranges of considerations even more relevant. You have to admit that at last Herbert has found his reader.

It is true that this conclusion asks for a certain modesty, a readiness to receive. Can poems you think you have understood pretty well since you first met them really have so much more going on in them? No doubt many will feel that in these explications and elucidations there is the risk that we may lose the poetry in the poetics—substitute *how a poem works* for *what it does* as our prime concern with it. There is, I think, truly a hazard here. It is connected for me with the ever increasing professionalism in the study of literature and with the coming in of another professional study, linguistics.[8] It is much easier to measure time lengths than sprinklings of grace. Moreover, the first is an examinable activity,

the second not. We may, however, combine apprehensions of this
order with a grounded opinion that ability to read poetry well has
(unlike literacy in general) been improving in recent decades. With
this, I would hope, belongs ability to discuss, sanely and sympa-
thetically, the validities of variant readings. If this is at all true, it is
something to be treasured as much as outbursts of critical brutalism
are to be discouraged. Our safeguard, in addition to models such as
I take this reading of Herbert to be, is a deepening recognition that
questionings about poetries must, when pressed home, aim more
nearly at the root of our being than any others. To be human is to
be a maker, the poetries are makings—well or ill, stupid or enlight-
ened, for good and for evil. They are makings of ourselves. Of this
doctrine I take Herbert's devotion to poetry to be an exemplar.

III Toward Autobiography

25 The Lure of High Mountaineering

"Red with cutaneous eruption of conceit and voluble with convulsive hiccough of self-satisfaction," the mountaineer strides into his hotel, back from his peak or his pass, no doubt jostling Ruskin in the doorway and so stirring him to this little masterpiece of descriptive vituperation. Today Ruskin is almost forgotten; in his place (no more welcome in his eyes than the climber with his axe and rope and uncouth footwear) now stands the tourist, very often an American, who, if he has not the same feelings about the figure that shambles noisily by, is usually as hard put to it to explain why a reasonable soul should want to do just this, or what anyone gets out of it that he should keep at it with such stupid pertinacity. To go up one mountain would be possibly an interesting experience, especially if it were the highest; to keep on climbing mountains seems to be mere silliness.

To describe a passion to those that do not share it is a difficult enough task, let alone explaining it. The passion I write of is eminently respectable. The pope and the new conservative member of Parliament for Cambridge—not to mention several kings and queens—have been among its devotees. It is a powerful passion, enthralling many until long past their sixtieth year. It is a serious passion, judged by the test that a considerable number of people have cheerfully lost their lives in its pursuit. They did not know, of course, that they would lose them, but they were perfectly aware of the possibility, and had decided upon the question of "Worthwhile?" And their fellow fanatics, when one of these calamities occurs, commonly treat it quite as a matter of course without raising questions of justification, unless carelessness or recklessness is suspected. Yet somehow this passion, more than most, does need

Reprinted from *The Atlantic*, 139 (1927), 51-57.

some explanation. It is surprisingly new, having come in only about seventy-five years ago; and its activities are to the outside eye peculiarly pointless. In this it perhaps stands alone. Games, though no psychologist will claim that he can completely explain them, have at least a good historic standing. We are never really puzzled as to why people play them even when we feel no inclination to do likewise. Hunting, fishing, yachting, gardening, camping, and the rest of the sports can plausibly be regarded as survivals, although of course this is not the whole story. Immemorial antiquity lends them sanction; though I doubt whether many yachtsmen or amateur camping parties were about in the sixteenth century.

To enjoy unnecessary discomfort or insecurity we must first be bored with comfort. These two sports in part appeal through their contrast with ordinary existence, and to some degree mountaineering shares this attraction. But while the positive lure of yachting and camping—that is to say, the part over and above contrast—links on to ancient and very widespread pursuits, the positive lure of mountaineering, including the impulse to go up to the top of the hill when the way is difficult, has a very meager history. Unless hunting takes them there, the natives never climb their mountains. Genuine mountaineering—Alpinism, for example—is an entirely new development, appealing only to a moderately sophisticated mind. It is, in fact, a strangely professorial pastime. What blend of what desires and delights will account for it, or what obscure needs and tendencies must we invoke?

Like other passions, this one has stages. And, again like other passions, it has degrees of impurity. We can study it here only at its ripest and purest. The novice, thrilling with anticipatory tremors at the largely erroneous picture which he makes for himself of his first serious climb, mixes in too much that is imaginary and has nothing to do with the matter. I have known one such novice afterward to confess that he "got the wind up" far more on his first big mountain than ever on the battlefield—and this was a man who saw a good deal of nasty fighting.

We must set aside also the confirmed habitué of the mountains, whose early ardor has declined—the man who goes on climbing moderately difficult ordinary mountains by the best-known routes in the company of guides who have such a reserve of mountaineering ability that only what the insurance companies style as an "act of God" could prevent the caravan from returning in safety at the appointed time. Let me try to describe instead what happens in the mind of the guideless climber, experienced enough to know what he is doing, when he is engaged upon an ascent which is just within his powers as the leader of his party.

He probably knows a good deal about his proposed climb. The idea of it may have been in his mind for a long while. He will have read about it, studied it, surveyed it from neighboring summits, perhaps. One of the incidental charms of mountaineering is the unexampled opportunity for detailed, intricate, concrete planning which it allows. The mountaineer fanatic spends hours, whole long winter evenings, gazing at maps and photographs and talking to the other members of his climbing party about the expedition. This planning as the day approaches grows more and more responsible. Here is another attraction. There are very few pursuits in which the question of competence comes more sharply to a head. A great ascent shares the glamour of an Arctic journey—a point will come when the climber will need his strength and skill to extricate himself. The factors upon which success depends are varied enough to need careful thought, yet not too numerous or too uncertain to be estimated. In this a big climb resembles a miniature campaign. It is a concentrated form of exploration, with the tedium cut out and the dramatic intensity heightened. The man whose mountain career begins and ends with scrambling up the Matterhorn or treadmilling up Mont Blanc under professional guidance misses so much of all this that he may well conclude that climbing is an overestimated pastime. Mountaineering is a craft which requires years to master, and the sense of increasing competence is no small part of its attraction.

Some of the branches of this craft are never mastered and have therefore an inexhaustible fascination. Weather lore, for example. The condition of the mountain and the difficulty of the ascent vary with the weather and the season in ways which may baffle the utmost sagacity. A stretch of glacier which early in a snowy year would be easy and would take but an hour to cross may a month later, after hot weather, be nearly impossible. Its ice is always cracked here and there, split by fissures which may be no more than a few inches or a few feet in width though hundreds of yards in length. When narrow, these "crevasses" are covered by the carpet of the surface snow and can be crossed if the snow is hard, as it is in the early morning, without anyone's being able to detect that the apparently innocent white expanse is actually stretched across what are in effect bottomless abysses of ice-walled darkness. These crevasses widen as the summer wears on. The snow that roofs them grows thinner; first a ripplelike hollow shows, then the ripple splits open; then the crevasse walls appear, smooth, shiny, blue black, overhung with treacherous bulges of unsupported snow. Here and there the snow roof is more solid, and a bridge is left across which a climbing party can pass, if need be, at certain hours and under certain conditions. But sometimes the crevasse can widen out without clearly revealing its presence, and only the sudden collapse of the snow roof under the weight of one of the party will show that it is there. The crevasse may be several hundred feet deep. Picture yourself walking on a snow blanket stretched across an opening in the dome of Saint Peter's and you will be able to understand one of the possibilities of glacier travel. This is why the party will be walking in single file as far apart as they conveniently can, and why they will be keeping the rope which links them to one another reasonably taut. Should anyone fall into a crevasse far enough for his head to disappear, it is no easy matter to pull him out again.

The quality of the snow, as much when it is lying upon gentle glacier slopes as when it is draped about the wild upper ridges, or is clinging in seemingly precarious fashion to the steep mountain walls, changes with the hour of the day, the angle at which the sun strikes it, the wind, the weather of the last few days. To plan an interesting expedition wisely, all this must be reckoned with. Early enough in the morning the snow will generally be good. This is why the climber usually starts with the first daylight. But there are other reasons. In the Alps, unless he has slept in one of the many Swiss Alpine Club cabins that are perched for his convenience high up, often upon tiny outcrops of rock surrounded by glacier, he will have two or three hours of steady preliminary walking, on a path if he is lucky, before the difficulties and the high mountaineering proper begin. He has to start early to economize time and to make use of the cool of the day, for he will have from four to eight thousand feet to ascend, and time is precious. Every big climb, and above all every new climb, is a race against the sun.

The weather affects the rocks of the mountain as much as the glaciers. A light sprinkle of snow overnight will give the peaks a fairylike silvery glitter, but will put serious climbing out of the question—not so much because it makes the rocks slippery as because it makes them so cold to the fingers. Only the easiest rocks can be climbed with fresh snow upon them. The slipperiness comes a day later when the new snow has melted and the moisture has refrozen to invisible ice—*Verglas,* as it is called—an abominable substance very difficult to deal with.

Often the descent will need special consideration. It will be late in the day, the snow will be soft, stones which in the morning are firmly bound by frost will be loosened by the sun and ready to begin their awful, hopping, bounding, whirring flight to the valley. Anyone who has loafed away an afternoon in the high Alps will have heard that faint growling, sometimes rising to a roar and rarely quiet for more than a few moments, which means that the miscellaneous debris of the mountains is slipping from them. A stone fall on a great slope is a horrible spectacle whether seen from above or from below, but especially when seen from below. Some mountain sides are death traps for this reason in the afternoon.

A prudent climber will rarely get too close to falling stones, but through bad luck or misinformation he may see more than he cares of them. He will be working down a ridge which stands up in low relief upon the great tilting side of the mountain. To right and left a wide, shallow, dusty gully, floored with worn slabs of rock and broken with zigzagging scree-littered shelves, may offer easier progress. A little rivulet of gleaming water staining the recesses of the rocks and sending a faint tinkle up to his thirsty soul may add to the temptation. He continues down the ridge. Suddenly from far above, where the upper cliffs lean forward and dominate the lower glacis, a single sharp report will sound. He looks up, ever fiber tense and quivering. For a moment nothing will be visible; then, exactly like a bursting shrapnel, a tiny cloud will flash out which looks like smoke but actually is dust. The falling missile has struck some scree-covered ledge. Usually the climber will see little more; he will have his head, and as much more of himself as he can, well and safely tucked away in the shelter of some overhanging boulder or cranny. But he will hear the whole slope, as it seems, leap to life, for the falling stone sets a myriad others in motion. Down they come, whirring and humming, taking enormous bounds and ricocheting across the whole width of the gully. By the time they pass him they will often be flying too fast to be visible. Only the scream of the air or, if a large boulder is fairly launched, a rumble not unlike that of an express train will tell him that they are past, and he can look down to see them splash into the snows below or leap into the open mouth of the crevasse which is nearly always there to catch them.

The prudent climber, I repeat, keeps well away from falling stones. Occasionally, however, circumstances may force him to run the risk of crossing such dangerous ground. He may be late in leaving the summit; hard pressed for time to work out the intricacies of the glacier before night falls, he may have no other way of avoiding a night spent *à la belle étoile*, an experience which is nearly always miserable and sometimes dangerous in itself. For a tired man may not be in a state to resist the great cold of the night high up without shelter, and the weather may be changing or the wind rising.

When for any such reason dangerous ground has to be crossed, the climber may hurry, but hurrying is otherwise something which he sedulously avoids. From one point of view he is the most leisurely of sportsmen; he takes a great deal of exercise, but he takes it as gently as he can. He cannot afford to hurry in an expedition which will probably take fifteen hours to complete and may take twenty. On the other hand, he cannot afford to waste any odd minutes. All successful parties develop an elaborate technique for saving seconds—at first a conscious effort, later on an unconscious habit. The beginner gives himself away by the time he squanders. He wants to stop to fix his puttee, or to put cream on his face, or to get out his gloves, or to put them away. A dozen little jobs arise and half a dozen little calamities befall him which the more experienced man foresaw the last time the whole party stopped to feed or to put on the rope.

But there is more in time-saving than this, difficult though this trick of not stopping seems to be to acquire. Consider the management of the rope alone. We are tied on, if there are three of us, one at each end and the third in the middle. There will be thirty or forty feet of loose rope between us. Most of the time we shall be all moving together. The rope must be kept moderately taut whenever there is any possibility of a mishap to any of the party. This is not so difficult when we are walking in the leader's footprints across a snowfield. But suppose we are working up a fairly steep face of rock. Fairly steep means an angle of about fifty degrees. This looks like sixty-five degrees until one measures it, and is usually talked of as eighty degrees. This face will not be smooth—few faces are. If it were, we should be moving one at a time, gathering the rope in and letting it out as required. More probably, like most big precipices that get climbed, it will be built up of a chaos of jammed blocks of all sizes at all angles, held in place by the weight of the blocks above. Over such ground experienced climbers can pass with great safety and speed, but the loose rope must be kept from catching among the innumerable spikes which jut out everywhere. To keep it free while himself moving with special care to avoid dislodging any of the rubbish with which all such faces are strewn, the climber must give a continual series of nicely adjusted flicks. In time this becomes automatic. Usually he will carry a few coils of the rope—enough to control it—in one hand, the same hand also holding his ice axe; he climbs with the other hand and with his feet and with a knee now and then.

This sounds like one of the dreariest and least inviting of imaginable exercises, and so it is until the knack has become second nature. But when everything is going as it should the very fact that all this tiresome detail is being dealt with without effort, by the mere sweet-running mechanisms of the nervous system, yields a peculiar exhilaration. I should ascribe a great deal of the fascination of mountaineering to this sense of successful technique. The good effect of doing anything that one can do well radiates throughout the whole personality. One's other faculties benefit, one is at peace with oneself, and the illusion of a complete mastery of existence grows strong. Add to this the slight tension which the situation, the drop below, and the constant need for care impose, and it is not hard to see how this routine part of climbing can acquire a charm.

More difficult rocks have another fascination. The technique of overcoming them without delay and without undue fatigue has much in common with the technique of the arts. Mediocre performers, for example, resemble one another in their procedure, but the masters of the craft develop individual styles. The difference between a breathless muscular struggle and an easy, balanced movement is often too subtle to be analyzed, but every golfer will understand how powerful the appeal of success here may become. And because the movements called for in rock-climbing are perhaps more varied and their nicety not less than those of any other sport, the spell cast is the stronger. To go lightly up a rock wall when the only hold is the friction of the forearm pressing against the sides of a vertical crack while the feet push gently yet firmly upon roughnesses not much bigger than a thumbnail is an achievement which allows a good deal of innocent self-flattery to develop. And if meanwhile the glance which is seeking for suitable roughnesses can travel past the poised foot and see nothing beneath but the glacier some hundreds of feet below, there is nothing in this to impair the pleasure, provided that equanimity is maintained. Calm control and alert, deliberate choice of pose are the essence of good rock-climbing; the exhilaration which accompanies it is as much made up of a sense that one's judgment is trustworthy and one's intelligence clear and unflurried as it is of any physical delights. And the final movement of such a passage, when the climber reaches handholds like the rungs of a ladder (no higher praise is possible), a roomy ledge to stand upon, and a spike of rock round which he can "belay" the rope, and so guarantee both his own safety and that of his companions who will now follow him, brings a quiet glow of triumph which is much more than a mere relief of tension or a sense of escape. A good cragsman, it may be remarked, can almost always retrace his steps and return to his companions if the passage should prove more difficult than he anticipated. It is, in fact, only on this condition that he is justified in assuming the responsibility of leading his party. There are plenty of borderline cases, of course, in which a climber may not be perfectly certain whether he should proceed or return, and it is just here that his judgment is tested.

Intelligence, not of a low order, is exercised at many points in any interesting ascent. The choice of route constantly demands it. A fine mountain is a succession of problems to be solved on the spot. Few who have not climbed can realize how very intricate a mountain face may be. Rocks by themselves can require varied enough evolutions, for most cliffs are more like highly tilted labyrinths, when you come close to them, than the solid walls which from a distance they appear to be. And often the choice of one fissure rather than another, of one shelf or shoulder or buttress rather than its neighbor, will make a difference in time to be counted in hours and spell success or failure for the whole expedition.

But the complexities of rock-climbing are matched by those of ice and snow. A broken-up glacier can present a maze which only a mixture of good luck and happy opportunism will unravel. It is a strange experience to come down in the late afternoon, one's heels sinking deep into a vast bulge of snow—like a swelling sail, but more dazzlingly white—to survey, as the slope curves over and what is below is revealed, the wild, contorted chaos of waves and chasms into which the glacier ice is riven as it descends. Through this chaos, often by a series of carefully planned leaps interspersed with thoughtful performances upon bridges of snow—an all-fours position which distributes one's weight over the fragile structure is not unusual—and as a rule by much chopping of steps along the slopes of the ice waves, an intricate way is forced. It is astonishing how often the way followed will seem the only one that is possible, and how rare it is for no way to be found.

I have lingered somewhat over the technical attractions of mountaineering because this side of the sport is the one least easy for the layman to imagine, though some knowledge of it is necessary if the climber's passion is to be understood. If I have said enough to show that a great climb is not a rash adventure but a campaign in which prudent strategy and skillful tactics have both been required, I shall have gained my purpose. I have said nothing about the view from the summit—the excuse which the nonclimber usually provides for the climber, who is often lazy enough to accept it. The view from the summit is as a rule no more interesting than the other views. And I have said nothing as yet about the beauty of the high peaks. Before attempting to say what little can be said about this there is another fact, less often mentioned, which must be indicated.

Few climbers are for long exempt from a certain modicum of anxiety—a watchful apprehension which rarely rises to the point of distress, but remains as a background of consciousness giving a special *dramatic* quality to each incident. It is tempting to speculate further upon this feeling, for it may have an intimate connection with the beauty which the climber sometimes sees. With fatigue or indisposition this somber tinge easily develops into a clouding dread, more or less well controlled. When this happens the whole expedition changes from a joy to a nightmare. For some climbers this is not an infrequent occurrence, though it may be but for a moment. With the unloosing of anxiety the whole character of the landscape is transformed. "The eye altering alters all."[1] There are always plenty of sights in the high mountains which are capable of taking on a hideous aspect. Gaunt, disintegrating black cliffs that can be contemplated without horror only by a mind which is perfectly in possession of itself; obscene convolutions of grimy glacier which stir nothing but nausea unless one is able to hold oneself in check; sinister gray curtains of ice, furrowed by stone falls, that hold no hope for any living thing for thousands of feet; monstrous gaping jaws of crevasses fanged above with sharp blue icicles and lipped with treacherous bulges of soft snow. Even the transcendental sparkle of the snow on the upper ridges turns easily to a mere grim glitter. The instant this anxiety slips loose, beauty vanishes. Naturally it does, for this holding down of tremors, this serenity amid stress, was its very source and being. Perhaps even the man who deeply feels the beauty of a great mountain from the valley is doing something similar. He is holding in control a set of feelings which if they broke loose would distress him. Let his equanimity be sufficiently destroyed, let some grief or harshness throw him off his balance, and he will not find peace among the hills, he will not see beauty in them, but only a hateful, discomforting presentation of that side of the universe which is least the concern of man.

The climber is not less susceptible to the ordinary beauty of the mountains, if I may call it such—this power they have to stir such subtly mingled feelings when they are seen from below; and his privileged enjoyment of their extraordinary beauty, the still more mingled thrill which they awaken in him when he is actually upon their ridges, does not, in spite of all that Ruskin had to say, betoken a lack of sensibility. In the best instances the closer, the more intimate, experience is an amplification of the other. It is possible, of course, to climb for a whole day, or for a week, or a lifetime, with scarcely a moment of the genuine awareness; just as it is possible to perambulate miles of galleries or listen to the best orchestras in the world without any result which is worth mentioning. But it is the claim of the mountaineer that the very conditions of his sport do tend to make a more fully awakened response likely. The passion, like others, can go astray, and bogus forms are not uncommon. There are collectors of peaks, for example, who know as little of the genuine worship as mere collectors of pictures. Fortunately, perhaps, they rarely know what they are missing.[2]

26 The Secret of "Feedforward"

It has all been like writing a book (and I have written many): as you come toward the end, you begin, you think, to see how you should have done it. This is an illusion, as with the book, because it becomes a different book in the writing, a different life. And it will be the same, I am sure, with this little essay. In spite of the generous limits allowed me, it will be impossible to do more than summarize my lessons, and, as I close it, I will realize that I have been trying to learn some of the more important of them over again.

Long ago, a banker friend, who had sat through many a big deliberative international meeting watching the doodling, told me that a doctor he knew had a custom of putting a number of little targets into his mazy web: bull's-eye, inner, outer, and off. After each contribution to the discussion, he would scan the deliberators, pencil poised, and mark on one of his targets where he thought the shot had gone. This impressed me, and for a time I tried it out. But not for long. I could not learn to feel sure enough beforehand about what was being aimed at. I found I had no such clear designs as those that the doctor must have entertained. But the attempt taught me this: how often I saw where I should be going only by setting out for somewhere else.

This situation is illustrated by a story a Catholic friend once told me. Whether he made it up or not I won't guess; it is a very Catholic story. It seems that Cervantes was calling on a painter in Toledo. On an easel were the beginnings of a picture. Cervantes asked what the picture was to be of. "Why, that depends," replied the painter, "on how it turns out. If it has a beard, it is Saint John the Baptist. If it has not, it is the Immaculate Conception!"

Reprinted by permission from *Saturday Review*, February 3, 1968, pp. 14-17.

Most ventures of mine—books and poems included—have been like this. They came along from fighting hard from the start to find out what they were. They were rarely set designs, fixed beforehand. When they tried to be so, they collapsed early or switched over to be something else. The typical venture for me is a poem which begins by setting itself a problem. It doesn't let me know what its problem is, and I suspect it usually doesn't know that itself. But I am sure it has one and that the solution will be the end—in both senses: goal and terminus of the poem. Often, but not always, the first lines to be formed get pushed down to become the final phrases. In its end is the beginning.

The process by which any venture of this creative sort finds itself, and so pursues its end, is something I have learned, I hope, something about. Indeed, I am not sure I have learned anything else as important. Although I never learned to play the doctor's target game, I realize now what a prime role belongs to what I have come to call "feedforward" in all our doings. Feedforward, as I see it, is the reciprocal, the necessary condition of what the cybernetics and automation people call "feedback."

Whatever we may be doing, some sort of preparation for, some design arrangement for one sort of outcome rather than another is part of our activity. This may be conscious, as an expectancy—or unconscious, as a mere assumption. If we are walking downstairs, a readiness in the advanced leg (but indeed in our whole body) to meet something solid under its toe is needed if we are to continue. Usually, on the stairs, this feedforward is fulfilled. There is confirmatory feedback at the end of each step cycle—the foot finds the expected, the presupposed footing. Compare pitch-dark and broad daylight as to the degree of awareness we may have of our feedforward. If the feedback does not come, if it is falsifying and not verifying, we have to do something else and rather quickly. The point is that feedforward is a needed prescription or plan for a feedback, to which the actual feedback may or may not conform.

Evidently, feedforward is a product of former experience: a selective reflection of what has been relevant in similar activity in our past. It can be crude and it can be delicate. Much of it, for economy's sake, must be routine (as in walking downstairs) in order to deal appropriately with the exceptional. Watch good tennis players and you see how exquisitely, how variously, and how ramifyingly feedforward and feedback are playing their game for them. We may well wonder how there can be *time* between all that must be exactly noted and all that must be exactly done. Nothing could better show us to what a degree feedforward can be developed. If with tennis, why not with more essential human abilities? Any exhibition of superlative skill can make us marvel that, in teaching, say, or in statesmanship, we tolerate so many underdeveloped performers.

As most examples suggest, feedforward and feedback need not be—indeed, commonly are not—fully conscious. Modern conjectural models of brain-mind activity suppose almost unimaginably complex systems of minimal unit cycles organized in hierarchies: cycles of cycles, of activity, all from lowest to highest levels guided by feedback. Of most of this we are certainly not conscious.

Against such a background it is, we all know too well, by no means easy to say, or to conceive, what this invaluable little word "we" is talking about. The question is one we are usually discreet enough not to raise. So, too, with "conscious." We may be ready to allow that between what is conscious and what isn't there may be many degrees, but what any "I" may have to do with what it isn't at all conscious of is again something we hardly know how to go into. Linger on this and we may well find the trouble spreading. Who can be clear about what an "I" and its consciousness have to do with one another?

What I have thought I have learned through reflection on the interplay between feedforward and feedback is the wisdom of making close friends with such doubts and, indeed, of carefully cultivating their acquaintance. By shying away from them, by wanting more certainty than I could have, I never, as I recall, gained in security—rather the opposite. When I closeted myself with my confidences and thought so to be secure in any view, I found this was that grim old sense of "secure" used in Judges 18, where the Danite spies exultantly inform the slaughterers: "Behold there is a people in Laish that dwell there quiet and secure, far from any allies"; adding as a whet: "And are ye still?"

The lesson was that in all kinds of ventures—in teaching of many varieties, in the design of instruction, in the exploration of remote cultures (Chinese, African, Indian), in composing as in trying to comprehend poems, in propounding theories of comprehension—things went best when I had least conviction of the rightness of the feedforward by which each step was being guided. Long ago, in 1919, C. K. Ogden and I, when writing the first draft of *The Meaning of Meaning*, used to joke about "finding too many convictions in a thinker's record" and to allude to archbishops and other leaders of the faiths as "notorious convicts." That was at a time when we were ourselves exuberantly convinced—particularly of the wrongheadedness of .other people. Later, I became, I have hoped, more of an adept in uncertainty.

This is not a matter of large-scale external prognostications: how a book or an opinion would be received—the doctor's target game. In that sort of guessing I was always aware enough of inability. No, it was the necessary step-by-step feedforward: the witting or unwitting or midway surmises by which, say, a word tried out in writing a poem would open or close possibilities for the following phrases—it was in this sort of thing that I had to learn how to be duly tentative. And, too, to be prepared for the way feedback from the outcome of a step would interact with my feedforward. The next steps, I had to learn, would often be fed forward by some combination of the fresh feedback with former feedforward. And the less *convinced* that had been, the more open it was to modification in the further venture.

This held, I came to see, not only in the peculiar process of trying out alternates and submitting to outcomes by which a poem finds itself, but in other crafts, too. In the design of instruction—say, in literacy or in a second language—the actual outcome, the ease or difficulty (better, the discernment or trouble) with which a learner takes a step, is much more instructive to the designer if he has kept himself as little committed as he can be to the *detail* of what he is trying out. Meanwhile, however, constancy and attachment to the *principles* of the design (as opposed to the minutiae of its implementation) are required. For these principles have (or should have) governed the choice of the detail; it is these principles which are really under trial (not some one of a number of possible embodiments), and unless the principles stay constant, fertile interplay between what is looked for (feedforward) and what actually happens (feedback) is precluded. The experimentation will not lead to the strengthening or weakening or emendation of the principles, which should be its main purpose.

As I elaborate this, the reader may recognize it as the celebrated open-mindedness, the suspension of judgement, and the
hypothetical procedure that figure in so many accounts of scientific
inquiry. If so, the resemblance to the process above sketched of the
composition of a poem is, at least, suggestive. And so is the resemblance to the process of learning to read or to speak a second language encouraged in any truly self-critical theory of the design of
instruction, the student is invited to explore an intelligible sequence
of oppositions and connections rather than to memorize what he
hopes teacher would like to hear from him. Indeed, all species of
mental activity deeply resemble one another.

I took to writing poems late in life, and, if I rightly recall,
was prevented earlier by a mistaken notion that good lines and
stanzas ought to present themselves to the poet without the labor of
achieving compromises between frustrations. Remember, however,
Coleridge's warning: "Let us not introduce an Act of Uniformity
against poets."[1] It may very well be that different sorts of poetry, in
different sorts of poets, come into being in different ways. Abstract
words easily hoodwink us. I have just been adding marginalia in a
skeptical commentary on one of my books, long out of print, published in 1926, whose title was *Science and Poetry*. Its new title
when it comes into life again in 1968 will be *Poetries and Sciences*.[2]
The old book was youthfully dogmatic, and in its very title evoked
some sort of dramatic confrontation between antagonists. The new
title is relatively modest and pacific. In 1926 I had no useful experience in writing poems of any sort. I had also little or no useful experience in any sort of experimental inquiry. In those days, I think,
I never asked myself whether the pages of *Science and Poetry* were
either, or what, if neither, they could be. If the question occurred to
me then, I must have been canny enough to put it aside. I was too
much committed to my preclusions to be a kind host to such que-
ries.

Feedforward is, as I see it, highly various. At one end of the
scale, it can be a highly articulate examinable process, the sort of
thing known as scientific hypothesis waiting to be okayed or destroyed by evidence. At the other, it may be hardly cognized or
embodied at all, even in the vaguest schematic image. It can be no
more than a readiness to be surprised or disturbed by one kind of
event rather than by another: green-lighted or red-lighted by it. As

suggested above, billions of hierarchically systematic cycles, through which we live and move and have our being, are guided in all they do for one another by concord or discord in their feedforward-feedback. And it is perhaps a reasonable suggestion that much in what we call ourselves and admit to be "us" includes these billions of concordant cycles. When our dinner agrees with us we seem to be digesting it. When it does not, we do not seem to be so much in charge. Or, as Tommy puts it when his mother told him not to sneeze so: "I don't sneeze, Mummy, it sneezes me!"

However such matters may be, feedforward has come to seem for me a notion indispensable to an adequate theory of conduct and a necessary part of an account of feedback. I labeled it so in *Speculative Instruments,* a title I took from Coleridge.[3] It was indeed one of the chief speculative instruments there discussed. Launching the label, I thought soon to meet some echo or comment. But no such feedback has come. This talk of it here is thus a rejoinder to that taciturnity. What matters, though, is how the quality of our conduct may depend on the character of our feedforward. And not only on its character as tentative, provisional, corrigible—so much stressed above—but on other characters to which these may be due.

Consider another and a peculiarly interesting example of feedforward: what you have it in mind to say *before* you have begun to put it into any sort of words. This feedforward can be very definite. It can unhesitatingly reject any and all of your efforts to say it. "No," you note, "that isn't it at all." Even when you have gone a long way toward finding a way to say it, your feedforward can still purse its lips: "Not quite, it should be better!" Note that here we do not have two fully developed ways of saying it before us to be compared. We have only a series of offered attempts being judged by reference to something else—this inevitably mysterious thing I am calling feedforward. In relation to this, the ways of saying it that have occurred to you are feedback: reports of outcomes of your attempts at saying it. And we may note further that sometimes it is the other way about—as when your tennis ball or target shot is out. Or when you really drop a brick and have to ask yourself: "What *could* I have been thinking to have said that?" These considerations apply to all modes of would-be communication: enunciating national policies, composing poems, addressing juries, poor David Balfour's *gomeril* behaviors in wooing Catriona, etc.[4]

This leads me into another feedforward problem about which, too, I do at least devoutly hope that I have managed to learn something—somehow or other and at long last. This is the recognition in our feedforward of diversities of "point of view." There is something known as tact, which some have and some haven't. It is widely esteemed, but in some matters despised. It can be unreservedly condemned by certain rather wooden-eyed types of moralists. What I am talking about is a swift, before-the-event recognition of how something will seem to people looking at it from angles other than our own.

This last has brought the point-of-view metaphor into sharper focus. It is so familiar that it can easily be supposed of no more consequence than the metaphor in the phrase "leg of the table." Look into it more closely, however, and it can seem to become momentous, nothing less than a set of hints toward a series of new concepts for the new education required for the current and the coming worlds.

Let us consider rather closely the literal sense, the original, visual situation from which this metaphor comes. Take some object —the Statue of Liberty, for instance—which can be gazed at from north, south, east, west, and intermediate directions, from below and above, from far and near. No normal person above a certain age has any difficulty in allowing that such objects must look very different when seen from varying viewpoints and distances. And some people, after seeing a suitable object from one or more angles, can form a fairly good guess—a not too insecure feedforward—as to how it will appear from other angles. Those who can do this—or think they can—tend to say "Surely this is something we all can do!" But not at all. When I was last working at experiments in depiction—at the Visual Arts Center, Harvard—this was one of the questions my seminar looked into. We found that for relatively simple, easily perceived objects—a twisted paper clip, a leaf, a key . . . seen from the north, say, at full leisure and under good conditions—comparatively few people were able at all clearly to imagine, describe, draw how the thing would look from east, west, or intermediate directions. And if the object were turned and then shown again, the estimates offered of how and how much it had been turned went often wildly astray. The participants, moreover, were design-school or fine-arts students with, it is to be supposed, more than average concern and ability with visual perception.

Among the aims of these experiments (which are not yet extensive enough to warrant more than speculative applications), two are especially relevant here: (1) to find out what educational techniques might be devised to help people in looking at things from all sides and in putting the views intelligibly together; (2) to explore further the educational opportunities in this metaphor from optical viewing and intellectual and moral viewing. Long leaps, no doubt, but there seems ground for a hunch that practice and comparison between one's own and others' performances can lead to improvement. And, for another, that increased interest in what *seeing* is like can, at the least, encourage the realization that to view a question from one side only is not enough. And, further yet, that to regard it fully and fairly even from one side only involves venturesome feedforward (verifiable and falsifiable) as to how it is likely to seem to others in other positions.

What I hope I have learned about this is to ask, more often and more searchingly, of utterances that claim some importance—political, poetical, practical—whether they seem to be guided and guarded by reasonable feedforward as to how people of very different prepossessions are likely to take them. And this leads to a gloomy impression. Far too many of the voices that make us glow or wince speak too often as though they had the thing itself—the whole thing and nothing but the thing—presented to them. And not just, in fact, a view of it: a view formed under special circumstances which only a minority of the auditors can possibly share.

I seem to hear this disability-derived confidence loading the channels in almost all spheres: in criticism and in politics of all parties as much as in preaching. In none of them can failure to inquire into the dissident position (or to try to) be a worthy, rather than a comicotragical, ground for a belief that one is right. "I just cannot understand anyone taking any other view on this" is a confession of a lack of competence. And I have at the end of this essay to be rather careful not to join these well-filled ranks. But, alas, why people are not likely to approve the overall view of viewpoint-dependence I have been trying to present is clear. The history of controversy as spiritual warfare—of religious and ideological and national, as well as factional conflicts—is there to explain it.

27 An Interview Conducted by
B. A. Boucher and J. P. Russo

Last month you mentioned that you were going to "utopia" in a short while.

Well, I think I said "a better world"; we don't know yet *how* good it will be. Anguilla is an island which used to belong to a group—Saint Kitts, and Anguilla. Someone called Bradshaw on Saint Kitts has been ruling there for donkey's years, and Nevis has voted unanimously against him but has not seceded. Anguilla has seceded and has applied to Britain for colonial status. It is very small, about five thousand *native* inhabitants. It had no luck at all —Whitehall in London wants to get rid of colonies, not acquire them. Also, no other power (they always talk about other powers, meaning the U.S.) will do anything unless Britain says okay. And Britain says nothing; so they've got to start again. Independence Day is January 8th, and I'm going to get there before the new year.

Might you be drafted as, say, a minister of education?

I should hope not. I don't intend to be anything; just a visitor. It is apparently an island with perfect beaches and might be an ideal position for a gambling hall.

But it's probably easier running utopia for five thousand than for—

Well, it hasn't been properly investigated experimentally yet, but I should say that five thousand was on the big side.

Interview conducted by Bruce Ambler Boucher and John Paul Russo on December 12, 1968, at I. A. Richards' apartment in Cambridge, Massachusetts. Reprinted by permission from *The Harvard Advocate*, 103 (1969), 3-8.

May we go back to a beginning? How did you become interested in Basic English?

I'm glad you asked me that because I can tell you. It happened exactly at eleven o'clock at night on November the eleventh, 1918, Armistice Day. Violence burst out in my Cambridge, the other Cambridge, medical students on the rampage. I renewed contact with C. K. Ogden late that night because he had suffered from damage and I was a witness and could help him. We stopped at eleven o'clock halfway down my little twisting stairs (I rented a couple of rooms from him in a decrepit old house next to the Cavendish Laboratory), somehow we stopped there and started talking about meaning. There had been an article in *Mind* and another play-up in, I think, the *Aristotelian Society Proceedings;* people had been talking about meaning and making an awful mess of it, and we'd been reading them by accident—neither of us knew the other was interested at all—and we started making comments on them. We stood there two hours on the stairway till one o'clock. I can remember a bats-wing gas burner above my head. This was out of kilter and every little while it squealed and I would reach up and try to adjust the tap of the burner. We went on and on, and the whole of our book, *The Meaning of Meaning*, was talked out clearly in two hours. One of the chapters was on the theory of definition; we found we could agree. It's a most extraordinary experience, finding you can agree with someone. Decades later it wasn't the case that we could understand one another *at all*. That is a useful thing to think of: that a first intellectual encounter can result in almost complete comprehension on both sides and twenty-five years later there can be almost complete malcomprehension on both sides and at every point. Anyway that was the start of *The Meaning of Meaning*, and its definition chapter was to lead Ogden into inventing and working out Basic English. It is a curiously pinpointed starting point, a two-hour conversation on definitions interrupted by a bats-wing gas burner.

Were you then teaching in Cambridge?

No. I was only doing what a lot of people do at universities, hanging about, hoping for a job. And I was suffering from what Ogden used to call "hand-to-mouth disease." For a nominal sum, he had rented me an attic and it was on the way down from this attic that we suddenly got together and went on having the most enormous fun, I believe, two people have ever had—writing *The Meaning of Meaning*. It doesn't perhaps look as though it was such fun, but it was much of it written in the spirit of "Here's a nice half-brick, whom shall we throw it at?"

Do you find your intellectual origins back in the radical philosophical tradition of the nineteenth century?

Well—well yes, but most eclectically. I turned by accident to philosophy because I couldn't bear history. Then, what I read in philosophy was a matter of chance. In those days at Cambridge, you had no assigned reading. You had no apparent awareness— quite contrary to the fact—no apparent awareness in lecturers that others had ever thought about these matters before. Whitehead, Russell, Moore, McTaggart, and the rest were all prophets, as it were, of various kinds. They would occasionally make a reference to someone—but it was in order to controvert.

What did you read for moral sciences then?

Anything that came my way—contemporary journals, *Mind*, the *British Journal of Psychology* . . . I was mostly reading everything *except* philosophy until about three weeks before the final tripos examination when I did give myself a good dollop of reading.

In particular?

Hmmm. Well, Mill, of course—you couldn't escape from Mill. I was devoted to both Mills. In fact, you often are the most devoted to the people you most disagree with. There's something insipid about agreeing with an author, especially when you're young. You feel it's your business to be *other*.

Did you read Herbert Spencer?

Oh, on the wing, but not much was absorbed from him. He's too murky a writer; I couldn't swallow much of that.

Did you begin your studies in Coleridge then?

Not until years later, not until I had published at least the *Principles of Literary Criticism* and *Practical Criticism*. If anyone looked carefully, they could see I didn't—then—know anything about Coleridge. I wrote about him here and there, but I obviously didn't know him. But after that I really did get down to that, largely from having to give a course on Coleridge. Lots of things happen to people from having to give a course.

Where did you teach Coleridge?

Oh, Cambridge. I accidentally began to teach at Cambridge early. In fact I taught the next year, and I was giving a course on the principles of literary criticism and another course on the contemporary novel to make a little money. Between the two I could survive. In those days an "on approval" in my status could collect fifteen shillings a course from any who came three times. It is not so now.

At what time was this?

Began about the eighth of October, 1919. That year was quite beyond anything you could imagine. It was World War I survivors come back to college. Not a bit like the end of World War II. There was an atmosphere, such a dream, such a hope. They were just too good to be true; it was a joy to deal with those people; those who got back to Cambridge from all that slaughter were back *for reasons.*

What was the extent of G. E. Moore's influence on you?

Enormous, and it shaped me in a thousand ways—*negatively*. I spent seven years studying under him and have ever since been reacting to his influence. I feel like an obverse of him. Where there's a hole in him there's a bulge in me—the object that comes out of the mold is the mirror image of the mold. He could hardly ever believe that people could mean what they said; I've come to think they hardly ever can say what they mean. At any rate, I never could understand what he was trying to tell me. Of course, I

acquired all the mannerisms immediately. The first sign of disciple-
ship is the mannerisms.

For example?

Well, you turn to the blackboard and write something up
not very legibly. Then, every time you want to refer to it for the
purpose of demolishing it—not elucidating it—you underline it or
cross it out so there is a great cloud of chalk dust around you in all
directions. Moore lectured at the universe through the medium of a
blackboard.

I did a lot of that sort of thing in my young days as a lecturer. I learned later not to.[1]

Did McTaggart have any influence on your development?

Oh, very deeply. McTaggart was a big-scale dreamer.[2]
Other notable philosophers—C. D. Broad for instance—devoted
years to trying to expound McTaggart. I was once taken by a
greater than either, G. G. Coulton, the medieval historian, up to
his attic window in the neighboring college, St. John's. He said
"Look, do you see that mulberry tree?" I looked down—it is in
Trinity's small garden—and he said "Do you see that track round
the mulberry tree?" I did, it was bare. He said "That is where Mc-
Taggart composed *The Nature of Existence*, walking round and
round that mulberry tree." He would take the whole morning
walking round and round the tree thinking out paragraphs of *The
Nature of Existence*. Then he would go in and write them down.

That is a good way to philosophize, I think. But you won't
find much of the garden or the mulberry tree in the book, more's
the pity. Funnily enough, Wittgenstein found another garden belonging to Trinity, altogether more remote, which was more or less
given up to him—it had been a sort of secret sanctum for the
Fellows. It's hidden in and beyond Trinity Fellows' Garden. Wittgenstein took to walking round and round there in his later years at
Trinity, and nobody dared go near.

*Many Cambridge philosophers between 1900 and 1935,
yourself included, ended up discussing language.*

I'm very glad they did because sooner or later enough discussion of language—it's a very queer kind of pursuit, you know, using language to discuss language—should mean improvements. What worries me about so much of these discussions is that they're not practically oriented. My own peculiar slant on language, I think, is that I regard studies in language as, for me, preludes to linguistic engineering.

Was Russell of much help to you in developing your "peculiar slant"? Did you have much contact with him?

Oh, some. Russell always to me was too much of a logician on this. His interest in language has been a logician's interest. That again is another queer thing. Mathematics and logic lead people away from the actualities into, well, surprising generalities. There's a story, probably apocryphal, that I'm fond of about the great mathematician Hilbert.[3] He was attending a conference in Copenhagen, and they took him to see the very celebrated bridge they have there. He admired it duly and then said "It's astonishing! Wonderful! It's exactly like the bridge at Hamburg." At which the local Danes, his hosts, were much affronted because there's no bridge at all like that in Hamburg. They said "How is it like a bridge at Hamburg?" Hilbert answered "Why it goes from this side to that side and the river goes under it." I feel that a great many of the perceptions about language that logicians develop are rather Hilbertian. Just a shade too abstract.

How did you develop your distinction between referential and emotive language?

Well, I suppose in the old days (in the time of *The Meaning of Meaning*) one was concerned to modernize the theory of knowledge, and we (Ogden and I) outraged everybody by saying that really what you were talking *about* was only connected with what you *said* by a complex causal relation. That was scandalous in 1919. It became commonplace as time went on. *The Meaning of Meaning* tries hard to deal with it, and if anyone's curious, he should look at appendix B. That's the place where the scheme is outlined most precisely.

So much for the referential use of language. Against it in those days we set up a thing called the emotive use of language. (We inherited the word "emotive"; I think it was Marty who launched it.)[4] What we tried to say has often been misunderstood. I've since written two articles that are published in what I fancy is my most intelligent book, *Speculative Instruments*. One is "Toward a Theory of Comprehending"; the other is "Emotive Meaning Again." Between them, they do, I think, say better what we tried to say earlier. If you add a piece called "Meaning Anew" in *So Much Nearer* you will have what I still want to propose. The referential use of language is the job of leading people to think about certain things—about *this* rather than about *that*—and to think in this sort of way rather than in that way. Reference is your main instrument for influencing people. You can also do it other ways. Poets, of course, are the specialists in doing it *other* ways. I'm writing a third book this year—after *So Much Nearer* and *Design for Escape*. It is trying to take all that further and has got a fancy title. I began my writings with *Principles of Literary Criticism* (1924) and I shall probably end them with *Principles of Language Control* (1970).[5] Nearly, but not quite the same thing, you know.

In what ways is this used as far as Basic English is concerned?

We are just now reconstructing not so much Basic English as the technique of its *use*. Here's a republication of Ogden's essential works that has come out this year: *Basic English: International Second Language*.[6] It's edited in London, by former disciples and colleagues of Ogden. It's actually the horse's mouth; there's nothing in there that isn't his; everything as Ogden would have it. I'm now busy on all this again with my colleague Christine Gibson, with whom I've been working since I came to Harvard.[7] We are trying to show what can be concretely done with Basic English, or something very like it as a means of avoiding and of clearing up muddles.

How did the Basic English movement begin?

It was an extraordinary piece of virtuosity on the part of Ogden. I can't imagine Basic English or any of its derivatives having come into existence without this peculiar thing. Ogden was a very good scholar, good enough for a chair in the classics and destined for one—but he was interested in too many other things, in everything else, in fact. One of the magical gifts he had was his capacity to rephrase almost anything. At one time he thought of launching himself as a sort of Universal Rephraser for anyone who found difficulty in putting his ideas into words. The draft prospectus ran: "You have the Ideas," "We have the Words." It wouldn't have been true that *they* had the ideas, but certainly Ogden had enough of both. And he created Basic English by interrogating his intelligent friends; he had hundreds of them; he belonged to seven clubs, at least, and could contrive not to be a club bore. He was very, very witty, a most unexpected, surprising man. He'd take off with anyone he thought he knew all about X and keep him up to three o'clock in the morning. By that time he'd found out what he wanted to about X and he could use it. What he was finding out was which words one *couldn't* do without, and he worked away on which words one *can* do without. If you can substitute a phrase of ten words for a given word, however technical and abstruse, then you can do without it. That was one of his rough working rules. There's a wonderful book called the *General Basic English Dictionary* in which more than 20,000 words are defined in Ogden's Basic 850.[8] The definitions, if anyone compares them with the pocket Oxford dictionary, are about of the same scope. They had to beat the pocket Oxford. That was his test.

Did the Depression have an adverse effect on implementing Basic?

It never hit England, you know, with anything like the same sharpness that it hit America. I shouldn't say that the Depression in itself made much difference to my designs one way or the other. Of course it must have done, but I can't trace it.

When did television become an important part of the design of Basic?

About the middle of the war, '42 or '43.[9] It looked like the heaven-sent instrument. You could put pictures along with words and sentences. If you can get the eye and ear cooperating, you can do anything, I think. Television looked like the divinely appointed medium. So I got a little grant from the Rockefeller Foundation and I went to Walt Disney's studio to learn how to make cartoons. I had taken to drawing before that and their artists were very helpful. The great thing to do is to develop a kind of universal simplified pictorial script in which you can express situations. And then you must put sentences and pictures that correspond to their meanings in certain sequences together. I still think that TV or satellite-distributed sentence-situation-depiction games are going to be the way to educate the planet. There's more power to the eye and ear together than to either of them apart.

> *To what do you attribute the lack of success with educational television?*

It has become professionalized. There are several professions involved there: producers and the strangely assorted teams that have to work together on a production. I saw enough of it to feel the internal organization troubles. It's very hard to overcome professional expertise. People's careers depend upon their having a say-so in matters about which they haven't thought at all. If you try to do anything new through a medium like TV, you run into that kind of prestige, "my qualifications, my future" thing all the time.

> *Do you foresee any means of overcoming the intransigence of the communications media, especially considering the critical need for mass education in Africa and India?*

Much can be done if things get *bad* enough. Things are going to get really bad rather soon, and so I'm hopeful. It's just like a war. When you get a really bad war (I don't mean a remote war, I mean a home-threat war) people start doing things they had said were impossible. I think there's going to be a world crisis quite soon: we must hope it won't take the form of mutual murder all round the planet, but there's going to be a crisis. There are local crises almost everywhere you look and getting worse all the time. When things are bad enough you have to do the impossible or be fired and have another man come in. Impossibles had to be done all through both the wars. The great thing during those wars was to get rid of the people who were supposed to know better.

You spent a number of years teaching in China. In view of your experiences there and the current anti-Western attitude of the Chinese, do you think a concept like Basic English would be tolerated by them?

It could happen; it did happen once, in fact. The Nanking government, just at the moment the Japanese invaded and put an end to everything, had set up—with the minister of education as chairman—a committee to put my recommendations based on Basic English into China wherever the authority of the government could be enforced. It was too good to be true, and I couldn't believe it had happened. By the time I got back to Peking—this all happened in Nanking—I found the Japanese had invaded in strength and all that sort of thing was over. Something like it could happen again given the right government setup. The Chinese could be very flexible indeed, as flexible as the Japanese have been. We were in Peking through the first six months of Mao's advent there (April-August 1950). While the present regime, for which I have had much regard, continues, I don't think this will happen. But its successors might find that joining up with the rest of the world is just as much the national need as being opposed to the rest of the world has been in Mao's later years. It's quite possible. Then Basic English in China might come back into its own. That is partly why we are working on it still. [10]

How did Bruner's Toward a Theory of Instruction *apply to your thesis in "Design for Escape"?*

I much admire Bruner's work. [11] I like, particularly, his three modes: *Enactive, Iconic,* and *Symbolic.* By using them as controls upon one another we can teach learners how to confirm or correct their own learning. You see again that I'm a linguistic engineer. And an educational engineer. I'm looking for new and better ways of making many more capable and useful people through verbal means. Everyone's got that in view, I'm sure, but I'm perhaps a bit impatient. There is the disaster that I'm always aware is coming on us. It may not be the third world war as we have been dreaming of it; it may be a general crumbling, a general inability to staff our ventures and to follow through. All partly because of the enormous increases of wealth that the rich communities are undergoing and the contrast with the ever increasing poverty of poor regions.

> *One of the premises of your recent "Design for Escape" is in fact the population problem.*

It is, and the fact that the gap between the rich section of the planet and the poor section is widening. Alas! The publisher has got it wrong on the cover. It isn't the case at all that world population is outstripping productivity. No, the point is that the poor parts of the world are getting poorer and the rich richer. That's one of the first premises—that things are getting worse.

> *If the rich nations are not able to construct a generally competent educational system for themselves, do you foresee any hopes of such a system created in Africa or Asia —in view of the crisis facing both in the next twenty years?*

I believe we can construct a worldwide educational system which will teach better than we have ever imagined. I could offer you evidence on that. Organizing it would be easy compared with swinging people round the moon. It would be much less costly and far more repaying. And sounder as a defense investment too. The program would be for (1) teaching English very, very smoothly and easily and (2) at the earliest possible point, not teaching it as English, but teaching it as the necessary vehicle of modern world views! That's the thing I care about most. You don't want to teach a language just as a language (except to linguisticians). You should use it as a means for letting people learn what they most need to learn, which is how to run a sane state and how to run an educational system which will keep the state sane and in being. And cope too with the frustrations and tensions which are causing such terrible trouble on our home front. There isn't an advanced society today, the United States, the United Kingdon, or France, that isn't in a terrible mess.

> *Our society has taken such sharp turns that one need in England and the United States may lie in a reinterpretation of our own culture—back to Milton's milieu, earlier—a culture almost as foreign to us as the Greeks or Romans were to our literary forebears.*

A good point, that, Milton being at about the turning point. After Milton, I think you'd agree, things become more intelligible. Professional instruction, as it were, in English literature might very well stop soon after Milton. There's obviously a case for people being taught how to read Chaucer; people don't get into Chaucer just by the light of nature, not as well as they do into Tennyson. I see no excuse for tremendous courses on Tennyson. I'm a great admirer of Tennyson, but I think courses haven't helped him and won't. Milton's the turning point. What most people need, though, with Milton more than anything else is to hear him really well read aloud. He's the most readable-aloud poet there is, magnificent beyond description.

Not too many seem to want to read Milton aloud or, for that matter, in quiet.

Oh, I don't understand why. I heard so many good people read Milton as they read nothing else and so much better. It's just that Milton makes them better readers.

Have we developed to a point in our own culture where we only need to study in schools those who would be inaccessible, much as the classics were to a man of Milton's time?

That's right, and then after that, let people enjoy what they care to enjoy, what they find within their own range of taste.

And yet, when I teach Pope's poetry, I often find that it takes us a good deal of time to ramble around the politics, science, philosophy, and social history of the period before we can appreciate Pope's titanic genius.

Pope is, you are right, a Titan and there is a place for footnotes and commentary of some sort there. But Pope at his greatest, the opening of, say, the second book of the *Essay on Man*, doesn't need any introduction. It's just the greatest poetry.

All of which brings us to the question—Whither English studies? We've heard you question the ways and means by which undergraduates and graduates are currently taught English.

It's hard on the poets to make everybody study them like this. I think that's the main thing I had in mind: that literature, one's own literature, is for enjoyment. As far as I can see, making it into an academic subject has not increased the amount of *enjoyment* taken in the poems, or the novels or the plays or anything. No, I'm against it. I think it's all right that a very small special crew should study the works and battle with one another. I'm very doubtful whether we want a great *number* of biographies or studies in detail. You see, what is a man who's done English as an academic, literary subject, what's he to do the rest of his life, except to write books-about-books-about-books and reviews of them? I'm agin' it on the whole; I think we're burying the valuables under loads of derivatives.

Do you think that the study of English has fallen into the same pattern as, say, classics?

I think that's a fair comparison. Of course, classics is saving itself by aiding anthropology, archaeology, history, and all sorts of fine specialities.[12]

Where do you do most of your work?

Well, if I can go to bed early and not get up I just reach for pen and block and turn the light on, and work in bed. From four or five o'clock on until breakfast time.

That reminds me of the schedule Leonard and Virginia Woolf were on—

I never knew that!

It's in his book Downhill All the Way. *They did all their work in the morning. But I think it was a little later than your schedule. They would end the day by noon or one and spend the rest of it amusing themselves.*

Well I seem to remember Ben Franklin believing that the day began at five o'clock; he also said a thing I never understood, "The early hour has gold in its mouth." I don't know what that means— nothing to do with dentistry, I hope.

Have you read the Holroyd biography of Lytton Strachey?

Poor Strachey! No. I decided I wouldn't. I felt I knew enough about Lytton Strachey though I never met him personally. But, heavens, I heard a lot in his lifetime. No, if I had time to read biographies of people I used to know . . . I think I'd choose other people. I don't on the whole read biography. I'm postponing that for future decades.

Wasn't he in Cambridge researching "Queen Victoria" during the first years you were lecturing?

Well there wasn't too much research. He must have read books on Queen Victoria and looked around. The thing that struck me about him was that King George V (so I heard) sent him an invitation when the book appeared. He replied, I was told, in the third person that Mr. Strachey regretted but his engagements prevented . . . and then rushed abroad.

You've visited China many times in the past. Do you think China is closer to achieving "the good life" on earth than we are?

Yes, I've spent years of my life in China. They have some enormous assets, and one is that they have had a deep, ingrained horror of violence. When violence occurs, it's recognized in their culture as a breakdown. Certain people in our community no doubt do feel like that, but too many don't think that carrying a gun is a sign of inferiority. The Chinese have felt very deeply that people who will resort to violence in ordinary civil and other occasions are *out*. That's a tremendous protection for a country; and it is one, we may hope, they still have. When you think of the numbers of people, the amount of moving about, and the amount of tension inside that great community, it's amazing how little loss of life their revolution has caused. Very economical.

So you think Mao Tse-tung has come closer than any Western nation?

He has a long way to go, and we have a long way to go. No, I'm not going to speculate; actually, the terrible truth is that no one, from John Fairbank here on down, knows nearly enough about what is happening in China. Our sources aren't good enough.

> *Turning back to "Design for Escape," one finds reference to a plan for world education. Whom do you see in charge of this project which would be ultimately responsible for shaping the lives of so many? is it the Coleridge-Mill clerisy?*

That's a terrible question; I'd hoped you wouldn't ask me. Well, everybody will be trying to be in charge, and the Futurity Foundation (see *Tomorrow Morning, Faustus!*) advisers, for example, will have been working to keep any others from muscling in.[13] I think the slowness with which a lot of these things advance, even on a front which is ready to move (that is, the electronic, technological, the physical channels front) is because of this "Who's going to get it?" Everyone wants to help the world; it is the most rewarding thing to do; but they're in such a crowd at the gate that nobody can get through. When you come to choosing programs, I'm rather of the feeling that something remarkably successful will be achieved locally somewhere, that the choosers will then decide "Oh let's just take that!" That's my strategy, so far as I have any.

> *Actually, how do you set up an administrative authority to run a thing like this?*

I don't think you can; at least they would all be as bad one as another. What I feel is that if there is a way of doing things which is obviously much better than what anyone else has to offer then, in a bad enough emergency, everyone will jump at it. I've been only concerned to produce something really better than anyone else has. It's the old mousetrap story, you see; the better-mousetrap story.[14] Only, the mice have to become insufferable first. Until then we all stick to our old ineffective mousetraps. I think we have a better way of teaching English, but while you're teaching beginning English, you might as well teach everything else. That is to say, a world position, what's needed for living, a philosophy of religion, how to find things out, and the whole works—mental and moral seed for the planet. In this way the two-thirds of the planet that doesn't yet know how to read and write would learn in learning how to read and write English, the things that would help them in their answers to "Where should man go?"

Notes

1 Art and Science

1. Responding to issues considered by "S" in the *Athenaeum* (April 11, May 2, 1919), Fry argues that the analogies between the methods and aims of art and science are "close." He takes exception not with S's basic analogy between shared generalizing and particularizing tendencies of art and science but with the extent to which the comparison may be usefully developed. Although a scientist may frequently be motivated by emotional concerns, many of his processes are purely mechanical and could conceivably be carried on by an "emotionless brain." Feeling, on the other hand, is an integral element of the artistic process. S claimed that the pleasure a scientist receives from the observation of natural unities and relations is an aesthetic one, and yet, Fry observes, the "inevitability of relations" remains even without the concomitant pleasure. But emotion *is* a prerequisite of true aesthetic harmony. Fry must admit that the "highest pleasure" in art is "perhaps" identical with the "highest pleasure" in scientific theory: a "unity-emotion," an emotion accompanying the "clear recognition of unity in a complex." (This unity-emotion is distinguished from a lesser but specifically "aesthetic emotion" by which "the necessity of relations is apprehended" and from the physiological pleasure of seeing certain colors or hearing certain sounds.)

2. Fry himself opens a loophole: "I suspect that the aesthetic value of a theory is not really adequate to the intellectual effort entailed unless, as in a true scientific theory (by which I mean a theory which embraces all the known relevant facts), the aesthetic value is reinforced by the curiosity value which comes in when we believe it to be true."

3. "If we accept the view that there are objective falsehoods, we shall oppose them to facts, and make *truth* the quality of facts, *falsehood* the quality of their opposites, which we may call fictions. Then facts and fictions together may be called *propositions*. A belief always has a proposition for its object, and is knowledge when its object is true, error when its object is false. Truth and falsehood, in this view, are ultimate, and no account can be given of what makes a proposition true or false.

"If we reject objective falsehood, we have, apart from belief, only *facts*. Beliefs are then complexes of ideas, to which complexes of the objects of the ideas may or may not correspond. When they do correspond the beliefs are true, and are beliefs in facts; when they do not, the beliefs are erroneous, and are beliefs in nothing." (Bertrand Russell, "On the Nature of Truth," *Proceedings of the Aristotelian Society*, n.s. 7 [1906-7], 48-49.)

4. The discussion relies on G. E. Moore's concept theory of meaning and his definition of a proposition as *"what* is apprehended . . . when we understand the meaning of a sentence." A proposition "is a name for what is *expressed* by certain forms of words—those, namely, which, in grammar, are called 'sentences.' It is a name for what is before your mind, when you not only hear or read but *understand* a sentence. It is, in short, the *meaning* of a sentence—what is expressed or conveyed by a sentence." A proposition is "quite a different sort of thing from any image or collection of images . . . [it is] something utterly different from any collection of words or of images of words—something which a collection of words may *mean* or *express*, but which no word or collection of words can possibly *be.*" (*Some Main Problems of Philosophy* [1910-11; first ed., London: George Allen and Unwin, 1953], pp. 58, 259, 72-73.) Richards' critique of the interference between overly visualized imagery and "meaning" in the reading of poetry may be influenced by Moore's distinction. (*Principles of Literary Criticism* [London: Kegan Paul, Trench, Trubner, 1924], chap. 16.)

5. In *Principia Ethica* (Cambridge: Cambridge University Press, 1903) G. E. Moore stated that goodness is "unanalyzable," known by direct intuition, and that there are some things "worth having *purely for their own sakes,*" which are "certain states of consciousness which may be roughly described as the pleasures of human intercourse and the enjoyment of beautiful objects" (p. 188).

6. In the second column of his essay Fry remarks that, however close are the analogies between the methods and aims of art and science, he is doubtful whether "at any point they are identical"; that psychologists must explore "a number of problems" before the field of analogy can be more profitably explored; that given emotional motives, the processes of science are purely intellectual ("mechanical") whereas the processes of art always entail feeling; that pleasure is not a component essential to our perception of the inevitability of relations in a scientific theory whereas pleasure is essential to the perception of aesthetic harmony; that "perhaps" the highest pleasure in art is in fact identical with the highest pleasure in scientific theory, that is, the emotion accompanying "the clear recognition of unity in a complex"; that there *may* be more than one kind of feeling in art. With these positions, excepting the last and possibly the next to last, Richards would at this point be in agreement. On the last Richards would say that there very definitely *is* more than one kind of feeling in art. See "Emotion and Art," essay 2.

2 Emotion and Art

1. William James's concept, first set forward in 1884, was "that the perception of the bodily changes *is* the emotion, not that the changes take

place because of the emotion," thus reversing the traditional assumption with regard to cause and effect. This point of view—more broadly, feeling follows action—was expounded independently a year later by the Danish psychologist C. G. Lange. See J. C. Flugel, *A Hundred Years of Psychology* (London: Duckworth, 1933), pp. 156-157.

2. See note 4 to "Art and Science," essay 1. In these two early essays Richards had already introduced the term "vehicle," which has had considerable currency in his later criticism. See, for example, *The Philosophy of Rhetoric* (New York: Oxford University Press, 1936), pp. 98-103, 120-123; *Interpretation in Teaching* (New York: Harcourt Brace, 1938), pp. 136-138; "Complementarities," essay 12.

3. For example, Clive Bell, *Art* (London: Chatto & Windus, 1914).

3 The Instruments of Criticism: Expression

1. The poem is D. H. Lawrence's "The Little Town at Evening," which appeared in the *Monthly Magazine*, vol. 1, no. 1 (1923). The review is possibly by the editor of the *Athenaeum*, J. Middleton Murry.

2. For the orthodox view, see Benedetto Croce, *Aesthetics as Science of Expression and General Linguistic*, trans. Douglas Ainslie (London: Macmillan, 1909).

3. The British economist and logician William Stanley Jevons (1835-1882).

4 John Watson's *Behaviorism*

1. "We dispossess the Inner Man," B. F. Skinner remarks, "by replacing him with genetic and environmental variables" (*Contingencies of Reinforcement: A Theoretical Analysis* [New York: Appleton-Crofts, 1969], p. 273).

2. Kurt Koffka, *The Growth of the Mind: An Introduction to Child-Psychology*, trans. Robert Morris Ogden (London: Kegan Paul, Trench, Trubner, 1924).

3. E. J. Kempf's studies on personality theory are treated in detail in Ronald Grey Gordon, *Personality* (London: Kegan Paul, Trench, Trubner, 1926). Richards refers to the work of H. W. Frink, *Morbid Fears and Compulsions: Their Psychology and Psycho-Analytical Treatment* (New York: Moffat, Yard, 1918).

5 Belief

1. H. G. Wells, "The Scepticism of the Instrument," in *A Modern Utopia* (London: Chapman and Hall, 1905), p. 388.

2. See I. A. Richards, *How to Read a Page: A Course in Effective Reading, with an Introduction to a Hundred Great Words* (1942; Boston: Beacon Press, 1959).

3. James cites with approval the British social scientist and literary critic Walter Bagehot's definition of belief as the "emotion of conviction,"

and psychologizes the belief-state as "a sort of feeling more allied to the emotions than anything else"; consent is "a manifestation of our active nature"; "What characterizes both consent and belief is the cessation of theoretic action, through the advent of an idea which is inwardly stable, and fills the mind solidly to the exclusion of contradictory ideas"; "consent and belief . . . connected with subsequent practical activity" (*The Principles of Psychology* [New York, 1890], II, 283-284).

6 Between Truth and Truth

1. In his "Beauty Is Truth" (*Symposium*, 1 [1930], 466-501), J. Middleton Murry focuses on the last lines of Keats's "Ode on a Grecian Urn," considering various interpretations that have been advanced. He takes exception to Robert Bridges' view that the poem is a statement on the supremacy of art over nature and cites widely divergent comments of Sir Arthur Quiller-Couch, T. S. Eliot, and Richards. According to Murry, Keats intended the urn to be considered emblematic of all Greek life and of its philosophy. Moreover, with its encircling frieze depicting figures frozen in the midst of activity, the urn "is the symbol of a possibility of vision." "All human action, all human experience, can be thus arrested in enchantment." No words can adequately reveal this vision of pure being; the phrase "Beauty is Truth, Truth Beauty,' '" with the force of the poetic context behind it, is Keats's attempt.

The function of art, as Murry expands beyond the poem, is to record "many moments in many minds of lucid contemplation . . . Art purifies the world of existence of its animal impulse, so that we may retain a possibility of a different vision," that is, a vision of pure being. In an appendix to the essay, Murry criticizes Richards' concept of a pseudo-statement, which had been introduced in *The Meaning of Meaning* (chap. 10) in 1923 and given its name in *Science and Poetry* in 1926. Murry maintains that the term is an inadequate and misleading coinage, concluding that the "cleavage into 'pseudo-statements' and 'true-statements' . . . does a certain violence to the facts." For Richards' definition, see *Science and Poetry* (London: Kegan Paul, Trench, Trubner, 1926), pp. 58-59: "A pseudo-statement is 'true' if it suits and serves some attitude or links together attitudes which on other grounds are desirable. This kind of truth is so opposed to scientific 'truth' that it is a pity to use so similar a word, but at present it is difficult to avoid the malpractice . . . A pseudo-statement is a form of words which is justified entirely by its effect in releasing or organizing our impulses."

2. "The Primrose Bank," in *Selected Poems of John Clare*, ed. Geoffrey Grigson (London: Routledge and Kegan Paul, 1950), p. 167: "With its little brimming eye / And its yellow rim so pale / And its crimp and curdled leaf— / Who can pass its beauties by?" Catullus 5: "Soles occidere et redire possunt: / Nobis cum semel occidit brevis lux / Nox est perpetua una dormienda." ("Suns may set and rise again; but we, when once our brief

light has set, must sleep through a perpetual night"; Walter K. Kelly, trans., *The Works of Catullus and Tibullus and the Vigil of Venus* [London, 1834], p. 12.) Meister Eckhart, sermon 94: "There is something in the soul wherein God simply is, and according to philosophers this is a nameless thing and has no proper name. It neither has nor is a definite entity, for it is not this nor that nor here nor there; what it is it is from another wherewith it is the same; the one streams into it and it into the one." (*Works*, ed. Franz Pfeiffer and trans. C. De B. Evans [New York: Lucis, 1924?], p. 235.)

3. *Mencius*, trans. D. C. Lau (Baltimore: Penguin Books, 1970), book 2, part A, p. 77.

4. Francis Bacon, *The Advancement of Learning*, ed. W. A. Wright (Oxford, 1885), p. 100 (book 2, 4.2).

5. I have been unable to locate the source of this reference.

6. William Empson does not consider the passage in *Seven Types of Ambiguity* (London: Chatoo & Windus, 1930); he discusses Keats's "Ode to Melancholy" as an illustration of the seventh type (pp. 205-206, 214-217).

7 Max Eastman's *The Literary Mind: Its Place in an Age of Science*

1. Irving Babbitt (1865-1933), professor of French and comparative literature at Harvard University, who with Paul Elmer More led the New Humanist movement, which was based on Arnoldian humanism with a highly ethical and rationalist orientation. The movement had gathered strength after the First World War but was waning at the time of Babbitt's death. (See Harry Levin, *Irving Babbitt and the Teaching of Literature*, The Irving Babbitt Inaugural Lecture, 1960 [Cambridge, Mass.: Harvard University, 1961], and Austin Warren, "Paul Elmer More," *Connections* [Ann Arbor: University of Michigan Press, 1970], pp. 129-151.) For Eastman the New Humanists are easy targets, perhaps too easy, and are once described as men who "have not even made up their minds whether they believe in God or not" (p. 32).

2. Eastman, *Literary Mind*, p. 32. The passages cited by Eastman are from Irving Babbitt, *Democracy and Leadership* (Boston and New York: Houghton Mifflin, 1924), pp. 212, 203, 272-273, 208-209, 200, 196.

3. Eastman, *Literary Mind*, p. 46. Eliot's "attack" appeared in his "Commentary," *New Criterion*, 4 (1926), 6.

4. Eastman, *Literary Mind*, p. 25. Gorham B. Munson (1896-1969), literary critic, whom Eastman labels an "American propagandist of modernism" (p. 86).

5. Ibid., p. 17. "Suppose that, instead of knowing all about Thomas Lodge's *Defense of Poetry* in 1579, and Sir Philip Sidney's in 1583, and about Ben Jonson's *Discoveries* and Sir William Davenant's theories in his Preface to *Gondibert*—suppose that Miss Sitwell knew a little something about the senses and the brain" (p. 17).

6. Ibid., p. 19.

7. Ibid., p. 7.

8. Ibid., p. 254.

9. Ibid., p. ix.

10. Although Eastman is critical of Richards in his "Note" (pp. 297-317), he elsewhere praises Richards as a "psychologist who teaches literature— the sole living example of the long-awaited species" (p. 57). Yet even "pioneer" Richards, Eastman warns, is haunted by the Arnoldian tradition. "He has brought with him, it seems to me, and built into his psychology of poetry, a relic of the literary man's reluctance to face the stark character of the division of labor between poetry and knowledge. Although acknowledging that poetry is not knowledge, he wants still to hold for it the high role of guiding our acts and adjustments. He thus becomes, by inadvertence, the advocate of a sentimentalism in poetry and a deprecation of intelligence in morals and politics, which I believe are foreign to his real nature. He has still to relinquish this last thread that binds poetry to knowledge" (pp. 292-293).

11. Percy William Bridgman (1882-1962), American physicist, philosopher, and Nobel laureate. Eastman challenges Richards' and Ogden's Baconian, confidently inductive conception of science and introduces Bridgman's operationalism as a means of undermining it. For Bridgman, the role of the experimenter himself is problematic since the "proof" of whatever "is" depends upon the operational conditions that the experimenter devises for the testing of whatever "is." The mental activity, including emotion and attitude, of the experimenter, thus, to some extent, may play a role in developing operations and experiments and so will indirectly enter into the definition of whatever "is." For Richards and Ogden, however, emotive attitudes may play a role in developing operations, but the test of truth of those operations and experiments is the adequacy of their description and explanation of hard scientific data, not the satisfaction of or incidental pleasure given to the particular experimenter's will or psyche. The passages cited by Eastman are taken from Percy William Bridgman, *The Logic of Modern Physics* (New York: Macmillan, 1927), pp. 2, 5, 7. For Richards and Ogden on science see *The Meaning of Meaning*, 8th ed. (New York: Harcourt Brace, 1946), pp. 158-159 and chap. 10.

12. Sir James Hopwood Jeans (1877-1946), British physicist and astronomer. His *The Universe around Us* (New York: Macmillan, 1929) is cited by Eastman on p. 253.

8 Multiple Definition

1. Basic English was designed by C. K. Ogden as an international auxiliary language, a second language "(in science, commerce, travel) for all who do not already speak English." It was announced, with its list of 850 words, in "The Universal Language," *Psyche*, 9 (January 1929), 1-9.

Ogden's purpose was to devise a simplified version of standard English for fact-stating situations that could be easily learned and quickly taught and that would be idiomatic, "clear and precise at the level for which it is designed." It is, one should note, an introductory level of English, which places no bar on developing beyond that level to more sophisticated literary uses. Richards played a key role in the Basic English movement from the outset, particularly in China. He wrote a general introduction in *Basic English and Its Uses* (London: Kegan Paul, Trench, Trubner, 1943) and contributed to *The General Basic English Dictionary* (London: Evans Brothers, 1940). He also translated edited versions of Plato's *Republic* (*The Republic of Plato* [New York: W. W. Norton, 1942]), Homer's *Iliad* (*The Wrath of Achilles* [New York: W. W. Norton, 1950]), and the Platonic dialogues on the death of Socrates (*Why So, Socrates? A Dramatic Version of Plato's Dialogues: Euthyphro, Apology, Crito, Phaedo* [Cambridge: Cambridge University Press, 1964]) in expanded versions of Basic. Basic was later called Everyman's English.

2. Joseph Butler, "Preface," in *Sermons* (London, 1729), p. xxix.

3. "When I wrote that passage I was consciously setting what I hoped would be an amusing and instructive problem for any likely well-read Reader. They are all landmarks or commonplaces of Poetics. If you can tell those who have urged the identification of each of them, that this would spoil the exercise. (Say I belong to an earlier, pre-Ph.D. epoch when such references were frowned on as leading only to exam-cramming: not conducive to reflection and fruitful re-reading.)" (Richards, personal communication, March 4, 1976).

4. For example, in Henri Bergson, *Matière et mémoire* (Paris, 1896), chap. 1.

5. "I regard that alone as genuine *knowledge* which, sooner or later, will reappear as *power.*" Quoted in Alice D. Snyder, *Coleridge on Logic and Learning with Selections from the Unpublished Manuscripts* (New Haven: Yale University Press, 1929), p. 73; the passage is from "The Science and System of Logic," *Fraser's Magazine*, 12 (December 1835), 629. Richards cites the passage at least three times in his writings: *Coleridge on Imagination* 3rd ed. (London: Routledge and Kegan Paul, 1962), p. 127; *How to Read a Page* (New York: W. W. Norton, 1942), p. 38; "Introduction," in *The Portable Coleridge* (New York: Viking Press, 1950), p. 44.

9 Meaning and Change of Meaning

1. Although some writers distinguished between "semasiology," now obsolescent, and "semantics," the words effectively remained synonyms (Allen Walter Reed, "An Account of the Word 'Semantics,' " *Word*, 4 [1948], 82).

2. Wilhelm Wundt, German psychologist and philosopher (1832-1920), developed the first psychological laboratory. In 1920 Bronislaw Malinowski included Wundt's *Die Sprache* (Leipzig, 1900) among those

works on psychology and language that give "insufficient attention . . . to
Semantics" ("Classificatory Particles in the Language of the Kiriwina,"
Bulletin of the School of Oriental Studies of the London Institute, 1, pt. 4
[1920], 35).

3. Hermann Paul, *Prinzipien der Sprachgeschichte*, 3rd ed. (Halle:
M. Niemeyer, 1898), Heinrich Gomperz, *Weltanschauungslehre*, vols. 1, 2
(Jena and Leipzig: Diederichs, 1908), and *Uber Sinn und Sinngebilde, Verstehen und Erklären* (Tubingen: Mohr, 1929).

4. Stern, *Meaning and Change of Meaning*, p. 163.

5. Ibid., p. 342.

6. Ibid., p. 70.

7. See above, pp. 76-77.

8. Stern, *Meaning and Change of Meaning*, p. 173.

9. Jean Piaget, *The Language and Thought of the Child*, trans. Marjorie Gabain (London: Kegan Paul, Trench, Trubner, 1932), p. 9.

10 Emotive Language Still

1. In a prefatory note to this article Cleanth Brooks wrote that
Richards' "distinction (made in *The Meaning of Meaning*) between the
'referential' aspect of words and the 'emotive' seemed to split in two, not
merely the world of words, but the universe itself, wrenching asunder fact
and fiction, science and poetry, thought and emotion . . . His present essay
may be considered an elaborate footnote on that distinction: an exploration of some of its implications; a caution against making it oversimple and
brittle. If it represents, as it does, an extension and a development of his
general position, it is only fair to point out that it is not a startlingly new
development. The essay may well send us back to read more carefully and
thoughtfully *Science and Poetry* and *The Principles of Literary Criticism*."
(*Yale Review*, 39 [1949], 108.)

2. Preface to *Lyrical Ballads*: poetry "is the impassioned expression
which is in the countenance of all Science."

3. Shakespeare, sonnet 66. Richards' punctuation is retained.

4. John Von Neumann, American (born in Budapest) scientist, economist, and philosopher (1903-1957), whose *Theory of Games and Economic Behavior* (which he wrote with Oscar Morgenstern) appeared in
1944 and whose work was highly influential in the development of the
electronic computer.

5. Charles L. Stevenson, *Ethics and Language* (New Haven: Yale
University Press, 1944), p. 80.

6. Matthew 10:34.

7. William Blake, preface to "Milton."

11 Semantics

1. In 1942 Richards introduced the use of specialized quotation marks.
Ordinary marks were, he believed, being overworked by too many over-

lapping responsibilities. With seven "specialized" marks, one could take best advantage of "this too serviceable writing device." "It gives us a compact means of commenting on the handling of language—more comprehensible, less ambiguous, and less distracting than the usual devices of parenthesis, qualification, and discussion. I believe it will abridge both the optional and the intellectual labor of the reader." (*How to Read a Page: A Course in Efficient Reading with an Introduction to a Hundred Great Words* [1942; Boston: Beacon Press, 1959], pp. 66-70.) In subsequent books Richards used specialized quotation marks, but in 1973 he expressed disappointment that his innovation had been completely ignored. (Jane Watkins, "Conversation: I. A. Richards," *Harvard Magazine*, 76, no. 1 [September 1973], p. 56).

2. Charles E. Osgood and Thomas Sebeok, *Psycholinguistics: A Survey of Theory and Research Problems* (Bloomington: Indiana University Press, 1965), p. 4

3. "Language about language must share some of the complexities of all language" (Charles L. Stevenson, *Ethics and Language* [New Haven: Yale University Press, 1944], p. 80).

12 Complementarities

1. Shakespeare's Welsh nobleman says of himself: "And bring him out that is but woman's son / Can trace me in the tedious ways of art / And hold me pace in deep experiments" (*I Henry IV*, 3.1.47-49).

2. For a close parallel to this statement see below, p. 257.

3. G. E. Moore, "A Reply to My Critics," in *The Philosophy of G. E. Moore*, ed. P. A. Schilpp (Evanston: Northwestern University Press, 1942), p. 535.

4. Vida Carver, ed., *C. A. Mace: A Symposium* (London: Methuen, 1962), pp. 70, 90, 46, 56.

5. C. A. Mace, "Some Trends in the Philosophy of Mind," in *British Philosophy in the Mid-Century: A Cambridge Symposium*, ed. C. A. Mace, 2nd ed. (London: George Allen and Unwin, 1966), pp. 104-105.

6. Niels Bohr, *Atomic Physics and Human Knowledge* (New York: John Wiley, 1958), pp. 1, 5-6.

7. Shakespeare, *Measure for Measure*, 2.2.118-121.

8. Bohr, *Atomic Physics and Human Knowledge*, p. 11.

9. Ibid., pp. 90, 2, 11, 21. Richards recalls a remark made by Mace in *The Psychology of Study* (London: Methuen, 1929).

10. I. A. Richards, *Speculative Instruments* (New York: Harcourt Brace, 1955), p. 114.

11. Louis de Broglie, "Sur la complémentarité des idées d'individu et de système," *Dialectica*, 2 (1948), 326: "deux conceptions en apparence incompatibles peuvent représenter chacune un aspect de la vérité et qu'elles puissent servir tour à tour à représenter les faits sans entrer jamais en conflit direct."

12. Niels Bohr, "On the Notions of Causality and Complementarity," *Dialectica*, 2 (1948), 318.

13. G. E. Moore, *Principia Ethica* (Cambridge: Cambridge University Press, 1903), p. vii.

14. See, for example, Richards' *How to Read a Page: A Course in Effective Reading, with an Introduction to a Hundred Great Words* (1942; Boston: Beacon Press, 1959), pp. 180-185.

15. C. A. Mace, "On How We Know That Material Things Exist," in *The Philosophy of G. E. Moore*, pp. 294-295.

16. W. B. Yeats, *The Collected Poems* (London: Macmillan, 1965), p. 42.

17. F. H. Bradley, *Essays on Truth and Reality* (Oxford: Clarendon Press, 1914), p. 218.

18. Gilbert Murray, *Five Stages of Greek Religion* (Oxford: Clarendon Press, 1925), pp. 100-101. Murray's footnote to the passage offers an ancient "complementarity": "Cf. the beautiful defence of idols by Maximus of Tyre, Or. viii (in Wilamowitz's *Lesebuch*, ii, 338 ff.). I quote the last paragraph: 'God Himself, the father and fashioner of all that is, older than the Sun or the Sky, greater than time and eternity and all the flow of being, is unnameable by any lawgiver, unutterable by any voice, not to be seen by any eye. But we, being unable to apprehend His essence, use the help of sounds and names and pictures, of beaten gold and ivory and silver, of plants and rivers, mountain-peaks and torrents, yearning for the knowledge of Him, and in our weakness naming all that is beautiful in this world after His nature—just as happens to earthly lovers. To them the most beautiful sight will be the actual lineaments of the beloved . . . Why should I further examine and pass judgment about Images? Let men know what is divine . . . let them know: that is all. If a Greek is stirred to the remembrance of God by the art of Pheidias, an Egyptian by paying worship to animals, another man by a river, another by fire—I have no anger for their divergences; only let them know, let them love, let them remember.'"

19. In *The Philosophy of Rhetoric* (New York: Oxford University Press, 1936), pp. 132-136. But "vehicle" was introduced as early as 1919; see "Art and Science," essay 1.

20. The passage does not appear, however, in a printed version of a lecture on Donne read at Princeton University in the spring of 1942, "The Interactions of Words," in *The Language of Poetry* ed. Allen Tate (Princeton: Princeton University Press, 1942), pp. 65-87. See, however, Richards' "Donne: The Extasie" in *Master Poems of the English Language*, ed. Oscar Williams (New York: Trident, 1966), p. 116: " 'defects of loneliness': chief of which is ignorance of what we are."

21. *Philosophy of G. E. Moore*, p. 677.

22. I. A. Richards, *Internal Colloquies: Poems and Plays* (New York: Harcourt Brace, 1971), pp. 162-169.

23. Werner Jaeger, *Paideia: The Ideals of Greek Culture*, trans. Gilbert Highet (New York: Oxford University Press, 1939), II, 198-365. Richards

and Jaeger arrived at Harvard University in 1939 and were both designated University Professors in 1944.

24. Alexander Faulkner Shand (1858-1936), British psychologist and philosopher, author of *The Foundations of Character* (London: Macmillan, 1914).

25. Samuel Taylor Coleridge, *Biographia Literaria*, ed. J. Shawcross (London: Oxford University Press, 1907), II, 12; "their irremissive, though gentle and unnoticed, controul".

13 The Enlightening Eye

1. "The Embankment (The Fantasia of a Fallen Gentleman on a Cold, Bitter Night)," in Alun R. Jones, *The Life and Opinions of T. E. Hulme* (Boston: Beacon Press, 1960), p. 159.

2. Arthur Rimbaud to Paul Demeny, May 15, 1871, quoted in Denis Donoghue, *Thieves of Fire* (London: Faber and Faber, 1973), p. 87.

3. In his "Ode: Intimations of Immortality from Recollections of Early Childhood," Wordsworth writes:

> Our birth is but a sleep and a forgetting:
> The Soul that rises with us, our life's Star,
>   Hath had elsewhere its setting,
>   And cometh from afar:
>   Not in entire forgetfulness,
>   And not in utter nakedness,
> But trailing clouds of glory do we come
>   From God, who is our home:
> Heaven lies about us in our infancy!

4. Justus Buchler, *The Main of Light: On the Concept of Poetry* (New York: Oxford University Press, 1974), p. 4.

5. Ibid., p. 94.

6. Ibid., pp. 93, 95-96.

7. Ibid., p. 97.

8. Ibid., pp. 101-102.

9. "On Linguistic Aspects of Translation," in *On Translation*, ed. Reuben A. Brower (Cambridge, Mass.: Harvard University Press, 1959), pp. 232-233. In a note to this sentence Jakobson refers his reader to John Dewey, "Peirce's Theory of Linguistic Signs, Thought, and Meaning," *Journal of Philosophy*, 43 (1946), 91.

10. Buchler, *Main of Light*, pp. 103-104.

11. Ibid., p. 6.

12. Ibid., p. 152.

13. Ibid., p. 14.

14. "Wörringer would not have gone far with 'abstraction' without recourse to 'empathy'; Nietzsche has Dionysiac clamour answered, successfully or not, by Apollonian order; Jung's *Psychological Types* is

largely a description of two, introspective and extrovert. If you emphasize one aspect, you are bound to look at its opposite." (Denis Donoghue, *Thieves of Fire* [New York: Oxford University Press, 1974], pp. 16-17.)

15. Buchler, *Main of Light*, p. 167.

16. Donoghue, *Thieves of Fire*, p. 46. "There is also a curious ambivalence in the relation between Prometheus, Satan, and Christ. Kenneth Burke has remarked that 'the Greek Lucifer had brought to man a part of divinity, but had brought it *divisively*, as an offence against the gods.' This is true, even though Prometheus's motive is good, from the human standpoint. Satan also brought to man a part of divinity, the promise of divine knowledge, though his motive was impure. In Christianity, as Burke says, 'Christ had become revised as an unambiguously benign Lucifer, bringing light as a *representative* of the Godhead.' In Prometheus and Satan the divine part is torn away from the whole, and the act is sacrilege: in Christ, it is 'integral with its source,' and the act is redemptive." (Ibid., p. 44.) The passages cited from Burke are from *The Philosophy of Literary Form*, 2nd ed. (Baton Rouge: Louisiana State University Press, 1967), pp. 59-60.

17. Ibid., p. 46.

18. Ibid., p. 50.

19. Buchler, *Main of Light*, p. 12.

20. Donoghue, *Thieves of Fire*, p. 41.

21. Ibid., p. 19.

22. " 'Which is within all things, Yājñavalkya?' 'You cannot see the seer of seeing, you cannot hear the hearer of hearing, you cannot think the thinker of thinking, you cannot understand the understander of understanding. He is your self which is in all things. Everything else is of evil.' Thereupon Usasta Cākrāyana kept silent." (*Brhad-āranyaka Upanisad*, in *The Principal Upanisads*, ed. and trans. S. Radhakrishnan [London, George Allen and Unwin, 1953] 3.4.2.)

23. Donoghue, *Thieves of Fire*, pp. 25-26.

24. Samuel Taylor Coleridge, *Biographia Literaria*, ed. J. Shawcross (London: Oxford University Press, 1907), I, 202; II, 12.

25. Samuel Taylor Coleridge, *Aids to Reflection*, in *The Complete Works*, ed. W. G. T. Shedd (New York: Harper, 1884), I, 119-120. (Richards' italics)

14 Gerard Hopkins

1. Hopkins to R. W. Dixon, October 5, 1878, quoted in Gerard Manley Hopkins, *Poems*, ed. Robert Bridges (London: Humphrey Milord, 1918), p. 104.

2. Ibid.

3. Robert Bridges.

4. *Poems*, p. 97.

5. Hopkins to Bridges, April 22, 1879, quoted in *Poems*, pp. 97-98.

6. "To seem the stranger lies my lot, my life . . .," *Poems*, p. 66.

7. "My own heart let me have more pity on; let . . .," *Poems*, p. 67.

8. *Poems*, p. 62.

9. Ibid., p. 63.

10. "The Leaden Echo and the Golden Echo": "so cogged, so cumbered" (*Poems*, p. 55).

15 The God of Dostoevsky

1. See "Jesus' Other Life," essay 22, a review of George Moore's *The Brook Kerith*.

2. J. Middleton Murry, *Fyodor Dostoevsky: A Critical Study* (1916; reprint ed., New York: Russell and Russell, 1966), pp. 28, 200.

3. Dostoevsky to Mme N. D. Fonvisin, March 1854, in *Letters of Fyodor Michailovitch Dostoevsky to His Family and Friends*, trans. Ethel Colburn Mayne (London: Chatto & Windus, 1914), p. 71.

4. *The Possessed*, part 2, chap. 1, "Night," sec. 7.

5. Ibid.

6. Murry, *Dostoevsky*, pp. 43-44.

7. Dostoevsky to Mlle N. N., April 11, 1880, in *Letters*, p. 249.

16 A Passage to Forster

1. *The Longest Journey*, chap. 23; *Where Angels Fear to Tread*, chap. 7; *A Passage to India*, chaps. 14, 22.

2. The passages occur in the middle and at the end of chapter 19.

17 Nineteen Hundred and Now

1. Alessandro, conti di Cagliostro (1743-1795), Sicilian magician, adventurer, and charlatan. The year before Richards had reviewed W. R. H. Trowbridge, *Cagliostro: The Splendour and Misery of a Master of Magic* (London: Chapman and Hall, 1910; George Allen and Unwin, 1926), in "Count Cagliostro," *Forum*, 76 (1926), 473-474. *Buncombe*, presumably "speechmaking for the purpose of winning the approval of a constituency." According to the *Dictionary of American Politics* (ed. E. C. Smith and A. J. Zurcher [New York: Barnes and Noble, 1957]), "the word originated from the statement of Felix Walker, representing the North Carolina district which included Buncombe County, that he wished 'to make a speech for Buncombe' during the later stages of the debate on the Missouri Compromise, 1820, when other members of the House of Representatives were impatiently calling for the question," p. 47.

2. Tolstoy, *What Is Art?* trans. Aylmer Maude (London: W. Scott, 1899), chap. 16.

3. James's radical empiricism, his "stream of consciousness," and his critique of abstract logical relations as explanations of mentality have their parallels in Bergson's philosophy. As he wrote: " 'Dive back into the flux itself then,' Bergson tells us, 'if you want to *know* reality, that flux which Platonism, in its strange belief that only the immutable is excellent, has always spurned: turn your face towards sensation, that fleshbound thing

which rationalism has always loaded with abuse.' " (Quoted in John Pass-
more, *A Hundred Years of Philosophy* [London: Duckworth, 1957], p.
108.)

4. Ralph Waldo Emerson, "Give All to Love": "Heartily know, /
When half-gods go, / The gods arrive."

5. In *Science and Poetry* (1926) Richards criticized Yeats for turning
"to a world of symbolic phantasmagoria about which he was desperately
uncertain. The uncertainty came in part from the adoption, as a technique
of inspiration, of the use of trance, of dissociated states of consciousness.
The revelations given in these dissociated states are insufficiently connected with normal experience." (2nd ed. [London: Kegan Paul, Trench,
Trubner, 1935], p. 81.) However, in *Coleridge on Imagination* (1934)
Richards reversed himself, admitting "I did not properly appreciate Mr.
Yeats' later work. I can plead that I wrote before *The Tower* was published." (3rd ed. [London: Routledge and Kegan Paul, 1962], p. 207.) And
in a note to the second edition of *Science and Poetry* (1935) Richards
wrote: "Who would have foreseen before *The Tower* Mr. Yeats' development into the greatest poet of our age or the miracles in *Songs for Music
Perhaps?*"

18 Herbert Read's *English Prose Style*

1. Sir Herbert Read (1893-1968), British critic, poet, and art historian,
one of the principal exponents of the modernist movement in art in Great
Britain. In 1919-20 Eliot contributed reviews and poems to *Arts and
Letters*, a literary magazine that Read assisted in editing. See Herbert Read,
"T. S. E.—A Memoir," in *T. S. Eliot: The Man and His Work*, ed. Allen
Tate (New York: Delacorte, 1966), pp. 11-37.

2. See "The Instruments of Criticism: Expression," essay 3, for a brief
critique of the Crocean aesthetic.

3. "Poetry" in the 1928 text.

4. Sir Henry Maine (1822-1888), British jurist and legal historian.

19 Notes on the Practice of Interpretation

1. To the British critic Montgomery Belgion's "What Is Criticism?"
Criterion, 10 (1930), 118-139.

2. *Principles of Literary Criticism* (London: Kegan Paul, Trench,
Trubner, 1924), p. 219.

3. "Doctrine in Poetry," in *Practical Criticism* (London: Kegan Paul,
Trench, Trubner, 1929), pp. 280-281. "Interferences of all kinds—notably
the desire to make the poem 'original,' 'striking,' or 'poetic'—are, of
course, the usual cause of insincerity in this sense," Richards concludes. "A
sense which ought not, it may be remarked, to impute blame to the author,
unless we are willing to agree that all men who are not good poets are
therefore blameworthy in a high degree."

4. "But between these two extreme wings of the psychological forces there is the comparatively neglected and unheard-of middle body, the cautious, traditional, academic, semi-philosophical psychologists who have been profiting from the vigorous manoeuvres of the advanced wings and are now much more ready than they were twenty years ago to take a hand in the application of the science. The general reader, whose ideas as to the methods and endeavours of psychologists derive more from the popularisers of Freud or from the Behaviourists than from students of Stout or Ward, needs perhaps some assurance that it is possible to combine an interest and faith in psychological inquiries with a due appreciation of the complexity of poetry."

20 Lawrence as a Poet

1. Coleridge to John Thelwall, December 17, 1796, in *The Letters of Samuel Taylor Coleridge*, ed. Ernest Hartley Coleridge (Boston and New York: Houghton Mifflin, 1895), I, 197.

21 Literature, Oral-Aural and Optical

1. H. M. Chadwick succeeded to the professorship of Anglo-Saxon at Cambridge in 1912. Among his works are *The Origins of the English Nation* (Cambridge: Cambridge University Press, 1907) and *The Heroic Age* (Cambridge: Cambridge University Press, 1912).

2. See Eric Havelock's *Preface to Plato* (Cambridge, Mass.: Harvard University Press, 1963), which, though postdating Richards' essay, presents his argument in its most complete form.

3. John Burnet, "The Socratic Doctrine of the Soul," *Proceedings of the British Academy*, 7 (1915-16), 235-259.

4. Plato, *Euthyphro, Apology, Crito, Phaedo, Phaedrus*, trans. Harold North Fowler, Loeb Classical Library (Cambridge, Mass.: Harvard University Press, 1966), pp. 561-571.

5. Rudyard Kipling, "The Fabulists, 1914-1918."

22 Jesus' Other Life

1. *Biographia Literaria*, ed. J. Shawcross (London: Oxford University Press, 1907), II, 12.

23 Beauty and Truth

1. R. W. Stallman, "Keats the Apollinian," *University of Toronto Quarterly*, 16 (January 1947), 156; excerpted in *The Critic's Notebook*, ed. R. W. Stallman (Minneapolis: University of Minneapolis Press, 1950), p. 189.

2. Geoffrey Tillotson, *Essays in Criticism and Research* (Cambridge: Cambridge University Press, 1942), pp. xiv-xv. G. St. Quintin's letter is

quoted from the *Times Literary Supplement*, February 5, 1938, p. 92. Tillotson continues: "Mr. St Quintin's 'alternative suggestion' must be given
its place in any discussion of the text of the poem. This is not the occasion
for any such discussion, but it is already clear that Mr. St. Quintin's discovery helps to confirm the authority of the text of 'Poems' 1820. Unfortunately the latest edition prints the text as it appeared in 'The Annals of
the Fine Arts,' a text which does not employ any quotation marks. If Keats
were responsible for the text in the 'Annals,' it seems that he deliberately
revised the pointing for 'Poems' 1820 in the hope, unfulfilled for over a century, that quotation marks would make his meaning clear. Mr. St. Quintin's understanding of the pointing, and therefore his discriminating of the
choice of meanings for 'ye,' and therefore his choice of the better one—this
chain of deduction has relieved Keats of a charge of pretentiousness which
everything else he wrote renders him unlikely to have deserved. If the Ode
cannot be allowed to end as well as it began and continued—the grammar
of the close is not self-evident enough to be happy—Keats is at least found
writing an admirable sense."

  3. Shakespeare, sonnet 60.

  4. Cf. Douglas Bush, *John Keats: Selected Poems and Letters* (Boston:
Houghton Mifflin, 1959), p. 350, and W. J. Bate, *John Keats* (Cambridge,
Mass.: Harvard University Press, 1963), p. 516.

  5. John Middleton Murry, *Keats* (New York: Noonday Press, 1955), p.
217. The first edition, entitled *Studies in Keats*, was published in 1930.

  6. "Stanzas for Music" (1816).

  7. *The Dialogues of Plato*, trans. B. Jowett (New York: Random House,
1937), p. 335.

  8. *Plato's Republic*, ed. and trans. I. A. Richards (Cambridge: Cambridge University Press, 1966), p. 118.

  9. Murry, *Keats*, p. 225.

24 The Conduct of Verse

  1. Robert Bridges, *The Testament of Beauty* (New York: Oxford
University Press, 1929), p. 9.

  2. George Herbert, "The H. Scriptures (II)"; discussed by Vendler on p.
198.

  3. A. E. Housman, *The Name and Nature of Poetry* (New York:
Macmillan, 1933), p. 33, quoted in Vendler, *Herbert*, pp. 4-5.

  4. *Coleridge's Miscellaneous Criticism*, ed. Thomas Middleton Raysor
(Cambridge, Mass.: Harvard University Press, 1936), p. 244; T. S. Eliot,
"George Herbert," *Spectator*, 148 (March 12, 1932), 360; both quoted in
Vendler, *Herbert*, p. 4.

  5. *Atalanta in Calydon* (London: Chatto & Windus, 1894), p. 43.

  6. Richards was working on an essay on de la Mare at the time of this
review. The piece was published as "Walter de la Mare," *New Republic*,
January 31, 1976, pp. 31-33. "Music Unheard" (*The Complete Poems of*

Walter de la Mare [London: Faber and Faber, 1969], p. 116) is reprinted by permission of the publisher.

7. Vendler, *Herbert,* p. 5.

8. For reflections on this theme see I. A. Richards, "Jakobson's Shakespeare: The Subliminal Structures of a Sonnet," a review of Roman Jakobson, *Shakespeare's Verbal Art in "Th'expence of Spirit"* (The Hague: Mouton, 1969), in *Times Literary Supplement,* May 28, 1970, 589-590; reprinted in Richards, *Poetries: Their Media and Ends,* ed. Trevor Eaton (The Hague: Mouton, 1974), pp. 39-49, under the title "Linguistics into Poetics."

25 The Lure of High Mountaineering

1. Blake, "The Mental Traveller."

2. For Richards' other writings on mountaineering, see the articles by him and his wife, Dorothy E. Pilley, in the *Alpine Journal*: "The North-East Arête of the Jungfrau and Other Traverses," November 1923, and "The North Ridge of the Dent Blanche," November 1931. In her autobiographical *Climbing Days* (London: Secker and Warbury, 1935) Mrs. Richards describes the progress of their major climbs and many others; she brings the record up to date in a "Retrospection" to the second edition (1965). On December 8, 1975, at the annual meeting of the Alpine Club of London Richards presented an address entitled "Mountains and Mountaineering as Symbols," forthcoming in the *Alpine Journal*. For more on Richards and mountaineering see Janet Adam Smith, "Fare Forward, Voyagers!" in *I. A. Richards: Essays in His Honor,* ed. Reuben Brower, Helen Vendler, and John Hollander (New York: Oxford University Press, 1973), pp. 307-317.

26 The Secret of "Feedforward"

1. Coleridge to John Thelwall, December 17, 1796, in *The Letters of Samuel Taylor Coleridge,* ed. Ernest Hartley Coleridge (Boston and New York: Houghton Mifflin, 1895), I, 197.

2. It was published by W. W. Norton, New York, in 1970.

3. Richards later admitted to being unable to find his source and, quite possibly, to bringing together on his own two Coleridgean words. (See p. 112.)

4. "Gomeril," or "gomeral," means "fool." " 'Why,' said he, 'I have proved myself a gomeral this night.' " (R. L. Stevenson, *Kidnapped* [1886], chap. 20.) Richards refers to the sequel of *Kidnapped, Catriona* (1893).

27 An Interview

1. Richards discusses his association with G. E. Moore and a meeting with Wittgenstein in an interview with Reuben Brower in *I. A. Richards: Essays in His Honor,* ed. Reuben Brower, Helen Vendler, and John

Hollander (New York: Oxford University Press, 1973), pp. 20, 26-27.

2. J. McT. E. McTaggart (1866-1925), British idealist philosopher, Fellow of Trinity College, Cambridge. McTaggart's "Time is unreal" was one of the objects of attack among the younger generation of realists such as Russell and Moore. McTaggart was Richards' first supervisor in moral sciences at Cambridge.

3. David Hilbert (1862-1943), German mathematician and logician.

4. Anton Marty (1847-1914), German philosopher of language and psychology. See Anton Marty, *Psyche und Sprachstruktur*, ed. Otto Funke (Bern: A. Francke, 1940), pp. 198-206.

5. The book did not materialize immediately, but several essays appeared subsequent to the interview on this specific problem: "On Reading," *Michigan Quarterly*, 9 (1970), 3-6, 24-25, reprinted in "Instructional Engineering," in *The Written Word* (Rowley, Mass.: Newbury House, 1974); "The Future of Reading," a speech delivered before the American Academy of Arts and Sciences, May 13, 1970, reprinted in *The Written Word*; and "Functions of and Factors in Language," *Journal of Literary Semantics*, 1 (1972), 25-40, reprinted in I. A. Richards, *Poetries: Their Media and Ends*, ed. Trevor Eaton (The Hague: Mouton, 1974). Later Richards and Christine Gibson published *Techniques in Language Control* (Rowley, Mass.: Newbury House, 1974).

6. *Basic English: International Second Language*, ed. E. C. Graham (New York: Harcourt Brace, 1968).

7. I. A. Richards, *Basic English and Its Uses* (London: Kegan Paul, Trench, Trubner, 1943); Richards and Christine M. Gibson, *The Pocket Book of Basic English: A Self-Teaching Way into English* (New York: Pocket Books, 1945), reprinted under the titles *English Self-Taught through Pictures* (1949) and *English through Pictures* (1952). For a bibliography of the books in the series see John Paul Russo, "Bibliography of the Books, Articles, and Reviews of I. A. Richards," in *I. A. Richards: Essays in His Honor*, ed. Reuben Brower, Helen Vendler, and John Hollander (New York; Oxford University Press, 1973). The bibliography does not include filmstrips, teaching pictures, long-playing records, and so forth, in the Language through Pictures series.

8. *General Basic English Dictionary* (London: Evans Brothers, 1940).

9. On September 6, 1943, Churchill received an honorary degree from Harvard University and gave an address on the common linguistic heritage of England and America and its import for the future. He had heard of Basic English and "some months ago" had established a government committee to issue a report on the feasibility of making it a common international second language after the war. "What was my delight," Churchill said, "when the other evening quite unexpectedly I heard the President of the United States suddenly speak of the merits of Basic English. And is it not a coincidence that with all this in mind I should arrive at Harvard in fulfillment of the long-dated invitation to receive this degree with which President Conant has honored me? Because Harvard has done more than

any other American university to promote the extension of Basic English. The first work on Basic English was written by two Englishmen, Ivor Richards, now of Harvard—of this university—and [C. K.] Ogden of Cambridge University, England, working in association. The Harvard Commission on English Language Studies is distinguished both for its research and practical work, particularly in introducing the use of Basic English in Latin America, and this commission, your commission, is now, I am told, working with the secondary school in Boston on the use of Basic English in teaching the main language to American children and in teaching it to foreigners preparing for citizenship." ("Common Tongue a Basis for Common Citizenship," *Vital Speeches*, 9, no. 23 [September 15, 1943], p. 715.) For Richards' reflections on Churchill and Basic at a later date see Jane Watkins, "Conversation: I. A. Richards," *Harvard Magazine*, 76, no. 1 (September 1973), pp. 50-56.

10. A thaw in Sino-American relations provided Language Research, Inc., with the opportunity to send over a large amount of Everyman's English materials (books, records, films) to Peking. (Everyman's is a later development of Basic English.) In 1938 Richards published *A First Book of English for Chinese Learners* (Peking: The Orthological Institute of China). It appears that some favorable references to Confucius in these materials are preventing their adoption by the Chinese.

11. Jerome S. Bruner, *Toward a Theory of Instruction* (New York: W. W. Norton, 1966).

12. For another point of view of the state of classical studies see Richards, "Sources of Our Common Thought: Homer and Plato," in *The Great Ideas Today, 1971* (Chicago: Encyclopedia Britannica, 1971), reprinted in *Poetries: Their Media and Ends*, ed. Trevor Eaton (Mouton: The Hague, 1974) and "The New 'Republic,' " *Nation*, March 28, 1942, 370-372.

13. I. A. Richards, *Tomorrow Morning, Faustus! An Infernal Comedy* (New York: Harcourt Brace, 1962), was first performed at the Loeb Drama Center, Harvard University, May 12, 1961.

14. Richards is thinking of the expression, commonly attributed to Emerson, "If a man make a better mousetrap, the world will beat a path to his door."

Acknowledgments

For permission to reprint previously published materials I am indebted to the University of Illinois Press, for a figure from Claude Shannon and Warren Weaver, *The Mathematical Theory of Communication*; Harcourt Brace Jovanovich, for a figure from I. A. Richards, *So Much Nearer: Essays toward a World English*, and for "Complementary Complementarities," from I. A. Richards, *Internal Colloquies: Poems and Plays*; The Literary Trustees of Walter de la Mare and The Society of Authors for "Music Unheard," from *The Complete Poems of Walter de la Mare*; and Viking Press, for "The White Horse," from Vivian de Sola Pinto and F. Warren Roberts, eds., *The Complete Poems of D. H. Lawrence*, copyright © 1964, 1971 by Angelo Ravagli and C. M. Weekley, Executors of the Estate of Frieda Lawrence Ravagli.

J. P. R.

Index